MW01051432

The Suffering of Women Who Didn't Fit

The Suffering of Women Who Didn't Fit

'Madness' in Britain 1450-1950

David J. Vaughan

PEN & SWORD
HISTORY

AN IMPRINT OF PEN & SWORD BOOKS LTD.
YORKSHIRE – PHILADELPHIA

First published in Great Britain in 2018 by
Pen & Sword History
An imprint of
Pen & Sword Books Ltd
Yorkshire - Philadelphia

Hardback ISBN 978 1 52673 229 3
Paperback ISBN 978 1 52675 153 9

A CIP catalogue record for this book is
available from the British Library.

Printed and bound in England
By TJ International Ltd.

Pen & Sword Books Ltd incorporates the Imprints of Pen & Sword Books
Archaeology, Atlas, Aviation, Battleground, Discovery, Family History, History,
Maritime, Military, Naval, Politics, Railways, Select, Transport, True Crime,
Fiction, Frontline Books, Leo Cooper, Praetorian Press, Seaforth Publishing,
Wharncliffe and White Owl.

For a complete list of Pen & Sword titles please contact

PEN & SWORD BOOKS LIMITED
47 Church Street, Barnsley, South Yorkshire, S70 2AS, England
E-mail: enquiries@pen-and-sword.co.uk
Website: www.pen-and-sword.co.uk

or

PEN AND SWORD BOOKS
1950 Lawrence Rd, Havertown, PA 19083, USA
E-mail: uspen-and-sword@casematepublishers.com
Website: www.penandswordbooks.com

To the late Brian Fowler, English Teacher, who nurtured my mind and selflessly shared his literary passions.

Contents

Acknowledgements		viii
Introduction		ix
Chapter 1	Engendered Madness	1
Chapter 2	The Hysteria Hysterics	40
Chapter 3	Maternal Mayhem	56
Chapter 4	'Correcting' Women	86
Chapter 5	Suffering Women: the 'Unfortunate' Sex	113
Appendix 1	A Token of Madness	123
Appendix 2	The Unsuitable Suffragette Mind	125
Endnotes		127
Further Reading		151
Index		161

Acknowledgements

I owe so much to a great number of people, many of whom know a great deal more than I on this serpentine topic. Partly through their sex, mostly through their ungendered intellectual rigour. In fact, there are too many female historians and writers to attempt here to name even a handful, but a number are referenced in the following text. I urge all readers to seek out their words and explore a host of others. To feminists too, howsoever defined, be they academics, lay or 'simply' women.

Thanks go to Heather Williams and all at Pen and Sword History who entrusted me with this challenging task; to not just extract facts from the historical jumble and cut through misogynist rhetoric in favour of truth but to put into some sort of order a seemingly endless trajectory of women's suffering established on such shaky foundations, most of all on account of their sex.

Of course, none of this would have been possible had it not been for the repositories and other, often digital resources that now assail both our minds and our times. Cautiously distilled, without them so little of this book would have ever got done.

Likewise my readers, both here and of previous titles and my ongoing blog (see Further Reading). Were it not for your eyes, minds and hearts, such works as these would have remained alone in my thoughts. To you all an immeasurable, heartfelt 'thank you'.

Finally, I owe a debt of unlimited gratitude to Claire, whose constant support, encouragement and bountiful patience have ensured that this modest attempt came to fruition, even as she kept the author relatively sane.

Yet last of all, in this centenary year of the Suffragettes and their heart-wrenching struggles I, like so many of my sex, owe humility and respect to their astounding successes. And, like so many twenty-first century men who bear no resemblance to, nor guilt for, the 'sins of our fathers', thank you for your legacy that we may write of your trials - and perpetuate hope. To the suffering woman, the vote; more still, her voice to be heard. In this, I trust, I have served you a little.

David J. Vaughan 2018

Introduction

A book such as this is, by necessity, little more than an introduction to the wide, changing subject of women and madness. Detailed and enriched though it is by cases and personal thought, it provides not a medical aetiology but a well-informed history of gender, insanity and socio-cultural responses. Its focus, however, is undeniably women who experienced the brutalities of madness over five hundred years. Many, no doubt, might expect a rigid chronological approach yet the subject, to this author at least, lacks a fair spread of material and would hide the real issues that define women and madness.

Thus Chapter 1, Engendered Madness, isolates often generic responses to the female 'Other', those suffering 'madness', and assesses instead what it meant to be labelled insane on account of her genes. From defining her gender to periodic control, domestic confinement to breaking her chains, almost all of her suffering came from the misogynist male.

In Chapter 2, The Hysteria Hysterics, the origins of this, its most famous eruption, are investigated, not just in the Victorian Age when it reached its nadir, but from much earlier times, starting with Hippocrates' wonders at the 'wandering womb'. We also look briefly at what it means to women today.

Chapter 3 takes her gynaecological make-up, a persistent focus, as the signal curse of her mind. Through each life-stage, from pre-menstruation to post-menopause age, madness found its peak in the volatility of child-birth, and the rearing that followed. Maternal Mayhem gives eye-watering accounts blended with the hopeless concern felt by those 'unfortunate' women who brought new life into the world.

In Chapter 4, Correcting Women, the male domination of lunacy 'treatments' through the ages invented and resurrected a series of mental, physical, even spiritual interventions of the most invidious kind. From natural remedies to the cruellest of surgeons, each concocted response was designed for 'moral correction'.

Summarising many of the points addressed in these earlier chapters, Chapter 5, Suffering Women, encapsulates the woman's lot in a world where she endured mind-based abuse. From her pre-ordained role as home-maker and brood mare, to a wife and companion, she was expected to be a goddess near the hearth and a (reluctant) whore in the bedroom. Like a fragile machine, designed for a purpose, she was driven by man and corrected when broken. In short, it coalesces the wide-ranging points revealed through this book.

Throughout history, dangerous warnings and means of restraint have kept women and madness as inseparable cousins. By employing religion, politics, medicine and law – not to mention social designation – those deemed strange or unstable were kept under control. Running through its centre, like a poisonous snake, the so-called 'golden thread' of non-reason, the female gender.

Not that for women it was bad all of the time. The same jaundice that denounced women as weaker also force-fed her great pity, leading to countless escapes from the rigours of law and social revenge. The distaste for hanging women, for example, reached its peak in the mid-nineteenth century – precisely when infanticide cases seemed to reach their crescendo.

Nor does the past hold a monopoly on misogynist errors. In the present, too, it is too easy to misread social and political landscapes, drawing error-strewn readings no matter how inadvertent they seem. This book takes no account of typically recent developments in gender or sexual identity, including transgender and asexual selections. Rather, its remit is to present the experience of women as *biologically* defined. Perhaps one day, another will follow that takes into account such wide social and gender-based alterations; one, for instance, that focuses on the generations who followed the present work's focus.

Nor does it escape the author's awareness – and fear – that this work cannot but be written through male (if not overtly masculine) eyes. Though they may wear a lens of empathetic feminism, ever-changing political ideals and social corrections present a trap into which the unwary male must fall. Such men who have ever broached this mercurial subject have unavoidably written of notions they could not thoroughly grasp. Yet has the reader too been affected by the sex of the author – is he, to them, a narrator or the protagonist still? In short, if I have been guilty of causing offence, I beg the reader's forgiveness for, in fact, the opposite intention was true.

This notwithstanding, it is my historian's objective, with a love for the subject, to draw together not a collection of cases, but to accumulate a set of influences, guiding principles and thought - often irrational - which have hijacked this most formidable topic during the past five hundred years.

Setting the Scene - Time, Madness and Women: three clinical themes

By covering half a millennia of 'reason', the current work has set itself the unenviable task of making sense out of the fluid and nonsensical – vacillating, temporary ways of viewing the world – and with them the confusing plethora of insanity labels, each causing those looking back to see either more clearly or, more often, to submerge beneath a thickening mist. Faced with recognised historical terms, such as Regency, Enlightenment, Renaissance and more, we have settled here on the more familiar arrangement: Medieval (1450-1600), Post-Medieval (1600-1700), Early Modern (1700-1830), Modern (1830-1900) and Post-Modern (1900-date). Such terms are, of course, liable to become intertwined, but a Herculean effort has been made for their consistent application throughout the whole of the text.

From this most basic of segregations, it will be seen how each era was ascribed its own trajectory of suffering and illness. Gender historian, Ludmilla Jordanova, wrote of periodic epidemics that have been used to define the prevailing social condition: 'each century is characterized by a great illness: leprosy – thirteenth century; black death – fourteenth century; syphilis – sixteenth century; and in the nineteenth century it was the ulcerated womb of women … that summed up the epoch'.[1]

Added to this list, indeed pervading through time – as Victorian alienist, Daniel Hack Tuke lamented – the mad, dear things, have always been with us. Each epoch thus chose its own means to define them; and its own ways to respond. Such stark reassessments, whether gentler or harsher, owed more to their mindset than conditional change. The medieval Bedlamites were a real example: these unconstrained mad 'licensed' to beg on the streets around Bethlem, were at one time sorely pitied with money yet, three hundred years later, extolled as the eponymous Byronian muse.[2]

Tuke's own impressive *Historical Sketch of the Insane*[3] provided a neat, if at times overly-poetic drawing of madness and the reactions it drew through eons of time. As he related, human responses to madness and its unique diagnoses were amended in stages since men (*sic*) first trod the Earth. From those Early Medieval disruptive humours, to demonic possession; the supernatural fears that defined a post-medieval; such that each eventually gave way to an Early Modern self-harm (or, immoral behaviour that led to nervous decay). A later, so-called 'hysterical age' brought its own wealth of conditions, as General Paralysis of the Insane (GPI) was blamed on lax nineteenth century pleasures.

The real situation was seldom clear-cut. Seventeenth century attitudes, for example, conflated several 'causes'. Religion, morality, sin, madness and gender all featured strongly; to experience a defect in one must have meant disrepair in another. In a pre-Victorian absence of organised treatments and institutional centres, save Bethlem and Norwich, early madness was beholden to extant social mores.

Instead, it was the people themselves who 'diagnosed' madness – who recognised its cases as 'different' – and responded in line with prevailing socio-cultural beliefs.[4] And yet, as so often, it was the women who suffered.

As Macdonald observed, religious beliefs and secular notions (the two halves of human existence) were easily blurred. So that 'the spirit of evil' met with 'the malevolent humours', to produce 'disturbing emotions' in the greatly disturbed.[5] Both natural and supernatural forces were freely accepted, for at least half of the timeframe this study observes. It explained the otherwise 'inexplicable' and anti-social behaviour, as astrology, astronomy and a belief in the Devil kept each remained rooted in diagnosing the mad.[6]

Down the centuries, ideas about women became no more forgiving, caught in a whirlpool of changing beliefs in the human condition. Ferocious debates on religious, secular and natural science defined successive eras of the mad female kind. Over half a millennium, religious teachings gave way to a reformed secularization, while scientist expression emerged from the wings of human endeavour, and yet each paradigm shift offered little for her.

Then by the end of this new work's chronological focus, there came a prosaic acceptance of being alive – as the mind, body and spirit were reduced to a collection of cells. Yet still, in the female context, little had changed except to get worse.

It is surely apt that the patron saint of the insane is a woman. Saint Dymphna, supposedly a high-status seventh century Briton, who was brutally murdered by her own unchristian father after he himself was heard to go mad. St Dymphna's Disease has ever since become euphemistic for madness.

In both pre- and early industrial societies, female madness was always acknowledged, if not its true cause or the rightful response. A key feature of how these 'mad' women were handled was how madness itself was seen to exist. It was possible, perhaps inevitable, that the subject's conversion into, say, the seventeenth century witch-hunts, revealed more about ignorant pseudo-religious beliefs than any clinical insight they may have claimed to behold. One thing was sure; it left women at the mercy of a powerful few – men.

Consistent attitudes to women and their place in the world offers only a parallel yet converging account with equally unsettling evocations. The unerring belief in the corruptibility of her gender had led to little abeyance in the male's need for control. It led not just to cruel and barbaric responses, but to an array of self-serving, self-interested male diagnoses of what it was to be 'mad'. Which is what we turn to right here.

From Humours to Wombers

It began from the earliest eons; from Hippocrates's belief in the four humours – phlegm, blood and yellow and black bile – to Galen's refined theoretical form. The dominance of each was believed to reveal a differing temperament in the human condition; so that a phlegmatic person was stoic and calm; biliousness brought on melancholia (black) or irascibility (yellow); while the over-heated blood also produced a short temper and irritable nature (choleric).[7]

So how did this relate to mental well-being and the earliest responses from the medical world? As Andrew Scull expertly apprised, from fevers to delirium (historically seen as cause and effect), 'emotional and cognitive dysfunctions' were blamed on a humoral imbalance. But not even the ancients found a consistent approach:

> 'Where Aristotle had seen the heart as the seat of the emotions and of mental activity, Hippocratic texts saw the brain as their centre: "men ought to know that from nothing else but the brain come joys, delights, laughter and sports, and sorrows, griefs, despondency, and lamentations"...
>
> 'If it was the head, not the heart, which ruled, the emotions, the encephalon was also where madness lurked: "It is the brain too which is the seat of madness and delirium, with the fears and frights which assail us often by night but sometimes even by day;

it is there where lies the cause of insomnia and sleep walking, of thoughts that will not come, forgotten duties and eccentricities. All such things result from an unhealthy condition of the brain…when the brain is abnormal in moisture it is necessarily agitated".'[8]

Nonetheless, it was the humours which governed mental disruption: 'too much blood [warmed] the brain, too much phlegm…[produced] a mania'. Too much black bile made a man (*sic*) melancholic – from the Greek *melanchole*, literally black-bile.[9]

From such somatic origins for mental conditions, it was perhaps inevitable that a woman's body should attract particular terror. The one thing she had, which of course all men had not, was her womb. Adding her supposed colder, moister condition, misogynist foundations were laid for her reputation as the inferior kind. To paraphrase Woods, women a long time before the nineteenth century were considered to suffer psychological problems *simply because of their feminine nature*.[10]

The world now had its earliest distinction in mental and emotional trauma: mania; melancholia; and the hysterical female (from *hystericus*, Latin for womb). Even later medics, like George Cheyne and his belief in frayed nerves being the root of all evil, drew humoral theory into their clinical thought:

'I never saw a person labour under severe, obstinate, and strong nervous complaints, but I always found at last, the stomach, guts, liver, spleen, mesentery or some of the great and necessary organs or glands of the belly were obstructed, knotted, schirrous, spoiled or perhaps all these together.'[11]

Yet without exception all would be challenged, cajoled, refined or dismissed, over the centuries that came.

A new direction of suffering and shame betrayed a continuous descent for the decried female gender. From the earliest expression of the volatile woman, through seventeenth century torture and being burned at the stake, the eighteenth century hostess of hell and damnation, to the Victorian expectation of the 'Angel in the House' (from Coventry Patmore's nineteenth century poem), to think for herself meant being labelled not only mad but deviant too.

To paraphrase again, this time Macdonald, in short '[each] century was a disaster for the [female] insane.'[12] It was no great surprise that a woman became the heiress of misfortune; outwardly troublesome, the pitiful sex. 'Medically unique but inferior… [her] health was determined by her femininity.'[13]

In the 1700s, both the Enlightenment era and the earlier Age of Reason had placed mad women in a negative light shared by other sources of shame: 'crime, vice and idleness' (including now women) were unreasonable, unreasoned, the very antithesis of nature (Bynum *et al* 1985: 80) to which they were supposed to belong. To be stable and sound, a woman was expected to conform to a 'norm' – that she was a product of fate, destined to breed and to represent nature.

Another hundred years on and a new breed of 'experts' – psychiatrists and alienists – now named specifically female 'insanity' conditions: hysteria; puerperal; uterine; and menstrual madness. Procuring the supposedly volatile sex to attain their own professional acceptance, in an uncertain place in these mutable times. Perhaps like never before, save the dark years of torturing witches, a redefinition of woman was attempted for society's 'gain'. Who they were, what made them tick and, above all, what to do when they failed, became a pivotal point in the alienists' world.

But the ones who knew themselves best – these 'fragile women' – had no option but to buy into it all. In this nineteenth century especially, popular opinion saw women who rejected their domestic existence risked being declared insane and committed to an asylum.[14]

But quite how had this appropriation of female madness come to take hold? In the late eighteenth century, the nature of madness was decidedly male; such as Cibber's statues of mania and melancholy that poured out their angst over old Bethlem's doors. In time it gave way, to a gentler, vaguely eroticised image, as madness became a typically female curse:

> 'In the course of the [eighteenth] century…the appealing madwoman gradually displaced the repulsive madman, both as the prototype of the confined lunatic and as a cultural icon.'[15]

The significance of the latter is reflected in this book's literal focus, as has been her descent into a blatant sexualisation of the female insane.

So was it all down to sex? One could be tempted to say so, were its *biological* meaning included, for out of such focus, madness reform proved to be a patriarchal response to the pitiable gender. While some could be classed as real advancements, like famed French physician, Philippe Pinel, who 'freed the insane';[16] or American psychiatrist Isaac Ray's bucolic approach to treating the mentally ill. [17] One undeniable example was the Quaker Retreat. Opened in York in 1793, its appearance reacted to unacceptable horror. After the mysterious death of a female inmate at the maligned *local* asylum, and she being a member of that peaceable group, the Tukes led by William, the redoubtable father, devised and developed their safe haven of sorts.[18]. That the victim was female was not unconnected.

A Woman's Lot in the World - an Early Discussion

Underlying this book is the treatment foisted upon and suffered by women, in particular those condemned to have lost use of their senses. Built too often on sand, all contributed to a woman's lot in the world. Such miserable truths are abridged in the following themes.

Firstly, her requisite role in bringing new life to the world, that rendered her unstable and dangerous due to her gynaecological riddles. From her adult development, 'a time of great stress', to her regular periods as a young, fertile woman; then 'heavy with child' and her hormones supremely chaotic, never more so than soon after birth when her mind was left wayward by her recent expulsion; or post-menopausal when she was further unhinged; all were yet more crudely translated into mental conditions. Phrases like maternal disquiet, monthly mayhem, the hysterical or the troublesome womb, removed her from the domestic home and the hearth to the lying-in hospital or worse the asylum. Yet only because the apothecary, the cleric, medicine, science and law, not to mention her family, said the strain was too great for her embattled mind to withstand.

Second to come, and indirectly related, rose the spectre of domestic confinement. As the 'Crimean Angel', Florence Nightingale had much earlier wailed, 'the confinement of women in the family [compared] to the circumstances of the lunatic in the asylum.'[19]

The all-too-lately acknowledged source of mental decay, the same home and the hearth, became a breeding ground for despair, of rebellious outbursts and misdiagnosed eruptions like the hysteric attack. And spawning new ailments, like uterine madness, or redefining the past such as neurasthenic despair.

Underpinning it all came the panic-struck male, frightened of masculine failure as much by the loss of her love, the very thing they most treasured: the source of their comfort, society and having a woman at home. The result was distasteful: an English*man*'s home may well be his castle, but it too often served as the *woman*'s impregnable cell.

For eons perhaps, yet never more obvious than during the long nineteenth century, the misogynist will had given women their rules. In all living matters – mind, body and soul – a woman could not think, say or do without seeking permission or being unfairly judged. From mental to physical and melding the two, control ruled then as it had threatened to do. The witch-hunting horrors might have belonged in the past, but her voice and her mind were still under restraint.

As Ben Griffin, author of *The Politics of Gender*, so eloquently though perhaps a little myopically bludgeoned: '[There were so] many ways in which women in the nineteenth century [and elsewhere] were oppressed by [the family and] laws that systematically and deliberately served the interests of men' (2012: 4). Expectation and law, with often unspeakable punishments, were simply designed kept the little woman at bay. And from this preposterous position, a woman's lot was defined. From the bedroom to the kitchen, the parlour to the hearth, Patmore's housebound angel was here to stay.

None less than Alfred, Lord Tennyson was driven to voice his toe-curling lament:

'Man for the field and woman for the hearth:
Man for the sword and for the needle she:
Man with the head and woman with the heart:
Man to command and woman to obey;
All else confusion.'[20]

But was change nearby? The suffragettes may have secured for themselves a political voice, but their inherited struggles reached far beyond those of acquiring the vote. Joined by members of the gender that for so long had abused –men like Karl Pearson, 'socialist and future eugenicist'[21] and John Stuart Mill, liberal philosopher and fighter for gender equality – the overdue ending of torment had finally dawned. Yet this, as in most things, was no more than a start.

The third theme occurred in the volcanic arena of sex and creation, perhaps the most scandalised aspect of this misogynist life. Coming again to a head during the dark 1800s, a contradictory expectation of women brought not just control but outright abuse. On the one hand demure, on the other obliged to service her husband; at the same time devoid of desire yet ready to please. In short, she had no interest in sex but was always prepared to give birth.

To be a mother and wife the man could be proud of was not just an aspirational target but demanded on pain. 'The good mother, like the submissive and sexually pleasing wife, had her role to play in [a] new [domestic] ideology by seeing to it that the family remained strong and intact…[and] a pillar of the state'.[22]

Such sanctioned control could often be found in the medical health guides. Manuals on marriage endorsed the procreation ideal. While men like William Acton, Dorsetshire surgeon, crudely cemented the view in his *Functions and Disorders of the Reproductive Organs*: 'I should say that the majority of women (*happily for them* [did he mean society?]) are not very much troubled with sexual feeling of any kind.' For those resisting such hideous proscription, allegations of madness led to institutional control.

Nymphomania, for example, was invented to define those who sought simple sexual pleasure of the non-breeding kind and resulted in horrific responses from blade-wielding surgeons with control on their minds.

As Acton continued:

'with these sad exceptions [of institutionalised nymphomaniacs], there can be no doubt that sexual feeling in the female…is [in any case] very moderate compared with that of the male.'[23]

He also observed how their 'love of home, of children, and of domestic duties are the only passions they feel.'[24] With an ironic eye, compare this to others' contemporary views of the 'frigid' wife, by which her self-expressed refusal to 'cohabit' was blamed for her husband's impotence – even his madness.

Much later again, during the Second World conflict, Beveridge the social reformer and economist, revealed that minds like his could never be turned: 'Housewives as mothers have vital work to do in ensuring the adequate continuance of the British race,' he laid down.[25]

While from the sexual demands, and from her proclaimed 'natural purpose', it was little wonder that she sometimes went genuinely mad. Others, less pliable, were simply labelled as such. The physical and emotional care of her spouse and her children remained the only requirements of the female sex.

Beyond the hearth and the home, women's madness was portended outside as well, as she sought to become more learned and wise. Educating the 'lesser sex', the fourth theme, was seen by many as stepping on the precipice of a slippery slope. Not just an abrogation of (domestic) duty but falling away to full mental derangement. Henry Maudsley, the juggernaut alienist and arguable father of mind-centred misogyny, feared the 'expense' women paid for their equality in learning. In particular, a race double whammy: of too much mental *and* physical exertion (the latter from her preordained motherly role); while the damage to both themselves and the species was a tangible risk – 'a race of sexless beings [who would] carry on the intellectual work of the world, not otherwise than as sexless ants do the work and fighting of the community'. In short, women 'cannot rebel successfully against the *tyranny* of their organization.'[26]

About the same time, Thomas Clouston, Superintendent at Edinburgh's Royal Morningside Asylum, vouched his support, seeing women who studied science leaving no innate energy for their 'true' purpose in life – reproduction.[27]

English and cultural historian, Lyn Pykett's, rightful denouncement of such a misogynist's stance ridiculed its purpose:

> '[the] argument against women being admitted to the public world of work and politics, and to the same education as men…[beheld] that the taxing of the brain would use up resources of energy which should be conserved for reproductive activity.'[28]

Yet almost two hundred years before, seventeenth century 'advice' too debarred women not just from learning but from reading as well, as one led to the other and both led to madness! For example, in 1645 John Winthrop, an English Puritan lawyer during the American witch-hunting era, attributed the insanity of the poet Anne Hopkins to her 'reading and writing…if she had attended her household affairs, and such things as belong to women…she had kept her wits'. A woman's place was the home, while literacy was only 'proper for men, whose minds were stronger'. Back in the hey-day of nineteenth century domestic confinement, female peers – that is mothers and no doubt 'maiden aunts' – forbade their daughters and nieces from reading a book.[29]

It was no surprise though, through the eons, that women had suffered nervous uncertainty, leastways according to men. Neurosis, as it became known, was considered not just to persist in the 'weaker' sex, nor especially during times of great social upheaval; it lay, in fact, in the woman's more fragile nature, and this was where its impact was most keenly felt:

> 'Overwork in the [so-called] modern system of high-class education in girls, whose physical health is unfitted for the efforts they are unwisely encouraged to make.'[30]

Fortunately, pioneering women, female medics especially, were quick to reply. Elizabeth Garrett Anderson, England's first licensed female doctor and stalwart of the Langham Place Group promoting opportunities for women, penned her calm, collected response to Maudsley's ridiculous rant. Correcting the misogynist medic, she wrote, 'the single aim of those anxious to promote a higher and more serious education for women is to make the best they can of the materials at their disposal'. And she demanded to know any evidence that supported his nihilistic view:

> '[where] has [it] ever been implied by any person working towards women's educational reform that the goal of their work is to dispose of all of their femininity and [in effect] become male.'[31]

Not for her, then, the idea that to better herself spelt certain mental decay.

If the woman proved particularly boisterous, there was always the madhouse – the fifth salient theme in our review of her lot. 'Women,' wrote foremost historian Hilary Marland, 'have been depicted as particularly vulnerable to confinement in asylums.' Yet it was not always so. '[I]n the eighteenth century male admissions to private asylums tended to outstrip those of women', and, according to Roy Porter, 'Georgian asylum admissions lend no support to the view that male chauvinist values were disproportionately penalizing women with mental disorders'. However, even before the Victorian era, 'increasingly large numbers of women were being confined in public and private asylums, thus reversing the previous situation as female admission in some institutions overtook those of men'.[32]

Yet more than a century before, in 1750, an early allegation appeared of wrongful confinement. Suspecting her son-in-law of incarcerating her daughter in a madhouse in Hoxton, north London, one Mrs Gold had the local Justice to thank after he extracted the husband's confession;, while at the same Parliamentary Committee held in 1763, other cases brought absolute terror. The propitiously named Mr La Fortune secured the release of one Mrs Hawley from a Chelsea asylum, but only on the strength of habeas corpus.[33]

The Committee had, in fact, heard that too many sane people were being confined as though unquestionably mad, including, it revealed, wives who had lost their matrimonial passion, and daughters who took unwise decisions on the subject of love. The go-to recourse at the time for such counterfeit cases was the Court of King's Bench, but this was where numerous 'troublesome wives' had been confined on invented, fantastical madness.[34]

Some eleven years later, the nation's legislature finally responded through the Madhouses Act (1774), though its eventual impact could be dismissed as little less than apathetic. Not only did it apply only to institutions near London (within a meagre 7 miles of its centre), it had no powers for revoking a license, regardless of how badly the asylum behaved![35]

William A.F. Browne, nineteenth century alienist and one-time President of the high-brow Medico-Psychological Association, had become the above court's fiercest (historical) critic, pitying the sane who were 'entrapped, imprisoned…[and] confined, in defiance of the most active interference made in their favour.'[36]. It was all a done deal when a wife was at stake.

Roy Porter had also unearthed several similar cases, including this sorry, sordid account of a not-so-merry wife of Windsor:

'I know of a Gentlewoman of substance who lived [in the town], who was flattered by her roguish Apothecary into the Management of her Fortune, and who had fixed himself in her Opinion and did all her Business for her, he decoyed her into a Madhouse not far from London on the Bank of the River Thames, where he took care that she was so ill used, that she, after a while, was made really mad in good earnest, and the Apothecary enjoy'd her Fortune, and took care that no Relation or Acquaintance of hers should have access to her, or visit her.'[37]

In August 1858, *The Times* newspaper led a new scathing assault on this frightful abuse. Citing four cases, all involving privately run houses, the once unspeakable practice was at long last being exposed.[38]

Supporting it all was a shadowy practice – the doubtful certification of the supposedly mad. From its murkiest origins in late Georgian Britain, around the time of the Madhouses Act, from 1845 it required no less than the signatures of two medical men. In the Lunacy Act of 1890, they were joined by a non-medical lawyer, typically a magistrate or other such figure holding power where the accused usually lived.[39] Moves designed to arrest unscrupulous behaviour only further exposed the scale of the problem. Mad-doctors and alienists, asylum keepers and wardens, all had a vested interest in declaring, then maintaining, a person or persons insane. And when the accuser was a powerful and affluent husband, who amongst them would be daft enough to question *his* mind?

Spurious certification and dubious medics now combined with manipulative husbands, fathers, uncles and brothers to put their 'mad' women away. The earlier, unregulated establishments had often added brutality to this already injustice. The private madhouses, or so-called 'lunacy traders', saw only profit, not patients; income not improvement. And the pseudo-prisons became the home of early wrongful restraint.

In 1714, the Vagrancy Act had initiated the two-justice requirement for certifying the detention of mad people.[40] As 'new' insanity conditions were being put forward – such as moral insanity and irresistible impulse – doubtful confinement became appreciably worse, as the nefarious practice was now easier to label. While these were perhaps used to secure welcome exculpation in the capital criminal trials, in the world of non-malfeasant allegations they woefully helped to secure wrongful 'arrests'.

The nineteenth century American physician, Isaac Ray, made the aforementioned W.A. F. Browne seem like a lamb:

> 'Of all the bugbears conjured up in these latter times to frighten grown people from the course pointed out by true science and true humanity, it would be hard to find one more destitute of real substance than the alleged practice of confining sane persons in hospitals for the insane.'[41]

A further move to correct or appease, according to viewpoint, was the 1840 Insane Prisoners Act, which brought in the legal requirement for two legal men as well as two medics to sign a lunacy certificate (though this allowed an untried defendant to be shut away on a whim, while the later Insane Prisoners Amendment Act (1864) further restricted the certification to two judiciary men appointed to the place where the accused was confined. [42]

Such dark abuses of privilege and liberty, while not exclusive to women, thus had a long, near-predictable history, a point highlighted by the *British Medical Journal* in October 1874:

> 'The Council of the [Lunacy Law Reform Association] have just issued their first report, in which they make a series of charges all round, of brutal cruelty, political influence, and criminal negligence on the part of medical men in signing lunacy certificates.'[43]

The national press were quick to endorse; citing real-life cases, such as that of Rosina Bulwer-Lytton, who they described as having been buried alive in a social tomb.[44] Meanwhile, the brilliantly candid Louisa Lowe condemned private asylums in particular as bastilles of wrongful confinement, where innocent women were kept 'out of sight…the victims…forgotten'[45].

While women like Elizabeth Packard, herself incarcerated on her husband's whim, only won back her freedom after relating her experiences to a horrified world. Dorothea Dix, an asylum reformer like Packard, became famed in the 1800s for exposing the unequal, some say non-existent, rights of the insane, and conceiving the first wave of American mental asylums.

During the later 1800s, certification abuses grew rife; it was a time when unscrupulous doctors joined forces with a self-serving husband to secure the confinement of the writer Sarah Wise's award-winning *Inconvenient People* (2013). It ignited an explosion of wrongful detention and, an outcry to match, albeit slowly,: that 'the sane were being sequestered in private asylums as though they were mad'.[46]

Finally, in the twentieth century, the philosopher Foucault – no supporter of institutionalisation – aligned the Georgian mad doctor and his predecessor, the medieval 'quack', with their nineteenth century equivalent, the asylum superintendent. All three, he shouted, were directly responsible for stealing away individual freedom.[47]

It is arguably worth stating that not all misogynist cruelty was as deliberately ill in intent as it was undoubtedly judged. Over the centuries, many of the clergy, medics, scientists, even politicians, believed they were doing genuine good:

> 'Unless we accept that they were all very uncomplicated sadistic monsters…then their doubtless multifarious views on what they thought they were doing must surely have some relevance in the history of psychiatry [if not feminist studies].'[48]

Throughout all ages, to paraphrase Porter, men from such disparate worlds as medicine and marriage, proffered complimentary sympathy toward the long-suffering woman.[49] What remained disturbing, of course, was their continued belief that the female species was 'constitutionally prone to irrationality'[50].

But why did this insult remain de rigueur for so long? Well before the nineteenth century's preoccupation with the corruptible female, early modern medical and socio-cultural responses fulminated against the 'weakest' of the two sexes:

> 'Within the humoral system women [were] constructed as the unruly sex: female bodies, composed predominantly of cold and

wet humours, are apt to go out of frame, and the balance of the ideal humoral body is constantly challenged by the ebbs and flows of the menstrual cycle [and] of childbearing.'[51]

'Women's relation to madness [was] inevitably gendered, conditioned by contemporary assumptions about women's minds and bodies. Women were thought less vulnerable to some forms of disorder, and more vulnerable to others; their weaker control over the passions and lesser degree of reasonableness might render them more liable to disorders of the mind, more easily thrown off balance by disappointments in love or personal crisis.'[52]

In the Georgian period alone, the fluorescence of nerves as the seat of all ills singled out women (and effeminate men) as those most at risk; from the Cheynian[53] era of 'sense and sensibility', to Showalter's opined 'proneness' to madness especially in higher Austen-esque circles. Such views of course had their origins in a time long forgotten: replacing the earlier obsession with the 'wandering womb'. As Blackmore observed in the earliest years of the eighteenth century, 'a more volatile, dissipable, and weak Constitution of the spirits, and a more soft, tender, and delicate Texture of the Nerves'[54] put women at risk.

By the Victorian age such prejudice was not only cemented in supposedly rational thought, it was raised up to a whole new, more unsettling level. That women outnumbered men in Victorian asylums almost two to one has been frequently cited as proof- positive for this gender distinction,[55] though it is fair to say others question the use of such interpretable statistics for reading the past. Whatever the empirical truth, that women were seen, feared and ultimately treated as the more dangerous sex, from anatomical make-up to uncontrollable passion, was and remains an indelible blemish on the history of madness and British gender-based thought.

No surprise, then, that in this centenary year of the Suffragette's successes, such social and political upheaval has once again burst onto the scene – and the streets – of a British masculine world.

Sources and Caveats

I must conclude this introductory chapter with brief notes about sources and caveats. By the theme's very nature, most forms consulted appeared in the florescence of insanity studies - namely, the Victorian era. Nevertheless, primary and secondary medieval and later sources do exist and have been consulted, as too those relating to the subject as it was read at the other end of the spectrum, the first fifty years of the twentieth century.

In academic and commentary writings, as in all, personal agenda, presupposition and latter-day thought cannot but fail to influence the focus and words of the opinions expressed. This is not to decry or undermine their inestimable value, simply to raise a cautionary note that whatever the facts, there is always contextual thought. In this, the present work is included.

From mind to body, covering not just madness but social condition, diverse titles such as *Psychical Research*, *Healthy Impulses to Crime*, *Malleus Maleficarum* and *The Insanity of Passion and Crime*, have become joined through their (often unintentional) contribution to the current debate. For an introduction to the many key themes, consult the Further Reading such as Tuke's 1892 *Dictionary of Psychological Medicine*, Porter's excellent introduction to Georgian culture and madness, *Mind-Forg'd Manacles*, and Scull's supreme *Madness: A Very Short Introduction*, as well as other, more feminist works from stalwarts like Showalter (*The Female Malady*), Walkowitz (*City of Dreadful Delight*) and Marland (*Dangerous Motherhood*).

As for images, I offer no apology for my extensive use of Wellcome Library, London for this title's pictorial offering. Their image collection, in my opinion, remains one of the best sources of related paraphernalia available royalty-free. I commend it to all.

Chapter 1

Engendered Madness

W e start this chapter by revisiting five hundred years of (mis) reading women, followed by the more awkward trajectory of defining madness itself. Coursing through these two strands is how an absence of the latter failed to desist control of the former. And how the 'understanding' of both was acquired without recourse to herself!

Defining Women Over 500 Years!

The (male) definition of womanhood has a long and arduous history, most of it constructed on masculine fear. 'Opinion-formers and policy-makers produced their own phantom *Doppelgänger*, reminders of [the] dangers lurking within, of what would break loose if law and morality broke down'. At the heart of this terror sat the corruptible woman. 'Late nineteenth century fears of demoralised, hypnotised, hysterical, or nymphomaniac women reveal male insecurities about precisely what *normal* women – your wife and daughter! – were really like'. A circumstance that revealed 'more about the crisis of personal beliefs and professional status of the [authority figures] ... than about their [targets'] 'diseases"[1] Yet the stage for this Victorian model had been set more than two hundred years before, and consistently targeted a perceived feminine guile:

> 'For pride and madnesse are of the feminine gender. They have reason for it. Man was made but of earth, Woman of refined earth; being taken out of man, who was taken out of the earth [a reference to Eve's creation from Adam's extracted rib]: therefore shee (*sic*) arrogates the costlier ornaments, as the purer dust'.[2]

In these clerical times, of medieval religion writ large through Puritanical fear, the language and castigation of women grew increasingly stark: 'By means of a whorish woman, a man is brought to a piece of bread'

(Proverbs 6: 26) – that is, a dissolute woman will bring a man to his knees. The blocks were now building for a means of control; the target of which was her facile mind.

Adams saw much to fear in their 'beauty':

'If you prayse their beauty; you rayse their glory: *if you commend them, command them.* Admiration is a poison, that swelles them till they burst [i.e. go mad].'[3]

Moreover:

'because the brain responded to the operation of the reproductive organs…the *mentalities* of the sexes differed as well. It was the totality of the physical and the mental differences that made up the essence [that] doctors [and others] confidently called woman's 'nature'.'[4]

This nuisance apparatus of human reproduction – and the masculine 'wisdom' on why women existed – created her reasons to fall. Energy depletion, in body and mind, left her prone to decay – especially 'up there' in the brain and the mind. While her gynaecological equipment – from the womb to the ova and her 'regular cycle' – made her not just more volatile, but more suited to nurture than to try to compete (the male's exclusive domain).

Maudsley's assertion that 'there is sex in mind' was rendered ever more derogatory by the epitaph, 'as distinctly as there is sex in body,'[5] extolling the thesis by condemning the female as unsuited to public 'offices in life' – i.e. those outside the home. Thus, a woman's mental collapse came when she undoubtedly dared to presume to know better than nature.[6]

An endless litany of sexist opinion saw control exercised on and withdrawn from the woman (had she ever possessed it), and it was achieved through what they said was medical 'progress', ably assisted by attitudes in both culture and law. Nineteenth century alienists like Prichard, Laycock and Beard (actually an American neurologist) introduced causes of the weak womanly mind, respectively homicidal mania; nervous diseases; and sexual (not just gender) neurasthenics. Beard made a career out of women's apparent neuroses, predicated on immoral living and his pessimist's view:

'The causation of sexual neurasthenia, as of all the other clinical varieties, and of modern nerve sensitiveness in general, is not single or simple, but complex; *evil habits, excesses, tobacco, alcohol, worry and special excitements, even climate itself* - all the familiar excitants being secondary to the one great predisposing cause – civilization.'[7]

Having labelled the 'Dark Ages' of nervous women just a half-century before, Beard unintentionally endorsed contemporary responses and insisted 'a large group of nervous symptoms, which are very common indeed, would not exist but for morbid states of the reproductive system' – though he had the good grace to extend the problem to both sexes. Nevertheless, he clearly believed in the origins of the woman's poor nerves: 'lacerations of the cervix and perineum, irritations, congestions, and displacements of the uterus and ovaries'…amongst others.[8]

As Cheyne avowed barely two hundred years earlier, history proved how it was middle class women who were found to be chiefly at risk, insisting it was the idle rich who suffered the worst of weak female nerves. While, as Woods has more recently stated, such women were particularly invested with purity, marriage and outward economic endowment, and having so much to live up to, their minds inevitably collapsed under the weight of their domestic oppression.[9]

By the long nineteenth century, the scene, having already been set, was now being ever fine-tuned to fearing the woman – especially one who had pride in her charms. The response, then, was to oppress and belittle, which none less than Charles Darwin redefined (and endorsed). In *The Descent of Man*, he wrote explicitly about woman's 'inferior state'. As he spelt out his perceptions of biological difference, he acknowledged evolution's preparation for the differing sexes; men were designed to excel at art, science and thought, while women's superior traits were restricted to 'intuition, perception and imitation'.[10] Such 'strengths', he argued, were 'characteristic of the lower races, and therefore of a past and lower state of civilisation' – an intended slur on a woman's role in the human existence.[11] Thus, for many, the misogynist's view was receiving endorsement.

Nature was where much of female suffering was given its justification. The implications were stark. 'Nature and society mutually illuminate each other,' Jordanova remarked. 'Gender functions in this way because it is… part of the natural world, the source of all morality and ethics…' Defining a woman and her role in the world, based on natural order, became so entrenched that declaring her mad seemed a quick easy-fix for condemning and subjugating the gender.[12]

By extending such fear, the pitied and now reprovable female – from girlhood to womanhood, through puberty, maternity and into old age – was more wont to psychiatric decay far beyond that of (most) men! But nowhere more so than in becoming a mother.

Maternal Collapse

Motherhood raised especial concerns in the realm of the mind. The forthcoming chapter on so-called 'maternal mayhem' elucidates this far more, but it is worth highlighting here how it became the ultimate focus of female suffering – from her physical danger in the 'dark' Middle Ages, to the oncoming ills of the nerves and her mind. According to many, her propensity to derangement arising from her capacity to bear children *was* indeed her unequivocal curse:

> 'During that long process, or rather succession of processes, in which the sexual organs of the human female are employed in forming; lodging; expelling, and lastly feeding the offspring, there is no time at which the mind may not become disordered; but there are two periods at which this is chiefly liable to occur, the one soon after delivery, when the body is sustaining the efforts of labour, the other several months afterwards, when the body is sustaining the effects of nursing'.[13]

A degenerative moral sense too, born of impaired and inferior faculties, her conduct and especially her self-control, all were seen now as prone to collapse. As Clouston advanced, as late as 1911: 'A certain lack of [self-control] is, I fear, almost expected in woman, and the highest degrees of it are not commonly expected in her…[it is] few who are not prone to yield in conduct to emotion, instincts and impulse.'[14] William Tyler Smith, a Victorian male midwife, went even further, and *guaranteed* a mother's insanity at the very moment she gave birth.[15]

Maternal madness could be 'traced' to several sources, as far as was seen by nineteenth century minds. And so great was their number, it was a miracle that any woman escaped being untouched by a perceived malediction. Amongst them were the following concocted conditions.[16]

Uterine changes led to an unstable brain – what Maudsley described as 'affections of the uterus and its appendages afford notable examples of a powerful sympathetic action upon the brain, and not unfrequently play[ed] an important part in the production of insanity.'[17] Blood decay, in both circulation and quality - Maudsley again, perhaps now revealing a misogynist's theme?[18] Melancholia reared up from weakened nerves, though whether from her natural make-up or from being confined whilst pregnant remained a moot point. And the curse of new mothers, puerperal insanity, the maternal mayhem *en vogue*. In simple terms comprised of mania and longer-term melancholia, the latter including lactational madness.

The same Professor Hogan, in an arguably overly feminist tract, recently lamented both the invention and misdiagnosis of maternal insanity conditions, typically puerperal mania. Insisting that such a tag of abuse ignored the real cause of the new mother's condition, she highlighted bacterial infection as the real blameworthy cause.[19] Hardly unheard of in pre-modern times, yet more unsettling was how motherhood itself was reduced to the woman's 'pivotal purpose'.

Not that such notions were confined to the Victorian era. The post-war years of the twentieth century retained its gendered perspectives. Psychotherapy also attracted stern condemnation, as self-labelled feminists compared Freud's psycho-sexualisation of women as another form of male-centric control.

Ahead of the emerging 1960s 'chemical culture', with first its American then European claims of magical pills, it was really the underground attitudes which were shifting the sands. Since the dawn of the 'chemical cosh', and the marketing of a new breed of sedatives and anti-depressants, more people, women especially, were effectively self-diagnosing via the medicine chest. Even in popular culture, this 'brave new world' was not going unnoticed; as heard in the Rolling Stones' hit, *Mother's Little Helper*, a rebuke on the increasingly popular diazepam drug, perhaps better known by its Valium trade name. Compare it with those nineteenth century cousins, laudanum and antimony, once the asylum superintendent's favourite for keeping her under control. The latter worked by keeping her nauseous but is now used in fireproofing fabrics![20]

Thus, from Darwinian theories to post-modern 'abuses', the 'inferior' mental state of the female sex saw her succumb to her subordinate nature, and her mental collapse during her maternal ordeal. From such a set of evolutionary circumstances, women had long-fought life's battle just to stay sane. These age-old misogynist responses to motherly madness perpetuated if not exaggerated earlier centuries' failings, bringing in a new wave of psychiatry formed on the old tide of gender control. Wrongful confinement may by the Sixties have become a thing of the past, but wrongful coercion remained another matter entirely.

Periodic Control

To witness the myriad ways in which men 'managed' their women is to see how the means, whys and wherefores of gender control fluctuated with one central exception; though each era had its own particular methods, connecting them all was a misogynist's fear. Whether this was born of her power, her sexuality or simply from not being men, women like the mad people they were suffered bias and bigotry on a towering scale.

One of the worst periods for fearing the woman is found in the seventeenth century, with its witch-scares, witch-hunts and, in certain areas of Britain, execrable burnings. Even when the accused woman escaped with her life, the physical and mental cruelty meted out must surely have taken her to the very edge of insanity.

Many latter-day commentators even suggest that much of what was claimed to be witchcraft was, in reality, madness itself. And it was what constituted witchcraft that paved the way for so many abhorrent reactions, as unsound mental behaviour was often distorted to Satanic collusion. Defining a witch – or a mad woman – provided the bedrock for decades of mental abuse. And in no area was this more keenly 'explained' than her innate sexual being:

> 'As [the esteemed academic] Roper explains in *Oedipus and the Devil: Witchcraft, Sexuality, and Religion in Early Modern Europe,* "Women were believed to be closer to the Devil, and they were therefore more subject to temptation and more enslaved to their physical natures than [were men]. In consequence, their bodies were naturally more suited to house devils"'.[21]

Modern commentator, Leslie Abshire, further observed how 'witches [were often depicted] as being sexually immoral creatures... related directly to the widely held belief that women were inherently more physical beings, falling victim to their sexual bodies and weak minds, and *in need of more guidance and control than [and by] men lest they fall prey.*'[22]

All this had led to the so-called 'two sex model', yet born of the male and enacted by him. Around the eighteenth century, both genders began to be treated as polarised disputants (previously, they had been regarded as twin elements of the singular human condition). 'Abnormal' women were no longer seen simply as aberrant to society's standards, but the antithesis of nature. Contravening God's laws, physicians, clergymen, novelists all used the two-sex model to denigrate the inferior woman.[23] And when madness was added, a palpable fear took hold.

Yet far from being confined to the same century that brought the Puritan perversions, such views found themselves de rigueur in the mid to late 1800s (if indeed not at all other times). Compare, for example, Victorian fears of the sexually deviant woman, to the warning handed out in fifteenth century Britain in the infamous *Malleus Maleficarum*, that:

'all witchcraft comes from carnal lust, which is in women insatiable…What sort of women more than others are found to be superstitious and infected with witchcraft; it must be said…that three general vices appear to have special dominion over wicked women, namely, infidelity, ambition, and lust. Therefore they are more than others inclined towards witchcraft, who more than others are given to these vices. Again, since of these vices the last chiefly predominates, women being insatiable, etc., it follows that those among ambitious women are more deeply infected who are more hot to satisfy their filthy lusts; and such are adulteresses, fornicatresses, and the concubines of the Great.'[24]

What is of greatest importance is how such (imagined) behaviour was translated not just into witchcraft, but as a sign of madness as well, so that a fine line was cast between female sexuality, sin and the lunatic asylum (or its earlier incarnation). To be an accused witch was undeniably frightful; to be accused of being a woman was potentially worse.

An example of where that line was crossed is similarly seen in *Malleus Maleficarum*:

'And by which they cause great suffering to both men, other women and children – that is, the entire race: 'First, by inclining the minds of men to inordinate passion; second, by obstructing their generative force; third, by removing the members accommodated to that act; fourth, by changing men into beasts by their magic art; fifth, by destroying the generative force in women; sixth, by procuring abortion; seventh, by offering children to devils, besides other animals and fruits of the earth with which they work much harm.'[25]

Arnold blames this 'pornographic' best-seller for 'joining the Bible to enforce the message that all women – not just witches – were evil, and responsible for [Original Sin]'.[26] She is almost certainly right.

Meanwhile, compare the inclusion of nullifying the unborn child with the idealised role of the natural mother. In the words of a presiding judge not of witchcraft but at an infanticide trial in 1885, it was 'one of the worst offences known and practised in this country'.[27] In short, abortion was the antithesis of being a woman.

Whatever the motivation, the history of women being deemed mad for nefarious purposes – from the scold to the suffragette – has been an evil ruse ever-present through the ages. In the eighteenth century, though no longer burning women as witches; and during the reign of the supposedly more genteel and liberal Georgians; numerous other horrific responses awaited those labelled insane by virtue of gender.

Mary Robinson, the celebrity actress, writer and monarchical mistress, tackled the unfair control of her sex through her novel, *A Letter to the Women of England Suitably subtitled: On the Injustice of Mental Subordination.* Addressing the tangible dangers of wrongful confinement – a hundred years and more before Bulwer-Lytton and Weldon (see Chapter 5) – Robinson's attack, published in 1799, arrived 'amid wide-spread controversy over the abilities, duties and rights of women' [as defined by the men]; while 'interrogat[ing] oppressive gender laws' with a sense of blind hope for a more egalitarian future, one when 'women speak and write...freely.'[28]

In the story, her fictional hero, Mrs Morley, having placed herself in harm's way for the sake of her female friend escaping oppression, finds herself squirrelled away in a private madhouse on the grounds of mistaken identity. The words Robinson skilfully crafted to reveal the horror she felt instilled in the reader a deep sense of fear and outraged despair: 'Her terror now became...[a] scene of desolation.'[29] As Robinson knew, such suffering did not only belong in the mind of the writer. Enforced, often illicit incarceration in an eighteenth century madhouse became seen as the pivotal mainstay of gender control. And anyone who supposed the 'new' Victorian public asylums would deter this earlier century's misdoings were all too quickly left disappointed.

At the centre of such a ravaging era of female confinement, ignoring for a moment the genuinely mad, was the male's menu of tricks and deceits; from spurious certification to unscrupulous doctors. Even beyond the establishments' walls, institutionalised sexism aided the woman's 'removal', a sickening mix of the laws on divorce, legitimised beatings, and sexual non-freedoms, including her role in the eruption of sexually transmitted diseases, especially syphilis and its causing General Paralysis of the Insane (GPI).

In the 1860s, new legislation on such contagious diseases had reinforced gender discrimination by tackling a particular problem: prostitution. Now a mere suspicion of taking part in that trade was enough to be cruelly subjected to a forced medical assessment, followed by institutionalization if her 'assessors' agreed.[30] It all smacked of the hunt, three hundred years earlier, for the witch's teat on which she suckled her sprites.

Yet another nineteenth century act (colloquially the 'Aggravated Assaults Act', 16 & 17 Vict., c. 30) brought little improvement, in which the law permitted only 'reasonable' correction of a troublesome wife! The laws before Blackstone's famous *Commentaries on the Laws of England 1765-69* had led to the controversial epitaph, 'rule of thumb', referring to the allowed maximum thickness of a cane or whip to be used in the 'salutary restraints of domestic discipline'.[31] Scarcely comprehensible today, it remains easy to imagine certain men in the past descending further, from meting out an 'appropriate' beating to having their wives placed in asylums, out of the way, all on the say-so, remember, of self-interested physicians.

Nor further back were her stakes any better. The spectre of cruelty for Georgian wives was revealed as soon as the knot of betrothal had been tightened, typically in church. Under the ancient law of coercion, a married woman escaped criminal censure as she was considered to be under her husband's control, even for the most serious offences.[32] Her debts too, upon marriage, were to be settled by her husband as soon as they married, 'for he has adopted her and her circumstances together'. Some might have said this was a good thing for women.

In exchange, however, she was forced to accept that, like his servants and children, he was entitled to 'correct' her, albeit with limited force - 'for as he is to answer for her misbehaviour, the law thought it reasonable to intrust him with [the] power of restraining her, [through] domestic chastisement'.

Certain transgressions in civil law further allowed him to 'beat her severely with whip and sticks' and, though this 'allowance' was mercifully abolished during the reign of the second King Charles, her husband remained free to 'restrain' her in cases of 'gross misbehaviour.'[33]

Meanwhile, not until the Matrimonial Causes [Divorce] Act of 1857 – despite continuing illicit confinement and home-based abuses – could women procure a legal separation except through a private Act of Parliament exclusively open to the fortunate few. And yet, in almost two hundred years

(1670–1857), the total number of successful cases thus brought numbered just ... four.[34]

And did things really improve for such a select group of women? Even when legal separation became a more accessible option other, emotional control was cruelly maintained; for example, through the ex-husband's rights to full custody of their children. Not until two further Acts, in 1873 and again thirteen years later, was the law finally changed. Even so, economic control remained up the misogynist's sleeve, at least until the Married Women's Property legislation (1870/1882) gave them the right to hold on to their money. Space has not allowed for a discussion of the differences in constituent law – even when, for example, Scotland's legislature was frequently years ahead of the rest of the British Isles.

Leading up to these changes, indeed doubtlessly helping secure them, a particular man's concern for a woman's position led to a welcome paradigm shift. John Stuart Mill, often co-writing along with Harriet, his life partner, tore open the topic with his 1869 acclaimed commentary, *The Subjection of Women*. Focusing on these very same issues, such as how a married woman's personal fortune became her husband's the moment the pair exchanged vows, Mill bewailed that 'the two are called "one person in law", for the purpose of inferring that whatever is hers is his, but the parallel inference is never drawn that whatever is his is hers.' Even worse, that 'far from pretending that wives are in general no better treated than slaves...no slave is a slave to the same lengths, and in so full a sense of the word'; noting how she was never 'off duty'. [35]

In perhaps the same way came the French historian Jules Michelet's now unpopular desire to prove how, some thirty years before Mill, 'woman does not live without man'; for they would surely 'die from illness or suicide if they [do] not enjoy the protection of a husband'.[36] From such unpleasant openings she reasserted Michelet's perpetuation of an historical myth: that men and women were different precisely because one was robust, while the other was weak. In other words, man was health, while woman was illness; she should remain reliable and calm, while he was wastefully wanton, expending his energies and wealth – things she could have used in maintaining the home! Whether intended or not, Michelet had established an argument for domestic confinement, and a societal need for her protection by men.[37]

Even the eighteenth century philosopher Rousseau obsessed about the dangers to, and of, women: from education, breastfeeding, virginity (versus being a good mother). And he furthered his often-shared personal notions of 'acceptable' female behaviour: from appropriate dress, to her being an obedient wife.[38]

Public Misogyny

Despite exceptions like Mill, such strident misogynist views were more normal than hoped for. From politicians to the media, medicine to the law, women had both a clear prescribed role and murky, described impositions.

The nineteenth century again provided the most explosive examples. *Westminster Review*'s reaction to the publication of *Adam Bede*, a new novel by George Eliot, the presumed male writer, raised a pivotal issue. When the book's character, Hetty Sorrell, is declared guilty of killing her infant, the publication's assessment laid bare the sexist preoccupations with unfortunate girls:

> 'With the exception of her extraordinary beauty, she might be justly regarded as typical of a large number of her sex: she was ignorant, vain and entirely wrapped up in herself.'[39].

Such disparaging views confirmed two things at least: firstly, the prevailing masculine view of the century's women; and, secondly, the context within which so many women, whether insane or not, had reacted to the pressures of life – in this case, by murdering her baby. Such was the woman's 'place' in this proto-industrialised Britain, that women – like men – were forced to conform to a new set of social ideals. The expectations of gender were used to create social constraint, by those of class and nouveau Victorian wealth. Unlike men, however, this caused her descent into a much deeper trough of despair – and a host of new remedial measures.

Nervous disorders, previously ascribed to the idle rich and their families, were now seen to dismantle the working class woman, whose intemperance and poverty were seen not as reasons for succour, but as damning signs of her own moral decay. At the same time, a wholly new invention, the middle-class worker, found both their bodies and minds stretched to destruction by rampaging progress and, as Darwin put it, a need to survive. As though not enduring enough, should a woman now fail to fulfil her newly imposed obligations of gender, then a plethora of strategies, tactics and underhand goings-on served only to make her robust situation exceedingly worse.

Even so, plausibly well-intentioned manoeuvres, by both medics and lawyers, took a woman's *vive la différence* and expressed it extremely in the criminal courts. No longer able to rely on the antiquated defence of her husband's coercion – especially if single! – an entire raft of responses constrained the female offender in male-styled expectations. In short, he placed her so high on a pedestal, just to watch her fall off.

Domestic Confinement

Perhaps one of history's singular displeasures at this contemptible notion – other than the non-emancipation of women itself – were her living conditions constructed by men; in short, her domestic confinement.

Contemporary colossi like Florence Nightingale, Mary Wollstonecraft and *Frankenstein's* Mary Shelley (Wollstonecraft's daughter) have long since been joined by a rousing chorus of outraged modern sisters (to be fair, also brothers); that not only did it limit a woman's already restricted outlook in life, it created an emotional cell in her physical prison.

Threat and violence had often kept the spirit subdued, but worse were the expectations of being a good wife and a mother. And those who sought an alternative path were tossed aside or pulled 'into line'. If the home wasn't enough, then asylums were used. As an increasingly recognised source of all emotional ills it was perhaps here though, in domestic confinement, that mental responses were born of utter frustration; and which led to pandemics and terror for the Victorian male. The rise of hysteria was perhaps the greatest expression, caused by pressures from without and expectations within. For now the matrimonial home was conjoined by the masculine statehood; both husband and government gathered round her dismay.

As the feminist Charlotte Perkins Gilman confirmed in 1898, resulting mental conditions came as no great surprise:

> 'It is not that women are really smaller-minded, weaker-minded, more timid and vacillating, but that whosoever, man or woman, *lives always in a small, dark place, is always guarded, protected, directed and restrained*, will become inevitably narrowed and weakened by it. The woman is narrowed by the home...' before adding with great insight: 'and the man is narrowed by the woman.'[40]

Griffin has more recently spoken of 'gender panic', when even traditional biological divides were called into question, typically during events such as war. That led to women stepping in as much-needed labour, creating new perceived strains on their powers. Men yet again awaited her fall.[41] However, the 'panic' Griffin spoke of occurred at the end of the 1700s, and the American War of Independence that she said brought cataclysmic effects. Her ground-breaking theory was interestingly simple: that the feeling for men at the loss of their nation led them to fear an entire collapse of their familiar lives. It left those responsible for society's morals, that is the men, facing an unwelcome lifestyle no longer so safe. While underpinning it all came the 'home and the hearth'. His domestic household – and his wife's place within it – became his much needed retreat, his very castle and home.[42]

While through modern eyes we see the startling sexism in such a patriarchal solution, many still contend that the women of the time were not wholly against the arrangement. If the sequels that saw women and girls locked away in asylums, and even more in their parlours, had at once been imagined, such tacit agreement may not have occurred.

Other modern scholars have separately presented the role of religion in domestic confinement, cementing gendered roles through the masculine church. 'Men were seen as better able to cope with the [world's] trials [in] the public sphere, while women were supposed to maintain [family] purity by remaining in the private sphere, where they could create a domestic environment in which…religion could prosper'.[43]

Added to potential statehood disorder and religious endorsement, the rapidly industrialising country brought its own societal threats. 'The cultural value attached to the home [now] increased, because it [offered] "the emotional and psychological supports which made working life tolerable".'[44]

Private imprisonment was thus being played out, and its impact on women's minds, emotions and freedoms were being increasingly felt. But as a new century dawned, the 'feebler female brain' began to wreak havoc, as women caught on to the notion they possessed far more power than they had been led to believe. At the same time, fear was employed to quell a female rebellion, and her 'wayward' mental condition was restated to suppress those seeking change.

The loudest expression, of course, came from the suffragette movement, synonymous with women obtaining the vote but revealing so much more about the female plight: an absence of liberties taken for granted by men, and the abuses and bedlam for raising their voice.

Enlightened Voices

Several masculine voices, however, had of course dared to speak out; the humanised few like Pearson and Mill. The latter especially had caused uproar in Victorian circles and, though much wider in scope than the insanity subject, the ghost of proclaimed female madness was seldom far from his thoughts. In many ways far ahead of his time, Mill[45] called for an alteration in the very marriage arrangement, and to the attitudes that were subjecting wives (and daughters) to domestic control:

'The true virtue of human beings is fitness to live together as equals…regarding command of any kind as an exceptional necessity, and in all cases a temporary one; and preferring, whenever possible, the society of those with whom leading and following can be alternate and reciprocal. However, the family is a school of despotism, in which the virtues of despotism, but also its vices, are largely nourished. Citizenship, in free countries, is partly a school of society in equality; but citizenship fills only a small place in modern life, and does not come near the daily habits or inmost sentiments.'

It read as a lamentable truth. But hope was at hand:

'The family, justly constituted, would be the real school of the virtues of freedom. It is sure to be a sufficient one of everything else. It will always be a school of obedience for the children, of command for the parents. What is needed is, that it should be a school of sympathy in equality, of living together in love, without power on one side or obedience on the other.'

There was no greater expression of this latent abuse than the sickening misuse of medical sanction and locking away 'errant' women – from the home and the hearth, she was transferred to that fake institution the asylum, a move which relied on fabricated mental 'complaints'.

A (Very) Brief History of Madness

On this devilishly difficult path to a diagnosis of madness, I start here with some general observations about non-gendered fears. Porter believed insanity to be a cultural response to 'The Other'; not just a medical diagnosis, but a condition arising from solely socio-cultural 'norms'.[46] As Dr Johnson said, 'madness was not unequivocal but an existential hazard of living in the world of opinion.'[47] Contemporary influences on defining and responding to madness were thus never confined to one period in time. Great similarities were seen between different eras, far more regularly than modern minds perhaps care for. The seventeenth century, for example, owed much to the Galenic and Hippocratic beliefs two thousand years before.

Hippocrates, the fourth/fifth century BCE Greek, and nominated 'father of Western medicine', identified the four humours (fluids) that he thought made up the human condition: black and yellow bile (from the spleen and gall, respectively), phlegm (from the brain) and the ubiquitous blood (from the heart). The disorder of each, singularly or together, spelt danger not just for the patient but for those touched by her ails.

The individual's temperament too, Galen in particular claimed, was forged from the relative strength of these humours. And by Tuke's time, in the nineteenth century, it was said that such temperaments and characteristics could be 'read' in a patient's physical features: including body shape, head shape, even the colour of their eyes,[48] leading to a physical smörgåsbord of potential insanity.

Thus, those sanguine and laid back were often short, with small bones, red-haired and blue-eyed. They were flighty, imaginative and, as a result, more open-minded, but equally open to madness. The nerve-jangled fretters, (melancholiacs) meanwhile, possessed large foreheads and pointed, angular features. Restless and changeable in mind, they were sensitive yet unreliable – and 'particularly [prone] to insanity, especially mania.' The cholerical were stocky, short, dark in features and perhaps so in thoughts. Their memory was long and, though typically calm, their passions erupted given the right provocation. Though little suspected of suffering madness, 'the question of the connection between temperament and insanity has never been adequately gone into.' Finally, the phlegmatic, who appeared to attract the least favourable assessment. Described as disproportionately constructed, thick of the arm and thick in the head, they were an unemotional cart-horse more than an excitable filly. Any mental decay was likely to appear as long-term dementia, rather than an acute disruption of fragile senses.[49]

Of the four humours involved, each was thus blamed for varying mental conditions. Black bile from the spleen left the individual prone to depression. An excess of phlegm was virtually expected in sixteenth and seventeenth century women, who 'by nature…[were] more phlegmatic, cold and wet… [yet] more susceptible to sudden [albeit short-lived] emotions'. They were also 'especially vulnerable to…pride, envy, detraction and inconstancy.'[50] Yellow bile, or choler, made the sufferer potentially violent, while an excess of blood – supposedly produced in the heart – left the patient more sanguine.

Even toward the end of the Victorian era, little more had emerged about blood's role in the creation of madness. Considered to affect that perceived seat of disrupted behaviour, the higher nervous centres to be found in the brain,[51] it was more corrupted in melancholia than in mania, though likely not as much as in cases of general paralysis, the latter especially in men. And in women's puerperal insanity, haemoglobin was found to be severely diminished.

Nerve complications from the woman's catamenial function provoked the perceived value of tonics in improving the blood ... though the remedies 'of choice' included not just iron and quinine, but strychnine, the dangerous poison.[52]

Then there was the brain itself, that critical organ for controlling emotions, one's reason and personal thought. From owning such a radical purpose, its perceived nature as susceptible to the disarranged humours was perhaps unsurprising:

> 'It is quite impossible to imagine any subjective condition or state
> of consciousness [set] apart from the brain, and there is no reason
> to doubt that throughout the whole nervous system the same action
> takes place from the simplest reflex act to the highest and most
> complex cortical process, but why some actions like the latter should
> be attended by consciousness and others not, it is very difficult to
> explain.'[53]

Predicting the likelihood of brain madness became a constant obsession. Definitive statements by Victorian alienists on issues such as the weight of the brain concluded insanity occurred in those that were lighter, while others saw exactly the same in the heavier ones. It seemingly depended on the alienist in question, and their nature of study, rather than the object itself and how much it weighed.[54]

Understanding the functions of the brain's cortex helped decipher which inner areas elicited an uncontrolled response in movement. Though this does not really address the present issue of defining disarranged thought – for example, one can be paralysed and think, just as one can be unthinking and mobile – nonetheless, it prompted Laycock into formulating his Treatise on the Nervous Diseases of Women in 1840.[55] His 'theory of reflex action...first applied to explain cerebral processes'[56] sat alongside that of another alienist, James Cowles Prichard, and his notion of irresistible impulse and the even thornier issue of the loss of free will.[57]

The jurist, Sir James Fitzjames Stephen, was typically opaque on the matter:

> 'In order that an act may be [accountable] it must be a voluntary act done by a person free from certain forms of compulsion.'[58]

In other words, it was possible to be considered insane even when a delusion or compulsion was not shown to be present.

A loss of reason (for example discussed by the seventeenth century cleric, Robert Burton)[59] caused an aberration of will, so that the imagination no longer exerted controlling forces which left the delusionary patient to believe what they thought. While Burton's own instrument of passions – the same imagination, or fancy – could be seen, others argued, in that century's witch-hunts in which alleged cavorting with Satan was in fact all in the minds of those making such claims.

In the 1700s too, grave concerns about dreaming meant it became a 'reasonable' fear, that they could in extremis lead to the loss of one's reason:

> 'A commonly cited example of this harm was the reputed power of imagination in women, either at the instant of conception or when pregnant, to "impress" whatever preoccupied their mind upon... their unborn [infant]. A woman who imagined ("conceived") a monster would indeed give birth to a deformed child.'[60]

What mattered most was how her resulting behaviour could be explained or excused. Near-farcical debates about irresistible versus unresisted impulse surfaced in a number of topics, especially criminal trials via the insanity plea.[61] It frequently featured in those cases involving the so-called 'much weaker'; in terms of the mind, this was usually women. An oft-cited example were those cases of murder which arose from lost love that had destroyed her weak reason. The male experts had a number to call on:

> 'In other cases – *female irregularities for instance* – individuals hitherto perfectly sane and in the full possession of their intellects are suddenly and without any assignable cause seized with the most anxious and painful emotions, and with a homicidal impulse as inexplicable to themselves as to others.'[62]

The same author cited a particular case:

> 'A lady...much tempted to the commission of crimes under this
> form of disease said that every act of violence whether in word or
> deed perpetrated on her children or those around her afforded her
> considerable relief.'[63]

How such impulses related to overpowering the will remained a debated
conundrum, as too the ongoing debates on will and volition, which even
today remain unresolved.

So much for the brain and Hippocrates' humours. Half a millennium later,
his countryman, Galen, adapted his theories, producing his own, more
pluralistic ideas. Thus this pioneer of anatomical dissection (on animals,
never on humans), disclosed various physical aspects such as how urine passed
through the kidneys (not just the bladder, as previously thought); how blood
was arterial (though its circulatory system was only discovered by Harvey
some 1600 years later); and, of significance here, mental (psychological)
disorders had a physicalist cause. In other words, the physical brain, hosting
the mind, could well be corrupted by illness or passion, leading to disordered
thoughts.

Such theories remained, by and large, well-received and acted upon as
unquestionable facts. Not until the seventeenth century at least was there
a critical change and, in Britain, it came from a small handful of 'experts';
including a particular trio: Thomas Willis, John Locke, and the poet,
polymath and royal physician, Richard Blackmore.

Thomas Willis, also a royal physician, to King Charles I, became the mid-
century expounder of nervous disorders, discarding deep-rooted humoral
theory for something far more prosaic – a disordered gut.

> 'By which he accounts for all these effects [disarranged thoughts], by
> the good or bad disposition of a leven or ferment;...while it remains
> in a regular state, is a great assistant and refiner of the...spirits, and
> when it is perverted, and becomes too sowre and austere,...[is] the
> chief, if not the sole cause of hypochondriacal symptoms.'[64]

Perhaps of even greater importance was his belief that the nerves rising up
through the spine and into the brain were the thing causing distress. Thus,
his conjecture on this neuroanatomy subdivided further his 'new' host

for nervous well-being, into these discrete areas of function: perception, imagination, instinct; as well as the vital centres and memory too. The brain housed it all, but the nerves made it work. And nervous disorders were ravaged with danger; as the science of neurology was finally born.[65] If only he had adopted moral therapy so quickly, instead of advising the beating with sticks as a cure for the mad.

John Locke, meanwhile, is regarded still as the grandfather of human 'experience', and the 'father of liberalism' and Enlightenment thinking.[66] He favoured a less mechanistic dissection of the mind-brain conjunction and replaced it instead with the concepts of learned behaviour and the innate (often flawed) responses to external command (stimuli). Enabled through his 'new' notion of the senses, and raising intuition (feeling) above reason (thought), he made human existence ever more fluid – and at last free to perform how it chose, for better or worse. From this, he observed, flawed thinking was what lay behind madness. He was strident particularly on matters of religion. His anti-Creationist stance, for example, freed the human spirit (for example, from the debilitating concept of Original Sin), and left humankind in a perpetual, individualistic balance. Yet if we were all meant to stand on our own two feet, who would be there (in seventeenth century England) to catch those who fell, women especially?

What too of judgements of value – if every man (and woman) were an island of thoughts, values and personal responses, who but God had the right to condemn? Locke believed he had the answer: 'A fool is he that from right principles makes a wrong conclusion; but a madman is one who draws a just inference from false principles...'[67] It was a neat dialectic, coming decades before those Victorian struggles that brought the M'Naghten Rules and the 'right-wrong' test.

Of these current three greats, Richard Blackmore came last, informed and influenced by the earlier two, as he took up their mantle. Accepting Willis' disrupted digestion, he extended its effect to the human mental condition:

> 'If the juices....contained in any of the bowels, degenerate, and become immoderately acid, sharp, pungent and austere, they urge and vellicate [grate on the senses, as fingernails on a blackboard] the nerves so much, and irritate and scatter the spirits in such a violent manner, that the whole intellectual and [physical] administration is violated and disturbed, while the mind is deprived of proper instruments for its operations.'[68]

He was thus paving the way for George Cheyne's definition of the fraught and delicate nerves, that suffered from indolence and reflected poor diet. But much more of this later.

Medieval Possession

There was, of course, an intervening hiatus between Galen and Willis – the unenlightened Middle Ages. Though (relatively) little is known about their responses to women and madness, one facet dominated the wondering mind: religion. Adopting superstition into a new pantheon of fear and loathing, the church became the dominant force in shaping the human condition. 'The Other' now became defined in relation to two fundamental beliefs; the Bible spoke truth, and errant behaviour was a 'crime' against God. In particular, a woman displaying unnatural behaviour, such as trembling, ranting and generally 'out of the ordinary' was deemed to have 'fallen'; she had succumbed to the Devil. Claims of medieval possession became a popular response to the clinically mad.

As a woman, considered more venal and volatile by nature, holding on to but all of her faculties spelt grave danger not just for the victim but for society at large. Underpinning it all was Original Sin, the creator of which was, of course, the first woman herself. As Eve misled Adam with forbidden fruit from the tree, women were thereafter condemned to suffer, including the pain that she felt bringing life into the world.

As Porter observed, for those failing to meet God's pure expectations, a human scapegoat was needed, which connected the mad with the Devil; 'the infidel, witches, Jews' all suffered condemnation; to which 'women' themselves were too easily added. Such early delineations of the human condition made it impossible to achieve anything but failure when one tried to live life as the Almighty intended. And it brought an unanswerable question; had Eve caused all Man to fail, so that all were but hopeless, or could the race attain redemption by observing His way? The latter left those suffering madness, in the Middle Ages especially, to be controlled not by their condition, but as profane, empty vessels possessed by Satan himself.[69]

From such a pitiless position, the tradition of beating the crazy was an almost inevitable 'cure': an exercise in literally thrashing out Evil. Incarceration and other abuses joined a panoply of brutal responses, so that the unruly, debased, unexpectedly violent could, as Willis insisted, 'be tamed only by a mixture of discipline and depletion, measures designed to put down 'the raging of the Spirits and the lifting up of the Soul.'[70] In the simplest terms, the mad were possessed because they had not the wit to resist the Devil's temptations: good or evil thus equated to being sane or mad.[71] In this, demonomania took life. And who more susceptible to hosting the Devil than that cause of the problem, those descendants of Eve.

Ousting Satan became paramount as a reaction to madness. Religious mania and the lesser known cacodemonomania (believing oneself to be possessed of the Devil and thus fearing perdition)[72] soon developed as self-help deterrents. Even the neurologist and social campaigner, Horatio Donkin, writing on hysteria some three hundred years later, emphasised the medieval approach to handling the insane: 'when these sciences [of understanding madness] were chapters in theology, it was consistent to regard hysteria as demoniacal possession.'[73]

From this medieval maelstrom, it became a regrettably short hop to those post-medieval obsessions: witches, witchcraft and the resulting patriarchal victimisation:

'The mad or those deemed to have cast spells on them to distraction might find themselves caught up in the mania for witch-hunting that periodically erupted in one community or another in a credulous Europe, and then they risked being cast into the flames. Thousands perished, and though by no means all witches were mentally ill (or those blamed for fomenting mental illness), still ancient folk beliefs about madness and possession...always created that danger.'[74]

Whether or not joining the crusade against such gender control, physicians and sceptics Johannes Weir (Johann Weyer) and Reginald Scot became sixteenth century trail-blazers for 'Reason'; condemning the notion of possession as a frightening mask placed on the face of enlightened psychiatry. The 'possessed' were in fact ill, and 'in need not of the faggot but of medication'.[75] Arnold has recently argued such a change manifested in the trial of the self-confessed (but disbelieved) 'witch' Ade Davie, whose judge at her trial, the same Reginald Scot, proffered a diagnosis of madness over any presence of witchcraft. He decried her belief as 'contrarie to reason, scripture and nature', and suggested instead that delusions and melancholia were her two separate and legitimate afflictions.[76] To avoid any doubt, he spelled out his misgivings in everyday language:

'If our witches phantasies were no corrupted, nor their wits confounded with this humour [melancholia], they would not so volutarilie and readilie confess that which calleth their life in question.'[77]

Richard Napier, astrologer-medic at the turn of the seventeenth century, was typically (though not always) inclined to agree. Recounting his numerous female patients who feared madness in the face of Devilish onslaught, worst of all was when Satan appeared disguised as a woman.[78]

According to Macdonald's analysis, Napier's records further suggested demonic possession per se was by then not so widespread, but in the seventeenth century's first quarter 'many ordinary villagers' still feared the Devil. Preachers and writers retained their conviction that Satan caused crippling ailments, and madness as well.[79] Even Napier himself recorded disproportionate numbers of insanity cases as the result of supposed Devilish illness, or possession or that new-fangled notion, enchantment by witches.

Even self-accusations of witchcraft plagued many of Napier's patients. And it wrought new means of controlling if not truly mad, then 'unruly' women.[80] As witchcraft and persecution became a predictable outcome, many have much later contended it was again nothing more than gender control.

It can be further conjectured that these constructed, variable factors created a dualism of states, as it defined as it were the Early Modern viewpoint of madness:[81]

Religious	:	**Supernatural**
Divine	:	Diabolical
Good	:	Evil
Normal	:	Abnormal
Sane	:	Insane

To which could be added:

Male	:	Female

Post-Medieval Witchcraft

'An epidemic terror seized upon the nations; no man thought himself secure, either in his person or possessions, from the machinations of the devil and his agents. Every calamity that befell him he attributed to a witch. If a storm arose and blew down his barn, it was witchcraft; if his cattle died of a murrain—if disease fastened upon his limbs, or death entered suddenly and snatched a beloved face from his hearth—they were not visitations of Providence, but the works of some neighbouring hag, whose wretchedness *or insanity* caused the ignorant to raise their finger and point at her as a witch.'[82]

Extending the dark medieval view of the female sex, many have since lauded the modern 'psychiatric "exposure" of witchcraft' as 'a typical patriarchal tactic for neutralizing a bastion of female power'.[83] Certain opinion on witch-hunts recorded the masculine need to rid itself of the powerful female,[84] no doubt inventing the precarious nature of her biological make-up to establish their view. Perhaps unlike any other historical era, with the possible exception of nineteenth century Britain, the witch persecutions that bedevilled a regressive seventeenth century sunk misogyny and terror to its unpleasant nadir.

A long while before, during the reign of Henry VIII, it was the law-making king who issued the first known statute with pertinent sanction:

'to practise or cause to be practised conjuration, witchcraft, enchantment or sorcery, to get money; or to consume any person in his body, members, or goods; or to provoke any person to unlawful love; or for any other unlawful purpose; or for the despite of Christ or lucre of money dig up or pull down any cross, or to declare where goods stolen be.'[85]

Though later repealed by his son, Edward VI, without a single case having ever been brought, it set out a growing fear that would erupt a century later, and into which were dragged those further unfortunate victims, the female insane. King James I (VI of Scotland) – *the* regal witch-finder general – forbade the insanity plea being made at the trials of witches. 'It is hardly necessary to say,' wrote Tuke, 'that the treatment of the unfortunate lunatics and epileptics who were judged to be witches by James I was nothing else than death, and he thus coolly comments on this punishment: "It is commonly used by fire, but that is an indifferent thing to be used in every country according to the law or custom thereof".'[86]

As the Crown had supplanted the Church as the nation's chief holder of power, the previous possession obsession was replaced with a belief in the conjuring witch. One of 'three instances in which matters long considered as being only ecclesiastical offences were made felony by statute – a small but significant effect of the Reformation…conjuration, witchcraft, and sorcery or enchantment.'[87] And as this was more likely to affect innocent women, it was easy to foretell how that gender would fare.

Their persecution was now claimed to have Biblical sanction: 'Thou shall not suffer a witch to live' (Exodus 22:19). The common Witch-finder General, and probable sadist Matthew Hopkins took it to new heinous, hanging extremes. The persecutor's own holy treatise, the *Malleus Maleficarum*, had appeared some decades before in 1486. Contrived by the Catholic paranoid sadist, Heinrich Kramer,[88] it was quickly adopted by violent extremists who sought scholarly sanction for tearing out 'female sin'.

Thus, these witches (women) were not mad, they were wicked; though they knew how to bestow insanity on those their balefulness sought. A catholic array of mental afflictions thought to be caused by a witch included melancholia, and epilepsy – though the latter was also acknowledged to 'arise from some long-standing physical predisposition or defect.'[89] Some two hundred of Napier's patients even *named* witches, as those responsible for bringing on the mental disturbance with which they then suffered.[90]

But were these accused 'creatures' truly possessed, performing Satan's malevolent wishes? Or were they suffering a malady far more prosaic? Were they, in fact, mentally ill? In grasping how the mad were being tortured for consorting with Satan prompted Tuke's much later assessment:

> 'It is indeed impossible to read the narratives of some of the unfortunate hags who were put to death for witchcraft, without recognizing the well-marked features of the victims of cerebral disorder'.[91]

Some modern academics have argued, offering greater or lesser endorsement, that the majority of those accused of witchcraft were indeed suffering mental disorders – hysteria and epilepsy especially, hence the frothing mouth and body convulsions. The higher propensity for women to become the accused was thus founded on two troublesome organs: the womb and the spleen (men, of course, possessing only the latter).[92]

Such hysteric connections have since been exposed by Scull in his clinical judgement. The American doyen highlights the case of one Elizabeth Jackson, charged with bewitching her quarrelsome neighbour, young Mary Glover, producing hysterical fits, starvation and blindness which lasted weeks upon end. Her succour at court was Edward Jorden, Royal College Physician, who testified that Glover's symptoms were real but that they were never the product of witchcraft. Unable to decipher its cause and denying the court (and Glover) a diagnosed treatment – how could he have done otherwise, the condition itself was not yet deciphered – Jackson was regardless convicted and sentenced to suffer her time in the stocks.[93]

Though she was later reprieved through the efforts of other, more influential supporters, Jorden felt driven to put his quill to some parchment and set about teaching the masses of his controversial beliefs; Glover's condition was not bewitchment, it was his own, newly labelled, 'Suffocation of the Mother' - akin to hysteria, the later century's curse. And women, he said, were more susceptible to attacks of this sort.[94]

Even as late as the late 1960s, esteemed academic criminologist, Nigel Walker, supported this case, 'mental illness…[incurring] reprisals from an unenlightened community'; believing those accused of being witches had suffered mental affliction; that they were 'unfortunates merely suggestible to the point of hysteria' or 'wished and believed themselves to have supernatural powers' and whose schizophrenia 'alarmed their neighbours and whose distortions of reality confirmed their reputation for dealings with the supernatural'.[95]

So too the 'incantations' and 'spells' from these self-proclaimed witches, which were dismissed as nothing but mistaken delusions.[96] The witch's confession – for so long a sign of discovered possession – became instead a symptom of the accused's melancholic beliefs. Not that the past had always agreed. Richard Napier, practising at the start of the witchcraft obsession, might well have rejected possession as causing individual madness, but he still saw a 'truth' in his patients' insistence that unrestrained witchcraft was making them ill. 'Very few accused witches were insane [even] by contemporary standards or our own', wrote Macdonald.[97] Yet despite rejecting the reality of witchcraft as a symptom of madness, some thirty per cent of Napier's patients who claimed to have been touched had, to modern eyes, certain mental conditions.[98]

What betrayed Napier's and others' inconsistent reactions was how he continued to resort to the occult to heal these 'supernatural' complaints. These included alchemy, casting horoscopes and 'conjuring up Archangel Raphael'. Nor was he averse to using amulets and potions to cure those with mental afflictions; the women (and men) who had attempted suicide, or who had turned their back on church teachings, led to numerous correspondents begging he 'engrave sigils for them when they were melancholy or anxious'.[99]

While the fact that so many of his patients were supposedly 'bewitched' women comes today as perhaps no great surprise. After all, during the Hopkinsian outrage, women were believed easier to bewitch by virtue of their 'inferior mental judgement'.[100]

Definitions of madness, just as with witchcraft and even Satanic possession, were still being shaped by prevailing thoughts and ideas. 'Contemporary social conditions and popular religion exerted a powerful influence on beliefs about insanity and methods for caring for the insane', observed Macdonald.[101] And tragic consequences followed its rejection in favour of bewitchment.

Take the case of Mistress Paul, who was 'tormented with a strange disease and pain that taketh her by fits…in such violent sort that you would think she would presently be plucked in pieces'. Or Mary Morgan, who was 'strangely taken out of her bed and thrice cast down to the ground.'[102] Whether Napier treated them as bewitched or mad remains a moot point. Certainly, 'many of the devices and prayers [Napier] used were meant specifically to be effective against both mental illnesses and the malevolence of demons and witches.'[103]

At length, witchcraft as a concept began to subside and with it, for a short time at least, the persecution of the insane and the woman. Its breakdown attracted competing explanations and included a secular medicalisation away from church teachings ahead of the increased reasoning of the Enlightenment and Victorian ages. Though this was not necessarily for the betterment of either the 'witch' or the mad as old ways died hard.[104]

Macdonald has shown how renewed religious enthusiasm (as Anglicans overrode the Puritan wave) rigorously rejected such supernatural nonsense. It led to a more empirical insanity replacing possession and witchcraft. As time marched further on, demoniac beliefs were reworked as themselves proof of 'a certain sign of madness.'[105]

It left an unpalatable view of the pre-modern woman, one which much later voices were loud to disgrace. The playwright, Joanna Baillie for example, in her 1836 play appropriately entitled *Witchcraft*, revealed a biological determinism as the misogynist's means of controlling female subversives, though whether their non-conformity rose from such persecution, or was its unacceptable cause, is another long-argued point.

The last conviction for witchcraft in the United Kingdom occurred not, as is popularly agreed, in 1712 of Jane Wenham, the famed Witch of Walkern. It was in fact some four years later, when mother and daughter, Mary and Elizabeth Hicks, the latter just nine years old, were hanged at Huntingdon, Cambridgeshire for calling up storms and ruining crops.

While in the second volume alone of Stephen's *History of the Criminal Law of England* (1883), no less than a staggering 120 cases were mentioned in just five short pages.[106] Yet this too barely scratched the surface.

One of the last executions in Scotland, meanwhile, did not come until 1722 and is of such great importance to the present discussion that it is repeated here verbatim through the following record:

> 'We find [the]...sheriff-depute of Caithness very active...in another trial for witchcraft. In spite of the warning he had received that all such cases were to be tried in future by the superior courts, he condemned to death an old woman at Dornoch, upon the charge of bewitching the cows and pigs of her neighbours. *This poor creature was insane, and actually laughed and clapped her hands at sight of 'the bonnie fire' that was to consume her.* She had a daughter who was lame both of her hands and feet, and one of the charges brought against her was, that she had used this daughter as a pony in her excursions to join the devil's sabbath, and that the devil himself had shod her, and produced lameness.'[107]

As religious intolerance waned, and Enlightenment waxed, the much-maligned, feared witch became the pitied old crone.[108] No longer capable of spoiling the crops or raising the Devil, the mad woman was after all nought but a weakling in need of masculine strength. From religion to the more secular ages, control of 'The Other' – be it lunatic, woman or typically both – became the predominant aim of a still fearful age.[109]

Cheyne and Nerves

The witchcraft furore had been sandwiched between post-humoral figures, like Willis and Locke, and the new Georgian sensation, George Cheyne. It was his later radical theories that eked out the nerves as the root of all evil. Through his magnum opus, 'The *English Malady*', published in 1733, Cheyne concluded the real causes of madness were the corruption of fragile and over-stretched nerves, brought on by idle indulgence and immoral lives. In this instant best-seller, he cited wealth, diet and too much spare time as the *curse extraordinaire* of eighteenth century society's gloomy. Defining melancholia as the illness of 'rich' tastes, he ascribed both status and class to an attack of the nerves, tapping into an emerging belief, not in the wayward organs (of women especially), but of the fragile nerves (of women especially!).

And it gave rise to such expressive examples as the writer Jane Austen. This was *the* age of nervous decay.

Even as Cheynian thought supplanted humoral medicine, a new holistic definition of madness had been drafted, that linked body and brain. Now a *physical* defect only could disorder the brain, from which all thoughts flowed, but where blame ultimately fell was the overstretched nerves. As Cheyne confessed: 'Warped nerves – those "bundles of *solid*, *springy* and *elastick* threads or filaments (like twisted catguts or hairs)" - explained warped thought.'[110]

In fact, he had seen the importance of the brain in experiencing such matters, citing his clients' displeasing traits to convey his disdain: 'Nervous distempers [are] under some form of disgrace'; regarded as 'a lower degree of lunacy'; or at the very least, in effect, 'put on'. Unknowingly predicting the following century's hysteria obsession, he addressed women's suffering in particular as: 'whim, ill-humour, peevishness…and in the [female] sex, daintiness, fantasticalness, or coquetry.'[111]

His female targets, however, could now be forgiven for smelling a sizeable and chauvinist rat. With the physical brain outwitting the ethereal mind and bringing with it new and strange (not to mention disturbing) responses, one of the notion's early adopters was not a psychiatrist but an obstetrician. William Smoult Playfair, a fervent supporter of Weir Mitchell's 'rest cure', proclaimed in the crudest possible terms that women especially suffered from various 'ailments' that, *after all*, were all in the mind. But there were more insults to come. Women were, according to Playfair, also physically weaker, and more susceptible to illness, and through their corruptible minds were freshly primed powder-kegs set to go off. In short, they were definitely not men!

Thus the Georgian malaise, like the humours before them, introduced a new danger for women, as the label of the moist, weaker sex began to take hold. In the two centuries that followed, in so many ways just another cruel era, female suffering – from invented conditions and hideous 'cures' – would descend to new lows.

Meanwhile, Cheyne's approach was one of the first to advise on the *prevention* of madness, not simply its cure. A pivotal 'free-thinker', he advocated moderation in all things, and a total avoidance of others. Remembered today for his vegetarian diet, his was a gargantuan hypocrisy for a man who once weighed *thirty-two* stones and matched only by the scale of his own sense of self-loathing.[112]

Throughout the next two hundred years, in Britain at least, the role of the nerves in madness remained a much-discussed point. Ailments like neurasthenia and hysteria shaped a generation of (mis)understanding and, of course, with it more male control. Even modern historians have often fared little better, in grasping the nettle, being 'particularly intrigued by these "functional" diseases...for they seem to show most clearly the cultural, social, and ideological factors which influence definitions and perceptions of disease and constrain the behaviour of both patients and their doctors.' Such diseases however, with resulting annoyance, lacked any physical disruption to be seen under the scope or a knife; 'physical symptoms predominated but... evidence for structural derangement was lacking'. And they set the trap for a classic example – the hysterical condition.[113]

Emotional collapse without such structural disorder was seized on by Thomas Trotter, a Scottish naval physician and ardent slavery abolitionist. In the would-be Age of Enlightenment, he devised the nervous condition from which women were far more likely to suffer and which could be 'blamed' for two-thirds of their multiple ills. Indirectly at least, he had re-opened the doorway to the 'unstable woman'.

Just a few decades later, Laycock and others manipulated this 'wisdom' *viz.* the brain and its disrupted control of physical actions. Creating his own exposition on the higher *voluntary* system and the lower *in*voluntary sector of everyone's brain, he devised the controversial exculpation of illicit behaviour which Prichard had alleged to be caused by an irresistible impulse.[114] Laycock was, in point of fact, defining a loss of the will, or the controlling volition – today remembered as his 'greatest' theoretical stance and since adopted by many.

His shared contemporary focus, however, was exposed in his much-admired treatise, 'fittingly' headed *A Treatise on The Nervous Diseases of Women*, published in 1840. In it, he highlighted nervous disorders of both the uterus and ovaries and spasm-inducing conditions like chorea (St Vitus's Dance), typically seen in hysteria *and* epilepsy, and equally mishandled, both being symptomatic conditions of nervous decay.[115]

Now another much-favoured misogynist mantra was quickly rolled out: that the weaker, more volatile woman would pass on her 'phancies' to her as yet unborn child. Her innate weakness created conditions like 'depraved' imaginings (dreaming) and somnambulism (sleep-walking), which both lay behind automatist action. They not infrequently led to the worst possible outcomes, even the committing of murder. It read like a throwback to the dark days of medieval 'possession'.[116] The discriminatory mind, this time the observer's not the afflicted, was something a certain 1950s French philosopher was quick to decry.

Foucault's Folly

Since the Middle Ages, the insane had been licensed to roam, much as the lepers were, to serve as a warning to the ill-living and the idle of mind. The now somewhat discredited Michel Foucault devised his own proposition of earlier madness, in which he wrote of the 'Great Confinement' of the seventeenth and eighteenth century's mad. This post-witch 'Age of Reason', as he chose to define it, featured his famed 'Ship of Fools' that carried 'The Other' on their perpetual journey, designed solely to keep them apart from the 'sane'.[117]

Prior to change, these unwanted outcasts had, in reality, been cast into gaols, Bridewells and prisons; a far cry from the preceding Tudor and Early Stuart eras when, according to Porter, there had been no real motive for interning the mad.[118] But under France's King Louis XIV (1638-1715), all would now alter. And it was he who introduced the notion of the non-itinerant madman, constructing great asylums into which the hare-brained were shelved. It was simply this that Foucault detested the most. It was, he argued, anathema to Reason, a system of brutalization that had never existed before. And he labelled them not as hospitals, or centres of respite, but as prisons disguised as something humane. Nonetheless, where Louis had led, an industrialised Europe would follow, removing the 'socially inept' from the new-ordered world, when trade, wealth and progress meant the 'driftwood' of nations were no longer set free.

Foucault's stark assessment has, in many ways, since been rejected. Porter, for example, saw a much more gradual confinement, using the private madhouses, workhouses and prisons since much earlier times. It was, he contended, enacted on a parochial basis, open to local abuses rather than the checks from a state-wide institutionalization.[119] Nonetheless, its impact on the victim was surely one and the same.

But two major concerns emerge from this divided opinion. Firstly, it highlights the dangers of looking backwards at all – every piece of modern opinion contains a political message, a personal agenda. 'Championing or demonising the past can easily serve modern agendas'.[120]

Secondly, all opinion is in any case judgement; what one era found unacceptable, another found sense. To paraphrase Scull, just how bizarre did one have to be before the madness label applied? 'As we shall see,' he wrote, 'social responses to madness, our interpretations of what madness is, and our notions of what is to be done about it, have varied remarkably over the centuries.'[121]

A classic example was the hysteria 'epidemic' of nineteenth century Europe. Though the term had existed since Hippocrates' humours, its 1800s explosion raised the contagion to new political heights. Was it the misogynist's proof of the unstable woman, or a genuine malady of the female mad? Was it, in fact, a condition at all or, as Barnes had conjectured, was it merely a symptom of something more grand; menstrual nerves? Howsoever defined, whether seen as an illness or simply 'put on' as an appeal for freedom, it commands the start of the following section; to what conditions exactly could the mad female succumb?

Finally here, even the more traditional response, of family members serving as full-time attendants for their 'sub-normal' relations, soon ceased to be an acceptable, modern day course. Not when they could be helping the burgeoning state, whether by going to work or rearing its next generation. What is more, as the mad themselves could not work, it was best for all if they were simply removed to a (low-cost), out-of-sight centre.

Diagnosing Female Madness

Many modern-day lists of past female conditions often include just the familiar few, hysteria, puerperal insanity and nymphomania amongst them. Yet the truth was more varied, diagnoses more nuanced. Before we proceed, it is first vital to establish the context in which such conditions were sited. That most basic assessment: of being a woman.

Numerous and fruitless attempts to secure a safe definition of female madness, and to agree on its treatment, revealed a pantheon of tasteless, often ineffective diagnoses and manufactured responses:

> 'Attitudes towards madness were never an island. They complemented wider images of self, rationality and social health, and they interacted with changing evaluations of such comparable groups of *threateningly marginal* individuals as slaves, witches and foreigners.'[122]

To which could be added, women.

It was this latest assembly that were forever feared most. The nineteenth century medical world 'took the view that merely to be in possession of a cervix predisposed one to insanity',[123] and it led to some 'accepted' women's conditions. Chief amongst them was the hysterical female, when Hippocrates' 'wandering womb' achieved its renaissance.

Conditions more broadly defined were aligned with declared female weakness – e.g. melancholia, described (in all seriousness) as being caused by 'lost love' and probably arising from *emotional or gynaecological weakness... an erotomaniac's lot*.[124]

When it came down to deciding whether someone was mad, being a woman brought its own unique definition. Since time immemorial, on account of her biological make-up and perceived weaker morals, the She of the race had suffered unfettered treatment at the hands of the He. Porter, citing naturalist Sir Joseph Banks (1743-1820), captured several aspects of this masculine thought: 'he [Banks] *diagnosed* his wife "a little old china mad", *considerately* adding, however, "but she wishes to mix as much reason with her madness as possible".'[125] With female madness, from defining its nature to patronising their plight, there were many masculine experts!

As a result, female conditions were variably labelled as acute or chronic, short-lived or long-lasting – often for life; all of course defined by their effect on the male. 'Treatments', such as they were, remained equally fluid, adjusted to suit those *touched* by her madness, yet seldom herself. This placed women in a socially manufactured abyss, frequently shaped by others' ideals; so that religion, morality and natural order were adopted as yardsticks against which their behaviour was critically measured. It led to indescribable suffering, but not just to the 'patient' – society too felt the effects of female abuse.[126]

Pre-nineteenth century madness, however, had been considered by many a male disease (women weren't insane, they were simply pregnant, or witches). But just as this shadowed the truth, nor was it right to label female madness a nineteenth century construct, the sole product of Victorian men.

According to Porter, defining female madness, indeed madness at all, came not from the medieval 'quacks' or the neo-Industrial alienists of the Victorian era, but rather the people themselves.[127] That is, madness was and always will be a social invention. Thus, it remained in the sceptic's domain to chart the very visibility of madness as the eras progressed. A political agenda has always been present. Nineteenth century accounts, for example, could be read as a misogynist's charter – using a new type of alienist psychiatry and the mid-century asylum explosion to control the worst excesses of the 'irrational' kind. Earlier periods though made this a more difficult notion, lacking as they did records, institutions and our own clear understanding of what went on in the past.[128]

As new 'experts' arrived, often taking an unpopular viewpoint and entombing it in technical jargon, such early diagnoses were not always met with a modern embrace. Burton's ground-shifting *Anatomy of Melancholy* for example was dismissed out of hand by Sir Thomas Brown as nothing more than a collection of 'vulgar errors'.[129] And professional disputes down the ages shaped the reading of madness, never more so than in the reinvention of the female condition.

Categorisation and victimisation of the vulnerable woman has thus been both consistent and varied over five hundred years. And through it all, her gender's own voice has been unforgivably absent! As Woods observed, to define women's mental maladies in the nineteenth century especially, was to diagnose *the unheard*. Only in the post-1950s has *any* attempt to understand female psychology taken account of these patients themselves.[130]

Flemish physician, van Helmont, asserted in the mid-1600s, 'women are more inclined to madness, depression, and bewitching or enchantment than men because of the influence of the "mad raging Womb"', before staggeringly claiming, 'the strong imaginations of pregnant women [were] responsible for birthmarks and birth defects in their children.'[131] Just as well that he advocated greater compassion! Dismissing the humours, he saw an 'inescapable truth' in the supposedly congenital nature of the 'hysterical' woman, feeding later ideas on inherited insanity and her life sentence of madness from her capacity for birth.[132]

His jarring views raised two pivotal issues. The likelihood of a woman to suffer 'communicated insanity' – that is, through either her familial genes or adopted behaviour, due in no small part to her fragile constitution,[133] which made her a danger to others, especially her husband and offspring. But also other women who fell 'prey to the influence of nervous contagion more easily than men.'[134]

The second critical issue was her preordained connection with nature, especially when it came to her wandering womb. It was what Smith neatly labelled 'a network of correspondences between woman, nature, passivity, emotion and irresponsibility.'[135] His views were immediately accepted by myriad others:

> 'On the one hand, the effect of these correspondences was that 'all women were seen to be closely bound to their biology, and the psyche was thought to be intimately connected with the reproductive cycle, the health or pathology of which directly determined their mental health.'[136]
>
> '[Which] meant that "with women, madness lay in [this] essential constitutional weakness"- *women were in effect predisposed to insanity*.'[137]

Underpinning such thought was the obdurate belief in the susceptible female. Writing his *Observations on Insanity* in 1798, John Haslam, apothecary to Bethlem, thought 'the probable event of the disease' (madness) was more likely in women.[138] As late as 1912, Lyttelton Forbes Winslow (ie not his father, the far more respected Forbes Benignus) decried it as 'the tragedy of woman'[139] and jurisprudent medic, Alfred Swaine Taylor, warned of 'disordered menstruation, owing to sympathy of the brain with the uterus' caused impulsive insanity, including an uncontrolled desire to murder[140] – a view he appears to have revised in later editions.

Women were thus considered more susceptible to unprovoked outbursts of sickening violence against objects, the person and often themselves. It was 'most frequently met…in imbecility and epilepsy, *and much more generally in women*.'[141]

More recent opinion has come to her aid:

> 'female violence was not about poisoning or planning the elaborate demise of lovers for reasons of *madness, passion or revenge*. By far the most common murders, attempted murders and manslaughters carried out by women were acts of despair and desperation, perpetrated not against other adults but those they cared for the most – their children.'[142]

Though deemed controversial by many, the nineteenth century sexologist, Havelock Ellis, gave his own warnings for the fragile gender. While men, he claimed, were more susceptible to brain-induced madness, women suffered more from emotional weakness and moral collapse. Likewise, they were more prone to melancholia, delusions – especially of persecution – and alcoholism; the latter often exaggerated by 'sexual excitement' – again all more so than men!

Within but a handful of words, he had ascribed the *maladie du siècle*, women's greater incidence of mental derangement – especially in the urban, more chaotic, and less moral cities. '[Nor is it] difficult,' he continued, 'to account for its growing frequency among women who are thrown into the competitive struggle for existence.'[143] Tuke meanwhile extended the role of the womb in the causation of madness, this time from a physical source: uterine cancer.[144]

But just *how* was this female madness defined? As Macdonald observed, during the Middle Ages some alleged tests for female madness bordered on the crazy themselves. Placing both herself and her family at the centre of 'normal', they spoke more of prevailing socio-religious ideals than any clinical understanding of mind-based disease:

'To demonstrate that a melancholy [woman's] sadness was pathological, one could say that [she] took no pleasure in...her spouse or her children.' Later quoting Napier's observations that a lunatic was she who "sayeth she hath no child or husband" or a "frantic woman [who] knoweth not her own children".'[145]

'Classical doctrine' had separated madness into various types, to create:

melancholy	:	quiet
mania	:	violent/unpredictable
delirium	:	frenzied/incoherent

the latter leading to certain death![146]

As we have already seen, Hippocrates' and Galen's defined humours led to early distinctions of mania, melancholia, epilepsy and hysteria, to reappear in the medieval West during the Renaissance in Europe.[147] That reinvigoration soon created the latter-day suffering, of that conspicuous group they termed women.

Some of the earliest definitions identified the melancholic female as a singular problem. Burton's *Anatomy* rather kindly aligned it to the double-edged sword of a genius mind.[148] But such 'positives' were rare and by later periods the goalposts had moved yet again. Variable causes – from possession to witchcraft, menstruation to nerves – obstructed real progression to understanding her mind.

What's more, in both medicine and beyond, delirium surfaced as a discreet, more dangerous ailment, defined by an incoherent, nonsensical rambling, but lacking the kind of mental fever that would indicate madness of the fully-blown kind.[149] Soon added were seventeenth century *moods* – grief, suicide, melancholia and morbidity, amongst others – and according to Napier's patients, was a period when English women at least had grown more aware of their own mental weakness.[150]

Climactic Insanity

Beyond the generic, female insanity was increasingly blamed on her eruptive life stages; puberty, adolescence, maidenhood, marriage and that most popular target, motherhood. Beyond which lay the scarcely less irregular age of the 'menopausal old crone'.

In the beginning, as puberty dawned, warnings of emotional turmoil began to emerge. The following is taken verbatim from Tuke's bible, or *Dictionary* (1892):

> 'The time of puberty and of the first appearance of the catamenia is one fraught with considerable peril to these nervous and sensitive girls, and they should be carefully watched throughout it. It is a time when all extremes must be avoided. They should not be allowed to over-fatigue themselves with tennis, long walks, or rides. They should not be exposed to great heat or cold, or anything which will check the menstrual flow or render it too profuse. They should not overtax the brain with lessons or competitive examinations, and a strict watch must be kept upon their sleeping, as an inability to sleep in young people of such an age is often a warning and forerunner of coming mischief, and if a girl sleeps alone it may easily be overlooked.'[151]

If puberty brought danger, adolescence could prove potentially fatal:

> 'A girl of seventeen or eighteen is far nearer to a fully developed woman if we compare her with one of twelve, and as her time of development is crowded, so to speak, into a narrower space, so is it fraught with greater peril to her. Dangerous as is the period of puberty to boys and girls, especially the latter, that of adolescence, between the ages of eighteen and twenty-five is far more so, and more break down and become insane.'

Its impact on her mind was often more feared even as she looked to her future:

> 'Many of the women... choose an occupation or calling; they also fall in love and marry. It is a time, moreover, when a girl's religious feelings are apt to be highly excited, and she is especially liable to hysteria and hysterical emotion in connection with such subjects. From all this it will be seen that when we have to deal with a neurotic girl...inheriting insanity, it will be of the utmost importance that the career chosen should be one fitted to the mental constitution, and that everything about them should be equally studied and regulated with the view of constantly warding off the threatened evil [of insanity].'

As maidenhood broke, so too her chances of surviving alone:

> 'The strangest vagaries of human nature which we perhaps ever witness are those which occur in young females in the early stages of womanhood; the whole nervous system, including the mental and moral nature, becomes so perverted that no circumstance of the most extraordinary kind may not then happen.'[152]

And, like a perpetual irritation, the perceived causes of mental decay in the Victorian woman focussed on her biological make-up and her maturing, increasingly dangerous sexual self.

Her next life-stage held the answer. To avoid it meant peril and almost certain insanity. Others before and long since have claimed its value in stultifying her predisposition to madness. In short, her mind relied on becoming a wife. Not that it was always plain-sailing. A new bride's propensity to collapse was duly divided into the following pitfalls: those slightly insane before marriage, but markedly so after; those single hysterical females who became wholly mad after; and those who showed no pre-marital madness but who become so, sooner or later, from new 'sexual excess'.[153]

Insanity *types* were produced according to which of these turned out to be true: delusions, delirium and/or nervous exhaustion; even acute mania, often triggered by irrational jealousy. If the marriage remained unconsummated, and any sexual excitation unrequited, mental (and marital) collapse was a danger – as well as a cause of divorce: '[when] the wife, as a rule, refuses marital rights…[then] trouble is started'; though there are plenty of cases when it is the husband who is divorced on similar grounds.

Given that marriage was so often seen at the time as a *cure* for insanity – hysteria, especially – it is even more unsettling when the marital state itself was thought to bring on her madness: 'The shock of marriage in some instances has been sufficient to start acute delirium which has ended fatally.'[154] 'The mental excitement of marriage,' wrote Tuke, 'culminating in sexual excitement, often excessive, is liable to act as an exciting cause of insanity in an individual predisposed to mental affection [i.e. most women]. Sometimes an epileptic fit [also] occurs.'[155]

But the last word for now goes to Walkowitz, or rather her cited members of the nineteenth century pressure group, *The Men and Women's Club*. In 1886, discussing the very real danger of repressed sexuality on the institution of marriage, they concluded that 'the impact of sexual restraint on female mental health' and a growing belief that the hysteria condition was the result of enforced celibacy in the marital home.[156]

Of course, if such a danger was prudently managed, conjugal relations maintained, the frequently resulting motherhood state brought its own raft of conditions, from puerperal mania to lactational madness. Stephen again exemplified Victorian ideas:

> 'Childbirth and its consequences, hysteria, disorders of the stomach, bladder, and liver, rheumatism in some cases, consumption and syphilis, may all in various ways affect the brain.'[157]

Finally menopause, the period when giving birth (at least as perceived in past eras) became consigned to the memory, feared for bringing new and terrifying forms of mental decay. As usual, it was the woman's biological construction, now in decline and all but redundant, that led evermore to the collapse of her mind. The ovaries in particular, those once-vital organs, were once again saddled with blame; causing mental disease, they had their own insane diagnosis.

The professed ovarian insanity persisted too in those women who had defied social convention by never entering marriage. Insultingly titled 'Old Maid's Insanity', the views of the alienist Clouston were unlikely alone. They are repeated here in full to convey their incredible message:

> 'OLD MAID's INSANITY – A form of insanity, so called by Dr Clouston, and Ovarian Insanity by Dr Skae (sic). It is characterised by a morbid alteration in the normal state of affection of woman towards the other sex. The patients are as a rule unattractive old maids about from forty to forty-five, who have led very strict and virtuous lives. The lady becomes seized with an absurd and reasonless passion for some particular individual of the opposite sex, very often her clergyman. She believes him to be deeply in love with her or accuses him of seduction or other misdeed in connection with herself, and uses the merest trifles as proofs of her beliefs. Recovery is rare, the insanity often passing into some other form.'[158]

Melancholic moods too left the older woman emotionally unstable. And its treatments were harsh. Leeches attached to the pubis were thought efficient in relieving her madness.[159]

In summary then, before we delve into the foremost epidemic of female insanity – leastways as historians have captured – a woman's exposure to madness had undeniably been a male-centric concoction. Indicators were everywhere, some apparently widespread: a deportment obsession, or taking pride in appearance; if it involved the hair especially, she was prone to mental decay![160] Even her peers, at least those of her gender, were often wont to enforce her inferior mental potential. 'Any girl that runs away with a young fellow, without intending to marry him, should be carried to Bridewell, or to Bedlam the next day.' (Lady Mary Wortley Montague cited in Johnson)[161]

But what of her lot, her defined sense of nature; the one thing that made her vulnerable and capricious. Due to her capacity for breeding, she was denounced as a 'product and prisoner of her [ovaro-uterine] system.'[162] As Cheyne revealed, her entire nervous system, including her brain, was not just influenced but *controlled* by what occurred in her reproductive organs. It led, so men said (and many females too), to an irrational being, volatile and untrustworthy, so unlike a machine.

Yet no-one could blame her; it was the way God had made her. '[The] peculiarities of her nature: the predominance of the emotional over the rational; her capacity for affection and aptitude for child-rearing; her preference for the domestic sphere; and her 'natural' purity and moral sensibility.'[163] Underpinned (or undermined) by those same organs of breeding, 'her life [was] one perpetual change.'[164] Her unreliability was writ large; and it placed her in a fearful position.

I finish here with a passing case history, taken not from a Victorian prison but from a seventeenth century home, proving that female abuse was no latter-day cancer. The victim, one poor Ellen Hixon, would have known this too well. Her 'symptoms', recorded in a letter to 'her' appointed physician, Richard Napier, betrayed the discussion. She was, he concluded, 'mopish, apish, foolish, untoward. Will not do anything that her parents bid her, *but at her own mind*'. As his biographer Macdonald later observed: 'households were hierarchical networks of dominance and submission...[a] sign of *mental abnormality* was [her] failure to acknowledge [her] superior [men].'[165]

Chapter 2

The Hysteria Hysterics

'These Fatigues, added to the Uneasiness of her Mind,
overpowered her weak Spirits, and threw her into one of the
worst Disorders that can possibly attend a Woman: A Disorder
very common among the Ladies, and our Physicians have not
agreed upon its Name. Some call it Fever on the Spirits, some
a nervous Fever, some the Vapours, and some the hysterics.'

(*Amelia*, Henry Fielding 1751).

For reasons presented above, the potential for diagnosing female 'insanity' was as endless in scope as it was brutal in nature. It is absolutely right however that this next chapter is devoted to the most renowned of them all. First recognised in the mists of antiquity, but now more closely aligned to Victorian England, we discuss next a phenomenon that eclipsed all others: the hysterical woman.

Hysteria's history starts well before the nineteenth century portrayal of over-tight corsets, ladies who swooned and uncompassionate males. Way back, in fact, to Hippocrates' humours and the 'wandering womb'. From its earliest mentions, the malady suffered for want of proper identification, in both its symptoms and even its title. King[1] pithily asked if it was 'a name without a disease?' While such a lack of identity epitomised its potential for being not a real condition at all. More a phenomenon, a pandemic, a social construction, we shall yet see that there *were* very real symptoms that led the (typically masculine) 'experts' to search for the truth.

But just what were its signs? And how did they lead to the spurious conclusion that it was a mind-based disease?

Its 1602 definition spoke of fits (such as chorea or St Vitus's Dance), swallowing, choking, a paralysis of the limbs, blindness and the body's unnatural distortion, 'turned rounde as a whoop, with her head backward to her hippes…[then]…turned rounde the contrary way, that is, her head forward betweene her leggs.'[2] At about the same time, it became linked with that scourge of all women, the Puritan witch-hunt; for if it were not a *natural* phenomenon it must have descended from a supernatural cause. Burn her! Burn her!

Edward Jorden's '*Suffocation of the Mother*' published in 1603 did little to remove the womb from being decried as the seat of the problem; though he did at least reject its occult connotations, something his counterpart, Napier, continued to absorb into his own thaumaturgical practice. When faced with Elizabeth, the supposedly bewitched daughter of the refined Lady Jennings, Napier courageously likened her symptoms to Jorden's more prosaic response: her witch-like hysterics were in fact Jorden's disease.[3] Likewise, John Cotta, the Northampton medic and despiser of supernatural 'medicine', inadvertently described the hysteric's condition in his *Short Discouerie of the Unobserved Dangers of Severall Sorts of Ignorant and Unconsiderate Practisers of Physicke in England*. As Macdonald summarized:[4] '[they] might become incredibly strong or perform acts of compulsive acrobatics. Their afflictions would always be impervious to the natural remedies of the most skilled physician.'. His lament would resonate even two centuries later.

In these periodic exertions to grasp the hysteria nettle, other voices began to dismiss if not the actual condition then its presumed causes. Van Helmont, hardly a reconstituted feminist, pilloried the label, 'an attack of the vapours', alluding to its ancient mistruth that hysterical behaviour came from poisonous gases escaping the womb. He also bemoaned how little still was understood of the woman's 'mad, raging womb' - and how it never stopped medical men turning a profit:

> 'Ah cruel wickedness, that would pacifie the furious or mad raging Womb, by a phantastical or imaginatory revulsion! Vain are the counsels, and helps of Physicians, which are adminstred without a knowing of the immediate Causes: For they know not how to apply a finger in the easing of the Malady, and they leave the whole burden on the Womens Shoulders, until they being strangled, do voluntarily give of or die, or by a strong fortune do return unto themselves, the circle of fury being measured or passed over. Frequent Visiters (*sic*) the while, do exhaust their Purses and Strength.'[5]

Though stopping short of normalizing her mental condition, the hysterical woman remained a feared anomaly, though at least not a witch.

During the following era, the Georgian condition – though its causes and styles were still not unravelled – became reintroduced to new medical theory. And now it became directly linked to the epitomised problem; her innate sexuality. In truth, this was no breakthrough opinion. Galen himself had ascribed a similar cause: '[He] held that sexual deprivation could cause the disorder [hysteria], and advocated intercourse for the married, and marriage for the single...'[6]

Cheyne's lifelong work on the nerves brought some much-needed reason, though with it came a new disproportionate sense of the fragile woman. And with it perhaps the origins of our own modern conception. Relying not on localised symptoms but the underlying systemic collapse from fraught nerves, it had led other physicians like Willis and Charcot to see hysteria, hypochondria and hystero-epilepsy (the latter's term) as products of poor nervous stock and her irresolute brain.[7]

Nerve-focussed he might be, but Cheyne himself also saw the menses as a viable source; withheld blood flooded her brain, causing hysteric collapse.[8] Only now he went further, imputing the hysteria condition specific to *class*: in particular, to the indulgent and idle upper elite (as he had and would with many of his theories). Things were only made worse by their efforts for social success, and the statuesque wealth that defined their eighteenth century status.[9]

Others who came later bought into his notion, but *re*-added gender as well. To be of higher rank *and* female, with great time on her hands...such women were acutely disposed to this 'nervous disease'.[10]

All in the Mind?

What arrived centre stage, then, was a new war to explain hysteria as a truly mental or physical condition. Cheyne of course, favoured the latter; the brain disordered from self-imposed errors – gluttony, excess, indolence, wealth. It was 'as much a bodily distemper...as the smallpox or fever.'[11] Willis too had favoured a physiological problem.

Thomas Sydenham, however, 'the seventeenth century hero of hysteria', saw its roots in a flawed *mental* state; suggesting, indirectly perhaps, that to suffer the malady, one had to be already mad![12] The future, as often, lay somewhere between, so that the hysterical woman was now seen to have suffered a unique kind of nervous disorder.[13] Being housed in the nerves meant it affected the mind: and hysteria – and that other 'indulgent' condition, hypochondria – became intimate bedfellows.

To still others, hysteria would soon become known not as bedevilment, or madness, nor a neurological curse; but cruelly dismissed as the 'paralysis of will'; and from that, claims of deceit and self-pity. In the nineteenth century, baronet physician Samuel Wilks was even less non-specific, boldly claiming that a 'want of will' defined hysteria not just in broad terms but with clinical fit. His belief in the nerves as the seat of the problem spoke of a 'nervous system…deranged *without*…organic disease', culminating in 'merely the extreme development of a disturbance to which nearly all men and women are liable'.

If this were true, why did women make such a fuss? To Wilks, the human system was more important than gender: 'It is a disorder occurring in those who possess a more than usually impressionable constitution.'[14] And most of his peers would have readily agreed, even as they turned their backs on the fool-making gender. Not that these male medics stood on their own in such outright rejection. The 'young gals' of Cheltenham Ladies College were threatened by Matron herself, with a cold water dousing and being force-fed evacuants to cure their silly hysterics.[15]

Imitations

Whether they liked it or not, certain 'related' events lent weight to the charges of it all being 'put on'. Now the 'mother of all ills' became equally well-known for encompassing all outlandish female behaviour. 'Hysteria epidemics' drew particular unkindness, dismissed as nothing but childish imitation, insubordinate women feeding each other's whims. Often this corresponded to religious passions, themselves blameworthy creators of over-reaction and which led to a curious example the world still speaks of today.

At a Methodist meeting in 1760 in Cornwall, several of the congregation suddenly leapt to their feet and shouted and hollered, 'What can I do to be saved?!' and began bounding and jumping, whereupon scores of others joined in to prove this would be no short-lived explosion. With scarce interruption, these 'Jumpers of Cornwall' kept going for over a week, such that they soon developed as a source of fascination and intrigue. Literally thousands of onlookers were drawn to the sight, only those who had come to observe found they were likewise afflicted, and the contagion grew such that even neighbouring chapels were reporting the same. Each person's affliction continued for several days at a time, their spasms mostly unceasing, not even to take of food or a surely much-needed rest. Cries of Hell and Damnation and strains for salvation tore through the air. And at its height, this titular 'compulsive malady' had affected upwards of 4000 women (and but a handful of men)![16] Even D.H. Tuke felt compelled to include the following entry in his late nineteenth century *Dictionary of Psychological Medicine*:

> 'JUMPERS—A name given to those hysterical fanatics who in their devotional exercises worked themselves into a state of frenzy, and began to jump about in a strange, uncontrollable manner. They appeared in Cornwall in 1760. The name has also been given to a family in Maine, U.S.A., which has evinced a like psychopathological condition, a sudden and peremptory order compelling immediate response on their part. The affection appears to have spread among the members of the family by imitation, and thus evinced a spurious hereditary character.'[17]

Unsurprisingly perhaps, nineteenth century alienists later seized on this bizarre episode and others like it, such as the American 'barkers',[18] were used to declare that hysteria was a social disease. Women and girls formed the largest number of those affected, describing their symptoms as that 'well-known' hysterical condition St Vitus's Dance.

Meanwhile, quite apart, an emerging passion for phrenology, in which a person's characteristics could be read in the lumps on their head, focussed on the so-called 'organ of *Imitation*' and its derangement thereof:

> 'it is well known that the occurrence of a paroxysm in one person, will often induce a fit in another, who never had the disease before. The general fact here stated has indeed been long known; but Phrenology gives it additional value, by shewing that the effect results in these cases from strong *cerebral* excitement, just as directly as if…any other passion or mental operation, carried to an inordinate degree, were the exciting cause.'[19]

As late as 1968, Walker regarded hysterics as 'notoriously imitative in their eccentricities'.[20]

While long before, van Helmont had ascribed *imagination* as a feature of the hysterical woman, especially when pregnant. Fantasy, he claimed, had 'a powerful influence on the womb', and '[she was] so greatly moved by her lust' that conceiving a child and the salacious nature it spawned were akin to self-induced harm: feeding the beast – her womb – that devoured her reason.[21] Claims of it being "all in the head" had been around a long time.

Some two hundred years after van Helmont, celebrity neurologist, Jean-Martin Charcot, ridiculed the idea that hysteria should have anything to do with the womb at all:

> 'the comprehension of hysteria as synonymous with *furor uterinus* (the furious womb) is the only one known in all classes of society; even among physicians, many have not yet been able to discard the idea that the uterus, or at least the genital apparatus of the female, is more or less the cause of this disease....[Think] that the best and easiest way [forward is] to forget that hysteria might possibly have anything to do with the uterus [whatsoever].'[22]

Opinions of the man change with the eras: a pioneer, a fraud; cruel or kind; the patient's best friend, or an exploiter of women. One thing is certain: his contribution to modern psychiatry is beyond even reasonable doubt. Yet his motives and methods were altogether more thorny, and nowhere more so than in this trickiest world of the hysterical female.

Many readers will be acquainted with 'Augustine', his patient-cum-stooge; or Blanche Wittmann, another unwilling puppet for his afternoon 'circus'.[23] Purported to show the onset of hysteria and his curative treatments, many have since dismissed them as little more than a crude self-promotion – a remote, bizarre advert for both himself and his revered institution, the Salpêtrière.

His lengthy entry in Tuke's *Dictionary*[24] is in many ways rightly lauded as the definitive word on hysteria, and by distilling his beliefs in the nuances of this 'most feminine of conditions', he identified his favoured causes.

With *hereditary* hysteria, he blamed its presence in the patient/victim on genetic and nutritional defects (including diabetes and gout). With no little surprise, he further castigated gender bias for extending the medical ignorance which had long surrounded the ailment. To label hysteria the *female* condition 'is a great mistake', he asserted. Though while (not) avoiding the genders, he homed in on their class. Poorer hysterical males, he insisted, were more likely to suffer alcoholic intemperance, while the women were the real hysterics; in the upper class, however, this position reversed.[25]

His detailed dissection of the hysteria condition has, nonetheless, added to his reputation for understanding the illness, and for even bringing hope to the world. Identifying at least three hysterical stages – convulsion, paralysis and the self-titled stigmata, he subsequently defined the hystero-epileptic condition, or convulsive hysteria. From here he coined the self-aggrandising phrase, the 'Attack of the Salpêtrière'.

The long-lasting attacks, at least those experienced by his own hysteria patients, allowed him to record various clinical pathways: from the near-ubiquitous body-bent-back *Parc-de-cercle* or *arc-en-cercle*, to the infamous *attitudes passionelles*, in which the subject, typically 'Augustine', adopts varied poses of crucifixion, ecstasy or erotic suggestion. Such supposedly involuntary postures led him to declare: 'one is sometimes surprised to see weak girls practising such gymnastics.'[26]

Among the superfluity of nuanced diagnoses, Charcot and others had given an array of evocative names to the symptoms they encountered: epileptoid, demoniacal, attack of clownism, spasms, sleep, catalepsy and his own hystero-epilepsy.[27] The sheer diversity of observed conditions surely called into question any single diagnosis of hysteria at all.

Treatments likewise revealed breadth and stubborn, age-old ideas. Manually pressing the synthesised hysterogenic anatomy notoriously included the woman's ovaries and the 'hysteric breast',[28] seemingly to counter the seat of the hysteria ailment. Yes, a woman's traditionally feared reproductive machinery was blameworthy again. Even her toilet was brought into question, with the newly identified ischuria, a condition in which her urine supposedly infiltrated her vomit.[29] The broken, volatile female was no doubt reconfirmed in the masculine mind.

Elsewhere in this *Dictionary* entry, various therapeutic responses were also suggested. Herbal and chemical ministrations included Valerian (for calming the nerves), though morphine should never be sanctioned (the increased risk of addiction in the hysterical female was too great). Hydrotherapeutics, electricity and massage offered varying degrees of success, while to counteract anaemia, a common hysteric's complaint, 'iron and arsenic may, as a general rule, be prescribed'.[30]

Fortunately, Charcot also proffered the use of 'moral therapy', although this included isolation rather like Weir Mitchell's rest cure, where the typically female patient was confined to bed for up to several months, as well as other acts of social removal. An undefined use of the moral approach had been recorded by Wilks, back in the 1870s.

One Mary B, a governess aged 30, had lost the use of first her left arm, then her left leg, and over the course of several months her eyelid and mouth. It left her tongue stuck out and she was unable to swallow all but the most liquidised food. The treatment administered succeeded in just five weeks, and Wilks was convinced this was merely through the power of suggestion. Any supporting 'medication' had been false, and her therapeutics placebos. Removing her from her 'stage' soon did the trick.[31]

Meanwhile, Charcot's new commitment to the alleged restorative effects of the hypnotic trance had become extremely well-known. Claiming only the 'biologically susceptible' hysteric could be genuinely affected, it confirmed, he insisted, the diseased state of her impressionable brain.[32] He had diagnosed hypnosis and hysteria to be a self-contained illness; in other words, one proved the other, and vice versa. But his assertions brought sombre rebuke from his many envious peers. By the last decade of the century, he had perhaps sensed the discomfort his views had encouraged. He reduced its usefulness while he admitted its risks:

> 'Hypnotism may be of some service, but not so much as one might *a priori* expect; it may be employed against some local symptoms. Although it may be true that in hysteria as such hypnotism prudently applied has not any injurious effects, it is quite certain that in the majority of cases the inconsiderate use or abuse of hypnotism has been followed by very serious complications. Suggestion may be employed without hypnotism, and may be quite as effective as in hypnotic sleep.'[33]

His increasingly avant-garde means of sharing his knowledge took on new, questionable forms. His ground-breaking use of medical photography, such as *Iconographie Photographique de la Salpêtrière*, can be lauded as helpful to medical knowledge, but his 'Tuesday afternoon pantomimes',[34] in which he supposedly hypnotised and 'corrected' the 'hysterical patient' – typically a partly-dressed woman – to modern eyes at least bordered on the perverse.[35]

His reputation had suffered. In recent times especially, scholars and commentators have openly questioned not just the inefficacy of his 'treatments', but their moral correctness.[36] But he is perhaps still best remembered today for his undeniable influence on understanding the mind. He certainly made an inestimable contribution to psychiatric opinion, drawing praise from his one-time student and fellow controversialist, Sigmund Freud. His legacy of responding to women suffering their gender-based 'strangeness' will however, for a very long time, result in rather more censure than uncontrolled awe.

The Hysteric Condition

As the nineteenth century progressed, hysteria the epidemic erupted like pustules that poisoned both the *lady's* condition and the *gentleman's* fears.

These terms are appropriate, because the majority of hysteria cases affected those who inhabited the more affluent classes. And led to the cynical observation that the hard-working poor had no time to fall ill. Also, in line with van Helmont's lament, a pandemic of such classic proportions and bourgeoisie purses was potentially too lucrative for the medics to ignore. It opened doors to a new raft of quackery, brutality and sadistic responses.

Lapping up the notion of hysterics as self-pitying actors, other men (medics and lay) tossed renewed condemnation. These 'manipulative, selfish creatures' they wailed, would have been better served by some 'fear and the threat of personal chastisement [(doubtless male-administered].'[37] Maudsley, perhaps typically, negated their behaviour as a 'moral perversion', and nothing less than a sham.[38]

Certain modern scholars devised that hysteria was, in fact, a 'spurious' invention of Renaissance and medieval minds, 'legitimated after the event by medical historians'. And became, in consequence, seen as a cultural construct, appropriated to fit prevailing social and even economic conditions aligned to domestic confinement. They argued it was a controlling 'philosophical' creation that went far beyond any medical origins it once may have had.[39] Whatever the truth, its demise as an accepted condition – if not its derogatory use in future generations – arrived gradually and with stealth, due largely to its renewed negative image. Fewer cases presented to the shrinking medical stable, amid those very fears of social rejection. Claims of 'moral feebleness' and 'unreality [of] symptoms'[40] sequestrated its worth.

The hysterical woman then was no more than a psychosomatic perplexion. Though it had long been used to label her insane, for many others it simply meant she was out of control.

Diagnosis

The seemingly endless attempts at forging a diagnosis outstripped even its own historical scions. From the humours and 'wombers', a more nuanced condition was devised and refined. The *globus hystericus*, or ball in the throat, became the definitive symptom, as a sense of choking and the inability to swallow brought on the avoidance of food and led to anorexia nervosa, a secondary yet fatal malaise sadly still known today. Chorea, or St Vitus's Dance, specifically referred to uncontrollable movements of the sufferer's limbs, producing erratic dance-like exertions with no reason or purpose. Sexual disorders, stigmata and even deafness were among a seemingly endless array of the hysteric's curse. [For a full and at times fanciful exposé of hysteria and its myriad traces, try Tuke's *Dictionary of Psychological Medicine* (1892), available free online].

Cheyne had noted disappointments in love as a cause of hysteria,[41] while Combe, through his phrenological leanings, favoured *amativeness* (the propensity to love or have fanciful sexual feelings) as a possible cause. After all, he wrote:

> 'females are especially subject to cerebral disease from this cause; and, according to the constitution and hereditary qualities of the patient, it takes the form of common nervous disease…That females should be most subject to insanity from this cause, was to be expected, from the stronger feelings of attachment and larger development of *Adhesiveness* [a proposed cerebral organ]… combined with the fewer sources of relief, and the impossibility of their taking any active steps to secure the possession of the object of their choice.'[42]

The tones of judgement and lamentation crescendoed together.

Early psychiatry doctors like Alexander Crichton believed in the hysteric's secondary ailments; in particular auditory delusions:

> '[a]ll delirious people, no matter whether they be maniacs, or hypochondriacs, or people in the delirium of fever, *or of hysteria*, differ from those of a sound mind in this respect, that they have certain diseased perceptions and notions in the reality of which they firmly believe, and which consequently become motives of many actions and expressions which appear unreasonable to the rest of mankind.'[43]

Perhaps belonging more under the imagination or hypochondriac label, phantom tumours were yet another hysterical symptom:

> 'In hysterical women there occasionally occurs a rounded prominence of the abdomen which is thought by them to be due to the presence of a tumour or to pregnancy. The cause is unknown, but the condition has been said ([by] Roberts) to be probably due to paralysis of the intestines, a consequence of *disordered nervous influence*. The treatment is that for hysteria; galvanism may be tried, and the bowels should be kept well open.'[44]

In the same publication, Barnes reduced hysteria from a condition to a symptom, of something far more specific – dysmenorrhoea, or menstrual disorders. At the same time, he bewailed his fellow physician's unenlightened responses:

> 'It is important to form a definite and rational idea of the terms hysteria and neurosis. Too often they are mere words used to conceal ignorance…Hysteria is not an independent entity. It is a symptom. If we cannot trace the symptoms and its cause, commonly underlying disorder of the sexual system, the rational course is to infer that our skill is deficient, and not to bow down before an idol of the imagination. This is certain, that, in many cases, *hysteria is the forerunner of insanity*. This also is certain, as the result of large clinical experience, that hysteria is cured by *removing* the causes of dysmenorrhoea.'[45]

Others believed it was simply a form of automatism, with its thrashing of limbs and uncontrollable arch (*arc-en-cercle*). Laycock, a great believer in the insane patient's irresistible impulse, in his 1840 treatise, *The Nervous Diseases of Women*, labelled hysteria peculiar to females on account of their nerves - a product of being a biological woman.[46]

In the following century, Winslow (the younger) perceived hysteria not as insanity at all, but an excuse for a crime: 'the nearest approach to involuntary viciousness is hysteria, which seems to be a pathological suspension of the will.'[47] As such, it led a woman to unspeakable transgressions, theft, stalking, even committing a murder. Winslow saw hysteria as a *cause*, an igniter of the by now more familiar conditions, including homicidal mania, kleptomania and delusional madness:

> 'One of the chief forms of mental disease to be found in women is hysteria. When so suffering, they become so absorbed in themselves, and believe so firmly that they are afflicted with every disease imaginable, that they often succeed in deceiving those around them. In such cases they are so sensitive that they brood over any sharp word that may have been spoken to them, distorting it until they feel that they have been cruelly wronged. Small slights are exaggerated to neglect and wilful unkindness, and they pass from discontent to happiness, from tears to laughter, with marvellous rapidity. Many crimes have been committed by women

labouring under a supposed wrong. The faithlessness of man plays an important part in the history of female insanity, and the delusion that certain public men are in love with them is a very common mental complaint among women. This form of insanity has often very unpleasant consequences for the objects of their delusions, as they are frequently persecuted by women who imagine that they have been encouraged in their feelings.'[48]

It is clear that hysteria was typically perceived as a woman's condition: from her biological make-up and her sexual organs, to an over-active, impressionable mind, including her desire to break free of social convention. But two issues arose from such entrenched 'diagnoses'.

Firstly, this view was devised by the patriarchal oppressor. Even Donkin said that 'it is a feminine condition', but unusually urged them to escape domestic confinement. As an early and rare feminist male, confused perhaps by the mores of his time, he was keen to see change, much as Mill had before him.[49]

Donkin himself had suggested that hysteria causes a mix of biological weakness and external control 'in her organism and her social conditions the potential factors of hysteria are present in a notable degree',[50] even as he controversially highlighted her sexual repression as yet another pivotal cause.[51]

In Scull's chapter on 'Mysteria', he presented the condition as a female malady. 'Was hysteria "real" or fictitious, somatic or psychopathological? Might it constitute an unspoken idiom of protest, a symbolic voice for the silenced sex, who were forbidden to verbalize their discontents, and so created a language of the body?'[52] Quite.

Whatever its cause, some still found the hysteric self-centred and unappealingly coy. 'In everyday life the selfish egotism of the hysterical woman is well enough known.'[53] While even mothers – who perhaps should have known better – saw the 'cure' for their hysterical daughters was to marry them off. Yet Sir George Savage – in both nature and name? – one-time medical officer at Bethlem, and Virginia Woolf's personal 'shrink', thought this not worth 'the risk'.[54]

Her mischief was, to many, exactly what defined the hysteric condition. Wilks, in 1878, included sexual misconduct, her inclination to 'steal or commit murder'[55] and how:

'when you see a paragraph headed "extraordinary occurrence," and you read how every night loud rapping is heard in some part of the house, or how the rooms are being constantly set on fire, or how all the sheets in the house are devoured by rats, you may be quite sure that there is a young girl on the premises.'[56]

The efficacy of so-called moral treatments were cited as proof of her insecure nature, the condition and symptoms purely imagined for the welcome sense of attention. 'Many a woman [will] pretend to be ill when she has no ailment whatever, and, in a further stage of this morbid state, to actually manufacture a disease.'[57] From such attitudes sprang outright derision:

'If the brain centres be compared to so many galvanic batteries always at work, we can understand how, with half a million of women in the country unmated, a large amount of superfluous force is either running to waste or doing mischief either to the producers of it or to others. If the energies are not used for the more direct purposes to which they are intended, they may find a very appropriate outlet in good actions towards the poor and helpless, or even in assisting the parish clergyman in his duties, no matter whether the aid afforded be of a substantial or a frivolous kind. Better than doing nothing and becoming a prey to one's own feelings, is riding, walking, or performing the routine of fashionable life.'[58]

Such gendered 'reasoning' was 'explained' by the female's loss of control; brought on by the loss of the will, her brain unable to control the lower faculties where it resided.[59] It led, *inter alia*, to uncontrollable movement and 'animal instincts'.

Modern researchers have selected understandably discordant women in history to refute much of the misogynist ownership of the hysteria condition; even surprisingly, if my reading is right, suggesting the ailment was real but that it was 'defined as their own'. The seventeenth century Duchess of Newcastle, Margaret Cavendish, one of the first women to question 'traditional medical views about female inferiority',[60] favoured Hippocratic and Galenic, that is uterus-based, causes of the hysteria curse. It should perhaps be remembered now that such inexplicable views were being written in contrary to the era's cruel treatment of 'witches', and its allegations of witchcraft.

Turning now to the other, salient issue, that hysteria was not to be found in the male, Charcot had already suggested to the contrary. A certain Dr Shaw, practising in the eighteenth century, advised wine, or 'the juice of the grape', as a remedy for *men* in such cases. He also recognised the oxymoronic nature of the term hysterical male, bearing in mind its philological foundations. Instead, he invented the term Hippo, after the ancient 'founder' of hysteria, to describe these male afflicted.[61]

Nonetheless, it retained the fragile female at greater risk of its menace. Through its nineteenth century heyday, it stubbornly refused to be treated as anything other than a woman's condition. The reasons were yet again at least two-fold in number. Firstly, that 'women were still seen as contributing a disproportionate share to the ranks of the sufferers…for the female frame, and the female nervous system, 'were simply a frailer, less robust version of the male.'[62].And secondly, 'real men' coped better with their emotional strains; only the effeminate succumbed, a view that erupted during the economic explosion of the Industrial age. Or so most people would have it.

Excellent work by Goodman, though, has questioned the exclusive female possession of the hysteric condition, by revisiting contemporary statistics from certain Victorian asylums.[63] Admission data and anecdotal evidence have been reviewed to challenge a:

'previous and popularly received consideration of the masculine experience of institutionalized madness. In removing…gender barriers, for example, in the hysteria condition, she agreeably [blurred] the lines of both gender weakness and the corresponding definition of the insanity condition. In this, she [has invited] us to re-evaluate our own perceptions of madness in the human condition.'[64]

More recent still, male hysteria has since been identified in the survivors of battlefield trenches. Re-labelled 'shell-shock', similar symptomatic conditions were observed by those treating those male unfortunates who might have escaped with their bodies but had jettisoned their minds. It is a view much embraced by twenty-first century thinking.[65] Originally termed War Neuroses, certain voices have reaffirmed the mind's role in the nervous condition;[66] while comparisons with neurasthenia have been all too readily drawn.[67] But will it ever put paid to the historic belief that hysteria was little more than the silly woman's condition?

A Male Response

From such a standpoint, the disingenuous benefits and unavoidable harms of largely masculine treatments came as little surprise. Each was undoubtedly crafted on a patriarchal attitude towards the unpredictable female (to many, a tautological statement). As Edward Tilt, English Victorian physician and writer, succinctly opined: 'mutability is characteristic of hysteria, because it is characteristic of women.'[68]

One of the more popular 'cures' was to remove the patient from her usual surroundings, recognising the strains she felt from her domestic confinement; and removing the gains of her 'putting it on'. Indeed, there is evidence that female hysterics embraced Silas Weir Mitchell's controversial rest cure precisely by acting hysterics to escape the drudge of their day. Meanwhile, Anton Mesmer, with his magnetic therapies through water-filled pools, known as *baquet*, were equally favoured.

Other, particular treatments invaded her body. Douches and water treatments were the Victorian equivalent of Cheyne's Georgian hydrotherapy treatments, occasioned at centres like his native Bath. Showers and cold baths were doubtless less popular, while ice water injections and labia leeches were considered much worse. Yet even worse was to come…

Hypnotism was considered by some, typically the most influential, as a means of overcoming the uncontrollable thoughts that had caused the hysterical outburst. Charcot, unquestionably its greatest exponent, believed in its therapeutic effect. Allegations of spiritualism and claims of charlatanism soon undermined its appeal, at least for those non-believers seeking solutions to the hysteria problem. While people like Savage, who dispelled the hypnotic trance as simply a hysterical female: 'wherever there were 'strange manifestations', he ridiculed, 'there was sure to be found a girl with hysterical symptoms.'[69] Winslow (the younger) castigated the spiritualist fervour as itself a distasteful cause of insanity, especially among impressionable, 'weak-minded hysterical women' and still others saw spiritualism as akin to that more accepted automatism condition. The automatic writing component of supposed supernatural contact was dismissed as an aberration of rational belief; a dangerous sham condemned in the harshest terms for opening up a portal to functional disorder: 'this way madness lies' revealed the fear from such psychological meddling.[70]

While hopeless despair was never too far away. George Young, eighteenth century philosopher and surgeon, related his own unpleasant experience:

> 'I have seen some women seized with an hysteric vomiting…tho' the minute before in perfect health both of body and mind; yet one slight affront has set them immediately a vomiting, with great difficulty of breathing, and the whole train of hysteric symptoms.'

And his response to it all?

> 'I confess I have, thro' ignorance, given hysteric pills, when I might as well have given pills to purge folly and make my patient wiser.'[71]

With more on her treatments to come later, the concluding remarks here must quite rightly be left to a woman. The following is an elegant summary of the hysteria hysterics:

> 'So what exactly is hysteria? How can we define it? It is mental instability, fits of rage, anxiety; things that can actually happen when you are suffering from an illness or trauma. In 1980, hysteria was removed from medical texts as a disorder unto itself, but it has remained present as a symptom of disease brought on by specific trauma, both physical and mental - Although it is now seen as a symptom or result of another illness, it has marked women for centuries: their volatile behaviour, their need to be tamed physically, their weak mental constitution. Although the myths of hysteria are fanciful, its real history not only reveals how it has been a tool to control women's behaviour and bodies, but shows the frightful neglect mental trauma has received throughout the centuries.'[72]

If hysteria had presented both society and medical minds with an insurmountable challenge, the underlying 'condition' – that of being a woman – caused brain-melting confusion and absolute horror, especially when her reproductive equipment was considered the scourge. And this is precisely what we turn to in the following chapter.

Chapter 3

Maternal Mayhem

Though this chapter features much more than the act of being a mother, a woman's potential to nurture caused her pain beyond reason. Emotional, physical, social *and* mental. As has already been shown, a woman's reproductive capacity had led to perpetual claims of her instability, illness, even criminal disruption. And it was her place in the annals of madness that attracted most scorn and masculine fear.

History's medics were too quick to laud their new, self-professed wisdom:

> '[t]he correlations of the sexual functions and nervous phenomena in the female are too common and too striking not to have attracted attention at all times; but, it may be confidently affirmed, that it is only within quite recent years that we have had adequate knowledge to enable us to discuss the problem arising out of these relations, with scientific precision.'[1]

That 'adequate knowledge' rendered women unstable.

Menstrual Misery

Madness, the moon and a woman's monthly menstrual cycle, had long been considered the most volatile conjunction. At the start of the twentieth century, experts from Britain and France may have dismissed the connection as a redundant, near-pagan belief;[2] but the idea that a woman's menstruation was associated with the moon, and the moon with her madness, long retained its disruptive appeal.

It was the effect of her period that had cursed women since Man walked the earth. In 1865, Alfred Swaine Taylor believed in the tripartite condition of moon-madness-menstruation, at least in his and others' medico-legal consensus - in other words, between menstruation and murder.[3] The non-alienist doctor, John Burton, certainly did, and he said so in the 1845 trial of Martha Brixey before she was found guilty of killing her employer's infant son:

> "I ... have frequently had occasion to attend young women who have been subject to temporary suspensions of the action of nature, and I believe any suspension of that action is calculated very much to derange the general constitution.'

Adding, with no little relevance:

> 'sometimes the effect assumes an appearance as though the patient was labouring under dropsy, and occasionally, instead of affecting the body, it affects the head ... dull chronic pains in the head and the region of the brain. This is attended with restlessness of manner, moroseness, and dullness of appearance. The patient is subjected also to fits of irritability and great excitement and passion.'[4] [Note the change in reference here from prisoner to patient.]'

Her predisposition to madness, simply from being a menstrual woman, was vehemently explained. Even senior French psychiatrist, Jean-Étienne Esquirol, reported no less than one-sixth of the physical causes of insanity arose from menstrual 'derangements'; and Sutherland drew the following conclusions from studying some five hundred lunatic women: idiots and cretins have a delayed monthly cycle; the epileptics suffer more fits; mania worsened and 'intense excitement' was 'almost continuous' in menorrhagia patients, leading to sexual promiscuity and obscene language; and melancholiacs suffered amenorrhea, as the 'the uterine functions [were] more or less disordered, and...suspended in the large majority of cases.'[5].

Others yet 'observed' maniacal responses to the suppression of the menses, from either the blood running up to the brain or from reputed asthenic insanity (weakened nerves). As late as the 1890s, the 'disordered' womb was blamed for its own variety of conditions. Dr Icard's treatise of that year – *La Femme pendant la Periode meustruelle* – condemned organic disease of the womb and the madness it created, such were its 'effects upon the intellectual faculties of the female.'[6]

Prevailing attitudes toward the biological-cum-mental weakness in the female gender was epitomised by the same French 'overstating' historian, in *La Femme*'s invidious quote:

'The menstrual function can by sympathy, especially in those predisposed, create a mental condition varying from a simple psychalgia, that is to say, a simple moral malaise, a simple troubling of the soul, to actual insanity, to a complete loss of reason, and modifying the acts of a woman from simple weakness to absolute irresponsibility. The tribunal(?) cannot appraise with any certainty the disposition of a woman who is the subject of menstrual disturbance.'[7]

Though Tuke may have dismissed the moon's role in her madness, in his same publication, French psychiatric physician, Antoine Ritti, insisted the female cycle was in itself an insanity cause, because it featured her blood. Defining circular insanity, he conceded, "Menstruation requires a special study'; which he then proceeds to deliver:

'In some patients this function does not undergo any change. In others, where the menses are of short duration, menstruation ceases entirely during the period of *depression*. In some - those who have attacks of insanity of double form of short duration with intermissions - menstruation establishes itself during the intermissions. In cases of monthly attacks (*fourteen days of excitement and fourteen days of depression*) the menstruation coincides with the period of excitement and causes then recurrence of all the symptoms of that period. Sometimes menstruation is suppressed during the period of excitement and reappears in the period of *melancholia*.'[8]

More than fifty years earlier, Combe had questioned suppressed menstruation as a real cause of female madness:

'A good deal of importance used to be assigned to suppression of menstruation…and to irritation of the sexual organs, as causes of insanity. But [others] have successfully shewn, that, in a great majority of the instances recorded as examples of this kind, the above phenomena were in reality the consequences, and not the causes, of the cerebral and mental affections.'[9]

Others later followed suit. In fact, Andrew F. Currier, medic and author, whose other works included *The Unrestricted Evil of Prostitution* (1891), went further, holding the view that the menstrual cycle – in particular its cessation – caused no physical problems, nor did it unsettle the mind.[10]

But what, then, when the monthly cycle desisted as a woman 'fell' pregnant?

Planning a Child

There is no attempt here to generalise the responses of mothers. As Hogan explained: 'experience is heterogeneous…there are different implications for the words "pregnancy" and "motherhood"…[t]here can be no "identity" divorced from the world the subject is experiencing' (quoting Moi, 1999: 81)…Therefore, to discuss women's experience of childbirth primarily as a pathological response, such as post-natal depression for example, is to reify a complex set of experiences to which women are subject in a deterministic, reductive and oppressive manner.'[11]

Nonetheless, throughout all periods, local society and social conditions both shaped and reflected prevailing responses to the impregnable woman. Unstable, erratic and devoid of her mind, her capacity for madness became an 'irrefutable' fact. Surprisingly, perhaps, it was built from late Georgian ideas:

> 'The natural processes which women undergo, of menstruation, parturition, and of preparing nutriment for the infant, together with the diseases to which they are subject at these periods, and which are frequently remote causes of insanity, may, perhaps, serve to explain their greater disposition to this malady [madness].'[12]

To be a 'natural mother and moral wife'[13] was (supposedly) the yardstick by which nineteenth century women were measured like never before, perhaps never more since. Underpinned by renewed moral and biblical teachings, an age of reason had given way to the re-emergence of unreasonable fear. Indeed, many have argued that no such oppression even existed before Victorian patriarchs reinvented the female.

Women were expected to be mothers, and mothers were judged by how they performed, their maternal duties now defining 'the hearth and the home'. Such presumptions gave rise to a series of protean assessments that seemed to change on a whim; and most, if not all, came from that constant thread of invention, the misogynist male.

Specific (and again variable) ailments, conditions, and 'remedies' were devised, instituted or simply invented to underpin the masculine need for the 'obedient gender'. Often in need of 'breaking in' and placed under control like a difficult horse, nowhere was this more acutely expressed than in the gynaecological circles.

The epitome of the issue undoubtedly arrived in the Victorian era. Sex, marriage (not in that order!), labour and motherhood were dissected, fought over and hijacked to demonstrate their effect on the volatile woman. The era's exaggerated misogyny crippled and plagued entire generations, at the same time baffling the madness debates. The unceasing conflict reached its zenith when the woman conceived.

Pregnant

Starting even before the foetus creation, the menstrual 'mother-in-waiting' was being prepared, in theory at least, for what was to come. Not just in the sexual sense, within the walls of the bedroom and through her missionary husband, but biologically too.

Her 'risk' of 'falling' pregnant raised dangers to an entirely new level. Indeed, a woman's mere inclination to become a new mother set off alarm bells in certain medical sections; such as Winslow (the younger) appeared to cast away all restraint when he cautioned against women choosing to carry a child: 'maternal instinct,' he wrote, 'is responsible for [all] women's crimes.'[14]

Moreover, the mental state of the expectant mother had an effect on the child once it was brought into the world. Combe offered strident opinion: 'A predisposing cause is the condition of the mother during gestation, which has often a striking effect on the future mental health and constitution of the offspring.'[15] So there it was; the young mother-to-be was responsible not just for her own health, and that of her husband, but of their child as well!

This combination of expectation (of her mental wellness) and her supposed proneness to mental disease, left her a patriarchal prisoner under the control of the men – her spouse, her doctor and, if things had gone badly, her alienist too. As Hogan[16] argued, becoming a mother was seen as the 'pivotal' purpose of being a woman – and yet, at the very time she delivered (in the wider sense of the word, i.e. on her expectations), she was deemed have sunk to her most fragile state. With a degenerative moral awareness, always exaggerated at her time of conception, her conduct, self-control and her worth to the child were all wont to collapse.

As Clouston remarked, 'a certain lack of [control] is, I fear, almost expected in woman, and the highest degrees of it are not commonly expected in her… [it is] few who are not prone to yield in conduct to emotion, instincts and impulse.'[17] In other words, women as mothers were always going to find trouble.

Such a propensity to derangement had, for some, an unequivocal cause:

'During [pregnancy and motherhood], in which the sexual organs of the human female are employed in forming; lodging; expelling, and lastly feeding the offspring, there is no time at which the mind may not become disordered; but there are two periods at which this is chiefly liable to occur, the one soon after delivery, when the body is sustaining the efforts of labour, the other several months afterwards, when the body is sustaining the effects of nursing.'[18]

When the pregnancy came, new types of madness were perhaps conveniently made – convenient, that is, to all but the mother. Insanity of Pregnancy, one such condition, was the least common of all the defined puerperal types. Typically comprising melancholia, and often associated with fear of being pregnant, symptoms were observed to include a broad range of cases. A dislike of her husband, her other children perhaps and, in extreme cases, ending up with a murder; while obscure cravings, such as coal and slate pencils was another result – if this was focussed on alcohol, there was 'no knowing to what this may lead'; a simple hysteria, leading to moral disorder, especially disrupting her family; and, as late pregnancy approached, even more dangerous inclinations, such as an open mistrust of her husband, a fear of some impending evil, or the loss of her child (i.e. taken away). Her chances of recovery too were depressingly thin.[19]

Many others concurred, going so far as to highlight the great number of types – and their sheer chance of occurring – that would cause the woman's systemic breakdown during the delivery. Citing Dr James MacDonald, one-time physician at Bloomingdale Asylum, they repeated verbatim his strident conclusion that 'the proportion [of insanity cases] increases from day to day, as we approach the day of parturition, and diminishes as we depart from it.'[20] Though, thankfully, the statistics do not seem to bear this out.

Lactation

Once the child arrived, and suckling began (if possible), yet another form of madness crashed into view. Lactational insanity, from its self-explanatory cause, was deemed to bring yet more serious dangers.

Similar to the warnings that plagued pregnant women, about their potentially deficit impact on the mental health of her child, the hereditary element was highlighted again, though this time from the milk she passed on to the baby. George Fielding Blandford, renowned Victorian psychiatrist, advised with apparently no sense of shame that women prone to madness (meaning all?) should never suckle their children:

> 'as a nervous, excitable woman, prone [the infant] may be, to varying mental moods, is not likely to be a good nurse, and it is of the first importance that a nervous child should be thoroughly well nourished either by a good wet-nurse or hand-feeding.'[21]

Renewed 'dread, fear, jealousy and suspicion' were joined by imagined attacks on her person, especially toward her organs of childbirth, which exponentially raised the chances of harming herself or her infant. Suicide was a particular risk, while delusions were rife and often accompanied by a pain in the head.[22]

But such 'clinical' thought, no matter how fanciful, was further undermined by a proclaimed class division: that is, women from a poorer start in life were more likely to fall to this mental decay. The prognosis for recovery, however, was considered typically good, unless she descended even further, and a number lost their grasp on reality, while some even died.[23]

Puerperal Madness

While the term adopted popular meaning, Prichard insisted puerperal insanity accurately defined a madness brought on either by giving birth to a baby, or while nursing the same.[24] Or, as Startup wistfully noted: '[when] stimulated by the physiologically disruptive influence of childbirth on the *already vulnerable female constitution.*'[25]

In common use, however, it described a *collection* of symptoms, occurring before, during or after labour. And it became harrowingly synonymous with mothers who killed. In the present context, puerperal insanity – a condition not really defined until 1820[26] – re-established women as the dangerous sex. It knew no social exemptions: rich or poor, educated or wanting, first time parent or with an earlier brood; the only prerequisite was being a mother.

As early as 1809, Haslam had entered the fray, referring to the putative condition as perhaps an inevitable canker:

'To shew how frequently insanity supervenes on parturition, it may be remarked, that from the year 1784 to 1794 inclusive, 80 patients have been admitted, whose disorder shortly followed the puerperal state'.[27]

The symptoms and problems he listed included an absence of sleep, flushed countenance with often a pain in the head, wandering eyes and remission of milk. As the mind became 'more violently disordered, it [milk] is totally suppressed.'[28]

Haslam also aligned the disease, however, with the woman's menstrual capacity, noting how in some cases a cure was beyond reach until she had reached her menopause age. Recovery, meanwhile, was often delayed until her amenorrhoea, with which it [had] flourished, settled down once again.[29]

Heavyweight Victorian alienists, Bucknill and Tuke, repeatedly highlighted a propensity for pregnant women and new mothers to become *fatally* mad:

'The excitement resulting from the puerperal state is so important, that it merits our special attention. It is a disorder which invades the sick-chamber at a time when it is most acutely felt; nor is it of very rare occurrence.'[30]

In other ways too, it reinforced the idea of the 'acceptable' woman, the puerperal maniac exhibiting behaviour and language they would not have otherwise used:

'In the acute form of the mania which succeeds parturition, we observe an intensity of mental excitement, an excessive incoherence, a degree of fever, and, above all, a disposition to mingle obscene words with the broken sentences; things which are rarely noted under other circumstances. It is true that, in mania, modest women use words which in health are never permitted to issue from their lips; but in puerperal insanity, this is so common an occurrence, and is done in so gross a manner, that it early struck me as being characteristic.'[31]

In his treatise on insanity affecting the mind, James Cowles Prichard – he of the irresistible impulse – devoted an entire chapter to the subject. Expressing both its eventual recession and its fatal potential – especially when accompanied by fever (rapid pulse) – he supported Scots physician Dr Ferriar's opinion:

> 'I am inclined to consider the puerperal mania as a case of conversion. During gestation, and after delivery, when the milk be gins to flow, the balance of the circulation is so greatly disturbed as to be liable to much disorder from the application of any exciting cause. If, therefore, cold affecting the head, violent noises, want of sleep, or uneasy thoughts, distress a puerperal patient before the determination of blood to the breasts is regularly made, the impetus may be readily converted to the head, and produce either hysteria or insanity, according to its force and the nature of the occasional cause.'[32]

He went on to recommend suitable treatments: shaving the head to cool the temporal region; immersing the lower extremities in hot water to stimulate warmth (with or without mustard or horse-radish added); the judicious application of leeches; and the use of blisters, a popular nineteenth century 'cure', to the head in particular. Emetics, ammonia and even some opiates were additional options. He did, however, urge the moral management of women, through complete isolation and being treated at home. The need to admit to an asylum was, he insisted, less frequent than in other insanity cases.[33]

Winslow the younger who, by now has surely painted his own unfavourable image, believed puerperal madness was all too common among women, and that as a result the asylums were full. He maintained it was a recurring condition, and certainly there were a number of cases where this proved to be true. But not all. The symptoms, he observed, of its impending arrival included neglect for the baby and a 'total indifference' to her husband's wishes! Nor was he alone in thinking it an often-hereditary disease.[34]

Such was its popularity among the psychiatric profession that many have since suggested puerperal mania sometimes 'got in the way', as a diagnosis at least. Underlying, non-medical conditions were being overlooked by this easy distraction, so that hunger, poverty, economic want and domestic abuse had been left unattended. Even the lack of bedroom agreement – i.e. consensual sex – was thought to bring on puerperal symptoms, which were blithely mishandled through the insanity plea.[35]

Certain modern scholars, meanwhile, have conjectured that the puerperal condition was ostensibly if not wholly, a nineteenth century invention, shaped for mastering gender. Marland argued that, in the nursery alone, puerperal insanity became the catch-all condition, the *folie extrême*, that defined the ungovernable woman. In its mid-nineteenth century florescence, it suited the male need for control; an invention for moral confinement of Victorian women, with their 'fragile nervous system and unpredictable [womb].'[36]

Perhaps supporting this view were the sheer number and incredibly nuanced conditions collated under the puerperal banner. One of the more obscure was *mania transitoria*, or ephemeral insanity. Though little recognised, even in its nineteenth century heyday, Savage considered it of some importance in the medico-legal debates. Why? Because the mother, once struck, usually in the first two or three days after labour, grew tense, her breasts became tender and firm, her bowels quite compacted. More importantly, she became a grave danger to her child. 'It must be remembered that in this state the mother may injure herself or her child, and in the latter case she may be quite unconscious of the act which she has done.'[37]

In the Criminal Context

Infanticide

In the Victorian era at least, a mother's insanity made an almost obsessive appearance in criminal courts, typically as a defence against murder, and raised her unstable image in the popular press. It was not without reason. As Smith has advanced, it was that rare condition where medicine and the law overlapped in their responses.[38] The outcome was often to the benefit of the murdering mother, but not all of society nor every individual case was seen to warrant such kindness.

Of innumerable examples, London's Mary McNeil struck a particular chord in 1856. At least three times a mother and nursing a new-born, in a fit of apparent madness she used a razor to cut two of their throats. She never once denied the offence, yet avoided the gallows on account of her puerperal mind, to spend the rest of her years in Bethlem's criminal wing.[39]

The more peculiar case of one Mrs Law, in 1862 Essex, proved not only had the child been at risk as she cut up not just her new-born but her husband as well. The successful defence presented her great loss of blood having exhausted her brain during her maternal confinement.[40]

Taylor, the jurist, reported the rather straightforward case of Mrs Ryder (1856), highlighting the likelihood not just of acquittal on the ground of insanity but the very real chance she would be returned to her family, due to the supposedly specific and limited risk she posed to the public, In the context of Victorian madness and crime, murdering mothers were rare incarnations indeed:

> '[In the case of Reg. v. Ryder]…there was an entire absence of motive in this as in most other cases of a similar kind. The mother was much attached to the child, and had been singing and playing with it on the morning of its death. She destroyed the child by placing it in a pan of water in her bedroom. The medical evidence proved that she had been delivered about a fortnight previously—that she had had an attack of fever, and that she had probably committed this act while in a state of delirium. She was acquitted on the ground of insanity: and [it was] remarked that [this] was evidently a case in which the insanity was only temporary, and the prisoner might be restored to her friends.'[41]

There remained however a cumbersome lacuna; when the child had reached a certain yet unspecified age. The defence of Celestina Sommer for the murder of her 11-year-old daughter brought howls of derision when it was suggested she might have escaped death on such ridiculous grounds. (Coincidentally, the child's last safe haven had been the home of her aunt, whose house was next door to Mary McNeil's).[42]

Infanticide, then, had become synonymous with female madness. The American psychiatrist and forensic pioneer, Isaac Ray, drew three major infanticidal conditions under one salient point:

> 'A curious form of homicidal insanity occurs in women, and seems to be connected with those changes in the system produced by parturition, menstruation and lactation. It is a little remarkable that with scarcely an exception, the victim selected by the patient is always her own, or some other, young child.'[43]

Child-murder had been considered since earliest times 'in the dramas of Sophocles, of Euripides, and of Aeschylus, all too often provoking the furies of madness: [recalling] a rampaging Medea slaying her children.'[44]

'I don't know how I felt about the baby.' Thus spoke Hetty Sorrel in George Eliot's classic, *Adam Bede*, the first work of fiction to tackle the infanticide horror.[45] She spoke the words as her form of confession, summing up for many what such women had felt: uncertainty, confusion, a loss of all reason; caught between the anticipated maternal instinct and its ragged rejection when reality arrived. Her innate inability to rationalise her own feelings had thus led to the gravest conclusion.

Certain latter day, typically feminist scholars have highlighted the double whammy faced by infanticide mothers; neither wicked nor mad, they were in fact both! 'Women offenders [were] depicted as doubly-deviant, transgressing gender…as well as legal norms.'[46] It was devised on the presupposition that the mother who killed had taken a dangerous leave of her senses.

Such stereotypical gendering of the law perpetuated circular thinking on women's insanity.[47] Nowhere was this 'mad or bad' argument felt more keenly than in infanticide trials.

For now, at the heart of the discussion, and newly adjusted for its political worth, the unforgivable or unfortunate culprit was the young, abandoned, unmarried mother, who had little option but to take the ultimate step. Preserving her income and reputation alike, she faced no choice but to dispose of her shame. Yet it was not always so clear-cut, especially when the murder was not of *her* children, nor was it restricted to the Victorian age.

Thus, a basic search of the unrivalled *Old Bailey Proceedings Online*[48] reveals some startling disclosures. Between 1674 (its earliest record) and 1836 – that is, from the Stuart era to Georgian – some two hundred and forty infanticide cases produced just seventy-seven convictions. Of these, a dozen were for neither infanticide nor murder, but concealment, a puzzling term brought in no later than 1623. Meanwhile, only *one* up to the year 1713 attracted the insanity plea. In 1675, for example, an unnamed defendant committed the particularly hideous murder of her newly born son. Several witnesses testified to her earlier signs of a fracturing mind and, though events leading up to the tragedy suggested malice aforethought, the jury at the Central Criminal Court declared her of unsound mind and pronounced her not guilty.

By the Georgian period, the insanity plea had become a more recognised tool, not that it always brought the help that was hoped for. In 1714, Mary Tate was acquitted 'as a Person not well in her Senses'. The following year, Jane Simpson was acquitted for want of a witness to confirm the child was in fact alive when delivered. The wonderfully named Pleasant Bateman was acquitted by a compassionate jury in 1723, who decided she must have been in the throes of a fit when her baby slid into the water closet and Frances Deacon was acquitted in 1733, whose only defence was that she was Irish and recently widowed and wished to return home.

Yet compare these with poor Sarah Allen who, in 1737, threw her newborn baby from the third floor apartment to the pavement below. Her insanity plea was straightforward, that she had been 'out of her senses'. Despite witnesses describing her as a silly, giggling girl, a somewhat empty creature, the jury remained unconvinced and sent her to die.

Or, too, the provocatively named Hannah Perfect, who in 1747 proved herself anything but. A 'very sober, honest girl' who, as a single, live-in servant, gave birth to her son, wrapped him in a petticoat and stifled its breath. An accusation of murder was dropped following witness accounts of her mental behaviour:

'Q. In what Condition was the Prisoner, was she in her Senses?

[Witness]. I think she was not in her right Senses.

Q. Was there any Behaviour at that Time that induced you to think she was crazy?

[Witness]. I think the Nature of a Woman, except she was out of her Senses, would not make away or destroy her own.

Q. Did you talk to her at that Time?

[Witness]. She talked to no Body, nor gave no Body any Answer.

Q. What Time might it be between your going up first, and the coming of the Midwife?

[Witness]. About five or six Minutes to be sure.

Q. How long had she been up Stairs before you went up Stairs after her?

[Witness]. About an Hour and an Half, Sir.

Q. Had you any Conversation with her afterwards?

[Witness]. No, Sir, only asked her how she could do so, but she made me no Answer.

Q. Do you construe by her Behaviour that she was stupefied; that she was in her Senses, or was not?

[Witness]. I believe she was stupefied.

Court. You believe she had not the Government of her Understanding?

[Witness]. No, I believe she had not.

Q. Is she a sensible Woman at other Times?

[Witness]. She is a very sensible young Woman.

Q. Have you had any Conversation with her since that Time?

[Witness]. Yes; and she said her Child came dead into the World.

Q. Has she since talked sensibly?

[Witness]. Yes, Sir.

Q. Do you think from the Condition she was in at that Time she was sensible what came upon her? Had she drank any thing that Day?

[Witness]. Nothing at all, any farther than common drink.

Q. What was her Behaviour in general?

[Witness]. She always behaved like a very sober, honest Girl; I never heard her speak an ill Word in my Life.'

The record had just one further entry: 'ACQUITTED', typed in capital letters.[49]

The Importance of Marital Status

Concealment

A court's response to the death of an infant was inerasably drawn by social convention. In 1623, for example, an act had been drafted through which unmarried mothers would be hanged if they concealed the death of an infant they had brought live into the world.[50] Until then, it had remained the law's responsibility in infanticide cases to prove that the child was alive at the time of its birth. Enacted in 1624, King James I's draconian statute now meant that demand was reversed: the *accused* had to put forward a witness who could prove that the child had indeed been born dead.

Another defence soon became vital; pleading 'benefit of linen' showed she had sought help in her labours. After all, 'why would a woman kill a baby when she had prepared for it or sought help to ensure it was born alive?' By the dawn of the 1700s, with the emergence of the legal adversarial process, not having sought help when pregnant, *and* the act of concealment, were finally removed from the list of capital offences. As the century passed, even proven infanticide was, in practice, less likely to lead to a capital sentence.[51]

By 1803 (43 Geo. III, c. 558), corrective measures were once again taken, so that a penal sentence applied even if the accused had been acquitted of murder. The 'Offences Against the Person Act' of 1861 prescribed the same punishment for *anyone*, not just the mother, if found guilty of concealing the birth - whether illegitimate or not.[52]

Murder

In the seventeenth century, particularly if single and pregnant, infanticide was seen as a woman's reaction to shame.[53] Contemporary records make for sad reading.

Mary Naples stood trial in 1681 for killing her infant, charged under the King James I statute (1624): designed to prevent '*lude* women from *murthering* their Bastard Children'. Seemingly an open-and-shut case, she was acquitted not, as one might expect, on the ground of insanity, for no such plea had been made; but because it was made known to the court that she was in fact *married*. Monarchical law could not be applied because women in wedlock defied the meaning of lewd.

Bringing together the two issues of marital status and the insanity plea, an Aylesbury woman in 1668 killed her infant while she and it were alone. Charged with cold murder, the jury were given leave to consider an absence of motive and its implied state of her mind. For here was a married woman, with no cause to murder her child, and no likelihood of her husband not being the father. Such violence in the absence of shame could mean only one thing – she had taken leave of her senses. The jury agreed and pronounced her not guilty, 'to the satisfaction of all [there] who heard it.'[54]

Contrast her favourable experience with just two of the scores of unmarried 'young wenches' who, being single, suffered the harshest of trials. Their condemnation was recorded in typically denigratory style:

'They were it seems *inticed* to Folly, and at last got with Child, and to cover one sin with a greater, most Unnaturally, and Barbarously, *Murthered* their Infants, one of them casting hers into an House of Office, and the other endeavouring to Bury hers in a Celler (*sic*): but being both discovered by certain *Symtomes* usually visible in that condition, upon strait search, the whole matter came to be disclosed, and they respectively Commited (*sic*). They had little to say for themselves besides the common Plea, that their Children were Still-born, but upon Reading the Statute whereby it is

The Fall of Eve: long held the creator of Original Sin and forever mistrusted for her 'venal and volatile' nature (1822). (*Author's Collection*)

Alia species q̄ nōiatur narbus ad ministratā a cirurgicis qn volunt menbrū aliquod incidere. ⁊ qn bibit solarẓ q̄d vr suffocās ei est tyriaca. Et idē auc. Rasis. Dixit mihi q̄dā ex antiq̄s babilonie. q̄ q̄dam pnella pmedit quinqȝ poma mādragore. ⁊ cecidit sincopizata. et tota effecta est rubicūda. et quidē supueniens effudit sup caput ei⁹ aqn nimis donec surrexit. Et ego vidi bōies q̄ sumpserunt de radice eius cā impinguādi. et accidit eis sicut accidit solẓ bōibus ingredientibus balneum et bibētib⁹ post exitum vinū multū. nā sacr⁹ fuit vultus coȝ nimis rubicundus. Et idem auct. dyas. Radicē mādragore multi dāt ad amorē.

folioȝ eius est simile mespili ⁊ est lofach. ⁊ citrini colo. bn̄s odore bonū. ⁊ intra ipȝ sunt grana similia granis piroȝ. ⁊ habet radices magnas mediocriter duas l̄tres adherentes inuicē exteri⁹ nigras ⁊ intent⁹ albas. sup q̄s est cortex grossus. Et hec species mandragore non habet stipitem

Operationes.

A Mandragora fortissimi odoris est. ab hōie ieiuno nō colligit̄ B Umisqȝ vis una est. Hec cum poleta trita fenotes oculoȝ ⁊ dolores auriū sedat. C Radix eius cū aceto trita ⁊ illita ignem sacrum curat. D Auicenna. Mandragora somnū puocat. Et qn ponit̄ in vino vehementer inebriat. Multisqȝ usus est ⁊ odoramentū. faciūt apoplexiā. E Lac eius euellit lentigines. et pannū line mordicatōe. Soluēdo āt educit coleˉa ⁊ flegma. F Radix eius trita et cū aceto imposita sup herisipilam sanat eā. Semen eius matricem mundificat. vl̄ vomitum prouocat.

Female Mandrake. The dangerous mad woman faced herblore and magic as itinerant cures (1491). (*Wellcome Collection*)

Ca. cclxxvij.

Mandragora femine. Seraȝ. auct. dyas. Et semie color est niger ⁊ nominatur landachis siue badachis aptlactuca. Mā in folijs ei⁹ est similitudo cū folijs lactuce. ⁊ sunt pinguia quis odoris. ⁊ extendūt sup faciem terre. in medio

(*Above*) Capricious and Crazed: twelve women driven to madness and blows over a pair of men's hose. Note the Fool(?) on the left (1464). (*Wellcome Collection*)

(*Left*) Medieval cell doctrine showing psychological functions. (*Wellcome Collection*)

A woman "defined" - all nature and curves (1631). (*Wellcome Collection*)

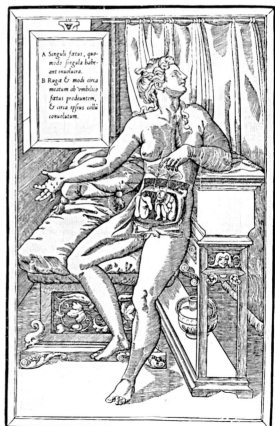

Double trouble? A sixteenth-century depiction of a rather full "wandering womb". (*Wellcome Collection*)

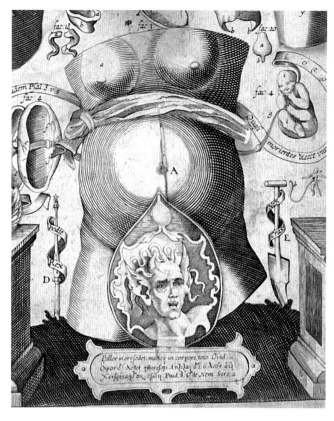

The seat of the Devil: the epicentre of female madness and social disintegration. (*Wellcome Collection*)

A woman consults her male sorcerer-cum-physician (c.16th century). (*Wellcome Collection*)

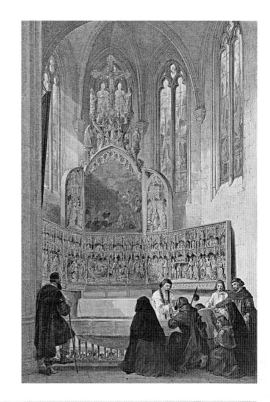

(*Right*) Pilgrims receiving the Eucharist in the chapel of St. Dymphna at Gheel. (*Wellcome Collection*)

(*Below*) "Curing their Folly: early seventeenth-century waters, druggs, conserves & potions, [purging] fancies, follies, idle motions" (1620). (*Wellcome Collection*)

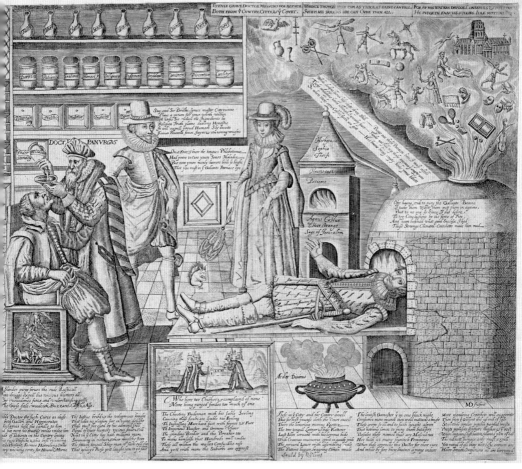

Barber-surgeon extracting stones from her head. Allegorical; symbolising insanity (1787). (*Wellcome Collection*)

Fetti's unintentional melancholic allusion to Maudsley's nineteenth-century fears for the educated female mind (16th/17th century). (*Wellcome Collection*)

Accusations of witchcraft ignored the real possibility that such women were in fact mad. (*Wellcome Collection*)

"Mad Margery", a young woman driven mad and living in the fields: patched clothes, flowers, straw, dirt, tears, and bare flesh betraying her madness (1790/1800). (*Wellcome Colelction*)

Is it to lavish fortunes store,
In vain fantastic empty joys?

Nº 9.

To scatter round the glit'ring ore,
And worship folly's gilded toys? Ah! no!

(*Above*) Pride comes before a fall: "inevitable vanity" predicted by some to cause female madness (1802). (*Wellcome Collection*)

(*Left*) Madness Confined (1775). (*Wellcome Collection*)

(*Above*) Dispelling the Demons: a melancholic woman strives to rid herself of the cause of her madness. (*Wellcome Collection*)

(*Right*) The 'unnecessary' Georgian man-midwife (1796). (*Wellcome Collection*)

A Man – Mid – Wife.

Knowing their limits: female accomplishments led to domestic confinement. (*Wellcome Collection*)

Mesmer's *Baquet* (18th/19th century). (*Wellcome Collection*)

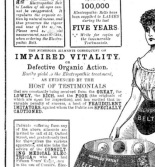

Third stage of Faradization: for "correcting" a woman's mental derangement and to rediscover her senses. (*Wellcome Collection*)

Harnessing innovative power for ailments of the female body…and mind. (*Wellcome Collection*)

Unrequited Love. Resisting her "betters" could land a woman in the asylum (19th century). (*Author's Collection*)

Libertas Amoris.   Freyheit der Liebe.

Cella amanti coelum est. S. Bernard.

Die Cellen oder Claußen, fer von allem welt=getümmel
Ist meine freud, mein süßigkeit, und auf der Erd mein Hümel.

An allegory of a woman's domestic prison and the madness it wrought. (*Wellcome Collection*)

(*Right*) Four stages of Puerperal Mania (1858). (*Wellcome Collection*)

(*Below*) Female dormitory in Bethlem (1860) (*Wellcome Collection*)

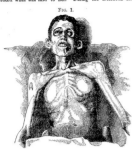

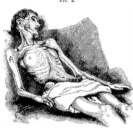

(*Left*) Anorexia nervosa (1895). (*Wellcome Collection*)

(*Below*) Moral Management of the Sex? Pinel Freeing the Insane by Robert-Fleury. Note the number of semi-nude female inmates (1876). (*Wellcome Collection*)

Padded Refractory Cell in Woking Prison - mad or bad? (1889). (*Wellcome Collection*)

Elizabeth Garrett Anderson, England's first licensed female doctor. (*Wellcome Collection*)

Charcot's "Circus" featuring Blanche Wittmann, the Queen of Hysterics (1887). (*Wellcome Collection*)

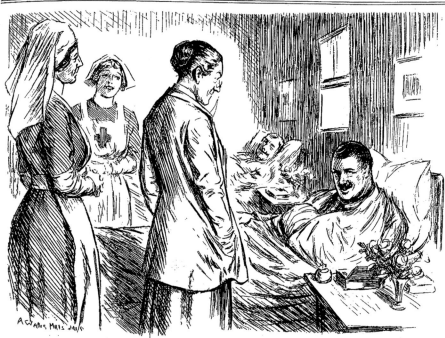

Eminent Woman Surgeon, who is also an ardent Suffragist (to wounded Guardsman). "DO YOU KNOW, YOUR FACE IS SINGULARLY FAMILIAR TO ME. I'VE BEEN TRYING TO REMEMBER WHERE WE'VE MET BEFORE."
Guardsman. "WELL, MUM, BYGONES BE BYGONES. I WAS A POLICE CONSTABLE."

Unkind Parody: Women in Medicine and the Suffragettes (1915). (*Wellcome Collection*) provided in such Cases that unless the same be proved by, at least one Credible witness, it shall be reputed and punished as Murder, and they were both Condemned to Dye.'[55]

The Nineteenth Century Crisis

It remained a sad truth that single mothers especially were still judged by their 'immoral behaviour'. As the nineteenth century dawned, their desperate infanticide act was being increasingly executed by married women as well. It gave rise to several, unsettling forces; was she single and wanton, or a victim of want (economic or social)? And if even the former, was hanging the right response to such an insane folly? Two pressures entered the mix: from those who sought an end to all capital punishment; and those Victorian alienists who presented themselves as the mad mother's salvation.

That *any* woman who murdered her offspring could not be right in her mind, led to a plethora of comment and outrage. For example, the *British Medical Journal's* rejoinder in 1865:

> 'In that particular form of mania…called puerperal – the mania of women, which sometimes follows upon childbed – the mother becomes melancholy, and is at times seized with an "uncontrollable impulse", ay! Even to destroy her own offspring – the doting mother murdering her own beloved child – and she is horrified with herself all the time, because of the dreadful crime to which she feels impelled. Does such a woman (becoming a murderess) deserve our deepest sympathy; or ought she to be handed into the hangman's hands?'[56]

But then the law did not readily accept the notion of puerperal madness and Victorian judges proved tough nuts to crack. Baron Bramwell, for example, one of its fiercest critics, harboured ideas of deterrent and sanction that more resembled the medieval coalition between the church and the state. He remained convinced that base wickedness existed when a young girl fell pregnant. How Bramwell would have welcomed the barbaric deterrents then around to such acts of 'temptation'.[57]

Many contemporary observers of a periodic moral collapse were aware of the crisis, in the middle decades especially. In Nottingham, for example, the number of discovered infanticide cases was so despicably stark that local coroner, Mr Browne, suspected they were in fact just the tip of the iceberg. He illustrated his concerns by reporting all inquests over which he presided, highlighting the large number of bodies found 'in privies, in the canal, or exposed in the fields or open places'.[58] Perhaps, he conjectured, it revealed the mothers' desperate efforts to detach her act from the norm; or to simply avoid being caught.

In his 1866 article, *Massacre of the Innocents*, maligned doctor and beekeeper Andrew Wynter, claimed that literally thousands of murdering mothers were escaping detection and even when caught, avoiding the noose. As he wrote in his hyperbolic language:

> '12,000 murderesses living in our midst, performing our domestic offices, ministering to our private wants, and doing women's work about the town, with the dreadful secrets locked up in their breasts.'

Though, surprisingly maybe, he blamed poverty, shame and the moral and financial irresponsibility of men for this crime.[59]

Not that the tragic act of killing your child has always been seen as the mother's rejection. In a radical treatise, Andrew Mangham has reconstructed thinking on what really led a mother to kill. Hers, he said, were reasons not confined to external or societal factors, but to what was going on in her mind. Using the case of Mary Ann Brough[60] as a live example, Mangham argued that the horrific violence she used in slaying her children in Surrey in 1854, before her defence pleaded irresistible impulse, was not anti-maternal but an [albeit unhinged] feature of the motherly instinct - what he calls 'a potential form of maternal necessity.'[61] Acting unreasonably for a reasonable purpose sat at the heart of the alienists' endeavours for exculpatory madness.

In the Criminal Context

Thus in crime, infanticide especially, a woman had long been dismissed as either fragile (the victim, of her circumstances and/or nature), or wicked (the 'Babylonian whore'). Alienists and death penalty abolitionists now added a third possibility: that they were truly insane.

To them, infanticide, whether concealed or not, whether its causes nuanced or not, *was* indeed madness. Jurist Stephen, unusually compassionate for one outside this alienist cause, stuck to the view that:

> 'women in that condition [puerperal] do get the strongest symptoms of what amounts almost to temporary madness, and…often hardly know what they are about, and will do things which they have no settled or deliberate intention whatever of doing…'

He even went on to suggest that the crime itself was not as bad as some:

> 'other kinds of murder. You cannot estimate the loss to the child
> itself, you know nothing about it at all. With regard to the public it
> causes no alarm, because it is a crime which can be committed only
> by mothers, upon their newly born children. Besides…there is the
> strong sympathy, which it is never safe to neglect and which always
> will exist, with the miserable condition of the woman.'

He had, immediately prior, summed up for the Royal Commission as to the
then state of the problem:

> 'I have heard many trials for child murder, and I believe that it is the
> almost universal experience upon that matter that it is exceedingly
> hard to get a jury to convict of child murder, and that if a conviction
> takes place it is very rare to have an execution.'[62]

In 1863, *The Lancet*, among a chorus of others, saw the need for change,
whether in the preventative law or in the social responses to these mothers
who killed, especially when suffering mental collapse:

> 'To arrest the wholesale massacre of children which is now carried
> on with impunity in this country is one of the most important
> duties of our time'…[and] a slur on our 'boasted civilisation.'[63]

And as Walker summarised over a century later, infanticide cases *demanded*
the presumption that the mother was mad.[64]

As the decades progressed, and the world awoke to a new century of order,
attitudinal differences between society and the law began to be felt. In truth,
this had happened ever since the mid-century epoch, when compassionate
(or ignorant) juries had begun to excuse or condemn mothers who killed,
often in the face of the judge's recommendations. When that failed to emerge,
the newly created Home Secretary's Mercy was increasingly applied, often
(usually) to the mother's relief – leastways her continued existence, for it
seldom brought the benefits such compassion suggests. These newly saved
mothers – as for women in general – had been 'transferred', not from male
control into female freedoms (so no longer possessed), but simply between
different misogynist masters, each having their own set of agendas. The male
prison director, like the asylum superintendent, had only correction in mind.

Nevertheless, from a new 1922 Act through to the last period of this book (ie 1950), a trend away from even imprisonment continued to gain renewed vigour. Slaying your own child was, for some mothers at least, an increasingly excusable act. Not even named as a murder, not even manslaughter per se, it was seen to lie beyond the innate requirements of the infamous M'Naghten Rules – now the accused might have known what she did at the moment she did it but still, unlike any other crime, find herself let off:

> 'All that she [the infanticidal mother] need produce [was] evidence that at the time the balance of her mind was disturbed by the birth or subsequent lactation: not that the disturbance was sufficiently severe to deprive her of knowledge of the nature and quality of her act, or knowledge of its wrongness, or the capacity to control herself.'[65]

When the Act was replaced sixteen years later (and amended 2009), 'the gap between the medical view of maternal mental disorder and its legal reconstruction'[66] was gradually closed. Likewise, when Diminished Responsibility was subsequently brought in, through the 1957 Homicide Act, it replaced infanticide both in its essence and, indeed, its inclusion as an insanity crime.[67]

Infanticide Cases

It might be of interest to provide just two examples here, in which the alleged lunatic mother was greeted with the full force of the law and/or social derision. The important dilemma they exposed was that, throughout the Victorian era, fierce, international debates broached the central idea; mothers in madness deserved greater compassion *versus* too many women were escaping scot-free.

First, the trial of Maria Clarke, in 1850s Suffolk, led to the harshest of hearings. Appearing at that county's Assizes, charged with the death of her illegitimate baby, she was found guilty and summarily sentenced to hang. Though suffering extreme poverty, and devoid of all solace, she had tragically buried the child alive.

While out walking that chill early spring, she had carried a spade and the starving infant for many more hours than she would ever remember. Destitute and alone she had, as presiding Judge Jervis bemoaned, arrived at her wicked decision – to rid herself of her status as an unmarried mother.[68]

Any chance of reprieve was essentially absent. Poorly defended, and Justice Jervis adhering to the Bramwellian school, the recalcitrant judge forbade interested parties, as well as the jury, any opportunity to consider her mind. Rather, he insisted, she had known the fault in her crime and in that alone had adequately proved that she suffered no madness. The M'Naghten Rules not even a decade in existence she was, he concluded, just utterly selfish. When compared to the accused's own 'confession', more humane commentators might have seen the grounds for compassion:

> 'I did not hurt the child…I kissed it and laid it in a hole, and went away and sat on a bank near a gate, and there I sat for a quarter of an hour, or twenty minutes. *But all at once something caught me up and told me I must be going, and then I went home in such light spirits as though I could fly*…I wanted them to let me go and fetch it; and if they had, I should have fetched my child and jumped into the pond and drowned myself.'[69]

As soon as her sentence of death was pronounced, local worthies harried the Home Secretary who, in either a fit of heartfelt compassion or disgust with the judge, commuted the sentence. It is not known how Clarke ended her days, but her history of insane thoughts, including repeated attempts at *felo de se*, were soon after made public.[70]

In 1903, Elizabeth Ann Sturgeon stood trial for murdering not her own child but Mabel, an adopted 'replacement'. That she had given birth to her still-born daughter just a few weeks before led her supporters to claim she had been suffering puerperal mania. And the Liverpool case drew wide international focus, for the victim this time was not the one to have caused the insanity state.

Evidence of Sturgeon's initial love for the child included how she had recruited a nurse, and the girl's 'sizeable wardrobe', awash with new, monogrammed clothes. Yet 'as the heat of [that] year reached its peak, Sturgeon began [displaying] some worrying traits'. These included rambling letters, such as the one she wrote to her father in which she claimed her husband was attempting to kill her. More bizarre still was her insistence that she, the child and the nurse spend the night in a nearby park, supposedly on account of the cool summer's night. As dawn rose over the city, she invented a reason to return home alone with the child and carried the grizzling child across the dew-covered fields… Mabel's lifeless body was discovered a few hours later, hidden beneath a heap of spent lime on scrubland close to a nearby church. Her small throat had been cut with what the police deduced was a penknife with an imperfectly honed blade.

Sturgeon was arrested quickly though she waited almost six months before standing trial. When it came, the case had already resulted in one damning report:

> '[Sturgeon was] ...inclined to be *hysterical*, and imagined things which did not exist. [While h]er [own] mother deposed that she was frequently queer and irritable, and influenza had left her mind weak.[71]
>
> 'Clearly something was wrong, but how now to proceed. The jury, returned a verdict of guilty - but advised a compassionate sentence, for she had, they agreed, "no control of her mind"... Branded a criminal lunatic, [she was] sentenced to be held at His Majesty's Pleasure'.

Yet, in a curious turn...Sturgeon's husband appealed to the Home Office for his wife's immediate release. She had, he insisted, suffered a mental derangement. Akers-Douglas, the Home Secretary refused, declaring her crime much too heinous. As *The Times* newspaper reported:

> THE DETENTION OF A CRIMINAL LUNATIC – Mr H.F. Neale, solicitor of Liverpool, yesterday received the following reply to his appeal for the release of Mrs. Sturgeon, a woman of independent means, who was at the last Liverpool Assizes convicted of the murder of the child she had adopted, though it was found that she was of unsound mind when she committed the crime:-
>
> 'Whitehall, Dec. 28, 1903. Sir - I am directed by the Secretary of State to say that he has had under consideration your letter of the 5th inst., asking for the discharge of the criminal lunatic Elizabeth Ann Sturgeon, and that he has made inquiry with regard to all the circumstances of this case, but he regrets that, in view of the serious nature of Mrs. Sturgeon's crime, it is impossible to entertain the question of her immediate discharge. He has, therefore, given directions that she should be removed to Broadmoor Asylum, where she will be well cared for and her mental condition carefully observed. I am, Sir, your obedient servant, C. E. Troup.'

'That she was at some time released is [however] borne out by her appearance in the census of 1911. Together with William, she had occupied a dwelling on the Wirral, "over the Mersey", living life as though nothing had happened, her past misdemeanours unknown. Like others before her – and, no doubt, many more since – the so-called 'puerperal insanity' had led to but a short-lived confinement – but to many, she had escaped her capital crime.'[72]

Throughout time, innumerable responses to mothers who murdered their children ranged from apathy to horror. Arguments for madness came later, growing in fervour since the 1600s and lasting until its nineteenth century peak. As time had progressed, and disheartened by the law's apparent lack of compassion, male juries took it upon themselves to acquit (or condemn) based not on any burden of proof, but on whether they themselves believed the defendant was irrefutably mad, at least at the time they committed their crime. Opinion had replaced intransigent fact.

Such virtual collapse of the system led to a drawn-out battle between hard-liners and liberals, a war from which many women's lives were either ended or saved. Such inconsistent responses were seldom seen elsewhere in the annals of crime, but taking an innocent life, by the one entrusted to care, was a wrong like no other. Exculpatory madness seemed an ineludible 'truth'.

Even so, it proved a double-edged sword. Whether saved or condemned, it was her reproductive apparatus, and its effect on her mind, that was invariably blamed. Far beyond the infanticide crisis, women of all backgrounds and ages, status and wealth, were maintained as the dangerous species, not because they were all of them killers, but because they were all of them women. The only difference in half a millennium was how her wandering womb had given way to her corruptible mind.

The woman's lot was still intrinsically poor.

Yet again gaining prominence in the long nineteenth century, another, non-filicide form of child murder had shaken the world to its core. Baby-farming rose to pandemic proportions, so that pleas of insanity were being frequently made on the basis that these supposedly maternal women could have resorted to horror.

In the case of Margaret Walters (alias Willis or Wallis), like Amelia Dyer much later, she was eventually convicted on one count of murder, that of a young, illegitimate boy. But it was estimated that she had already killed somewhere in excess of another two dozen. When the police had raided her lodgings, yet more were released in malnourished condition. Any insanity plea Walters made must have fallen on deaf ears, as she was found guilty of murder and hanged at her prison. The year was 1870.[73]

A more recent case, in twentieth century France, caused international terror. Jeanne Weber became infamous as the serial killer of several children, likely including her own. Arrested in 1908, she was convicted of multiple murders, and had been renamed in the press as *l'Ogresse de la Goutte d'Or* (The Ogress of the Golden Drop).

Her (obvious?) mental problems appeared to begin some years before, when she was first arrested for vagrancy and placed in Nanterre asylum near Paris. However, alienists there refuted her madness and thrust her out on the streets. After the scandal, she attempted suicide on at least two occasions, both times escaping any serious injury. But in 1908, time finally ran out. Rearrested in May, she was eventually convicted of the deaths of five children; her daughter, her son and three of her nieces. Only for the court to declare her insane. Her habitual drinking was suggested as a possible cause.

In what then became a startling use of insanity physiognomics, the famed Italian physician and criminologist, Lombroso, on being shown Weber's image and asked for his psychiatric diagnosis(!), announced, 'her microcephalic skull, her flattened forehead and her virile physiognomy' make her a 'hysterical epileptoid and cretinoid certainly from a family of morons'. Despite no further evidence, she was incarcerated for life, first in Maréville Asylum then in another, Fains-Véel, in the Meuse.

Such a bizarre case in the end had a fairly straightforward conclusion. On 23 August 1918, after being confined for ten years, Weber manually strangled herself – previously thought an impossible act. And the success of her final assault, on herself, was recorded as her 'crisis of madness'.[74]

Non-Child Murder

Nineteenth century responses to the populist's *femme fatale* ranged from her being feared as evil, to being feared as mad. When any obvious provocation was lacking, she was labelled one of the most irrational criminals committing the most inexplicable crime. Perhaps it was this reputation for madness that brought so many attempts to excuse other, non-child murders; typically those of her spouse, but often too some other family member.

Startup has observed that the use of poison in such cases gave rise to a societal fear that there was an epidemic at hand.[75] Illuminating the issue in terms which reflected 'her lot': 'stealthily at work where least suspected, betraying the trust placed in her, abusing her privileged position within the home.'[76]

Unlike the growing sympathy for infanticidal mothers, murderers of spouses received no such reprieve.[77] The act's very nature demanded malice aforethought; her motives were often pecuniary gain; while, all too often, genuinely disturbed women who resorted to murder were being cruelly mishandled in spite of their minds.

Not all bad behaviour arising from female madness took such murderous forms. A raft of other felonies and less serious misdemeanours attracted the insanity plea, often on supposed menstrual misery, disordered menses or catamenial madness.

Incendiarism, or pyromania, was put forward by Taylor as 'a variety of monomania in which there is a morbid disposition of mind leading to impulsive acts of incendiarism without any motive.'[78] It was believed to occur especially during puberty, a period in a girl's life when her maturing organs rendered her prone to emotional disruption. However, Bucknill and Tuke dismissed it as definitely *not* an insanity condition.[79]

Wilks, however, put it down to a bout of hysterics, and reported the case of Jane Ashmore, a Rochester servant, in September 1876. On no less than three separate occasions, she had set her master's parlour alight, later claiming no plausible motive. Over three successive nights, her employer had detected smoke rising up through the sitting-room floor, and each time found the room beneath consumed by fire. Ashmore confessed, was tried at Maidstone Assizes, where she offered no reason or motive.

Kleptomania, more readily ascribed to menstrual problems, was defined as 'an irresistible impulse to steal', especially found amongst pregnant and high society women.[80] Ann Shepherd, for example, escaped all punishment in 1845, after stealing a feather boa on account of her 'temporary insanity' brought on by her 'suppression of the menses'.[81]

Baker, however, thought that unless accompanied by intellectual weakness, the accused should be held wholly responsible. He enforced it for mothers:

'The state of pregnancy cannot be held as an exculpatory plea in cases of stealing unless supported by other evidence of mental derangement.'[82]

Compare this with Marc, the French forensic psychiatry author, who identified theft resulting from 'disordered menstruation' and shared the somewhat avant-garde notion that stealing sometimes arose from a repressed sexual desire.[83] Menstruation thus joined pregnancy and drunkenness as triggers for a felonious irresistible impulse.[84]

One of the more unexpected crimes to arise was female treason. Perceived more as a masculine problem, in 1786 Margaret Nicholson threw herself at George III armed with only a cake knife. Wrestled to the ground by his staff, she was carted away and appeared before the Privy Council who, without trial, despatched her to Bethlem.[85] A century earlier and she may not have been so 'lucky'. During the nominal Barebones Parliament of the seventeenth century, Commonwealth statute was passed so that 'women were no longer to be burnt' – even for treason. Instead, they were 'but hanged'.[86]

Earlier still, Henry VIII, one not readily remembered for his compassionate nature, misused his authoritative power and changed the lunacy law – just to rid himself of a nuisance. Having consigned Lady Rochester, Anne Boleyn's sister-in-law, to an imprisonment that drove her literally mad, he selfishly declared that the insane *could* be executed and promptly chopped off her head. The law until then had protected the crazed.

Finally, other non-criminal mania included the more unusual trichotillomania – a disordered compulsion to pull out one's hair, from the head to the pubis. It was first recognised in the mists of time, Hippocrates recording the practice of Delearces' depressed, grieving wife who 'groped about, scratching and plucking out hair.'[87] Hence the phrase, 'pulling your hair out' when feeling frustrated.

Away from the criminal courts, indeed a century before their eventual domination of the insanity plea, it was a person's wealth that meant more in their community standing. It was not just gender that separated the wheat from the chaff; the respected and 'poor' became the more important distinction. But then even wealth and possession attracted inhuman maltreatment and when both gender *and* class crashed together, the effect on the mind was thought a danger to all.

In the so-called upper classes especially, problematic neuroses were seen to have their florescence through the eighteenth and nineteenth centuries – amongst women, especially. From their well-to-do nerves (a sign of good breeding, though more prone to decay), to Cheyne's *English Malady* of 'melancholy, lowness of spirit and disturbance of appetite', the Georgian discovery of the central nervous system and its role in 'the female experience' – and the maladies they wrought – refocussed a physicalist cause for the mad woman's behaviour.[88]

The Mad Criminal's Gender?

A cacophony of voices down the millennia have pitched in with why women sometimes turned wicked. In the colliding worlds of medicine and law, stalwarts like Bracton, Griesinger, Hale, Ray and Coke, often diagnosed madness in criminal terms.

'Coke mentions the subject of madness,' recorded Stephen, the arguably enlightened jurist, 'only in the most casual and fragmentary manner. [Though] Hale has a chapter upon it which seems to me to be marked by the ignorance of the age in which it was written (the seventeenth century), and…omit all the difficulties of the subject.'[89]. Difficulties which, many might argue, still plague us today.

Half a century earlier, Griesinger, whom Scull labelled 'the founding father' of a new wave of German psychiatry, gave his own theories, in which he focussed on the pathology of the brain, insisting 'mental illness' was in reality a disease of both itself and the nerves. Yet he created a pessimist's charter, as very little if anything was offered by way of a cure.[90]

Over time, madness was adapted to 'explain' the criminal woman. In all kinds of jurisdictions and in all types of courts, definitions of exculpatory insanity became the biggest, singular focus for those who used gender corruption to predict – and excuse – almost all types of crime. And when the insanity plea was applied, a subtle new dawn of gender-based responses was quickly pushed forward. No longer was a woman punished because of her gender – as she had been in the seventeenth century witch-hunts or the Inquisition they mirrored – rather now she was pitied for precisely that reason, that she should be *managed* as the regrettable flaw.

As early as the thirteenth century, the first known petitions were heard in cases of alleged *temporary* madness; such as the Suffolk man found guilty of killing a woman while in a 'furious' state.[91] From Bracton to Hale, to appropriate Walker's excellent title (1968, Chapter 2), and covering the four hundred years that stuttered between the thirteenth and seventeenth centuries, the work of leading clerics, jurists and latterly medics shaped the changing legal responses to miscreant women. And though much more a theoretical wisdom than an earth-shifting advancement, in hindsight it was still an achievement of sorts, and a step forward towards progress and change.[92]

Mad women (and men) at the start of the 1500s may not have agreed. In an age when serious yet non-fatal crimes were excused from the sentence of death, other punishments were applied which today are abhorrent. For those declared insane, their pleas considered 'proven' by juries, were subsequently 'corrected' by beating, whipping and chains. According to Sir Thomas More, the future Lord Chancellor, writing in 1533:

'Another [insanity case] was one, whyche after that he had fallen into ye frantike heresyes, fell soon after into playne open fransye byseide...afterwarde by betynge and correcyon gathered his remembraunce to him'. But the punishment stopped working. '[I] caused him as he came wanderynge by my dore, to be taken by the constables and bounden to a tre in the strete before the whole towne, and there they stryped him with roddys therfore tyl he waxed wery and somewhat lenger.'.[93]

By the mid-1600s, Sir Matthew Hale's 'The History of the Pleas of the Crown' – only unearthed from his papers long after his death (1676) – included ground-breaking thought and conjecture on the crimes of the 'mad'. Eventually published in 1736, it served the legal profession, if not the medics, for a further two hundred years. He had previously argued the progressive value of investing more power in the hearts and minds of the jury (and away from the monarch): a critical opinion that implied lay men and women held greater compassion than those nominally responsible for the law of the land.[94]

Such early responses to those found 'not guilty on the ground of insanity' (a phrase not introduced until the Act of 1800 (40 Geo. III, c. 94)), included the Aylesbury woman who, in 1668, whilst '[in] a temporary phrenzy' murdered her child, newly born, but who was then simply set free; that is, she was likely 'return[ed] to her husband' where, it was hoped, she recovered her senses.[95] Or the 'distracted' woman in Great Staughton, Huntingdonshire who, according to formal accounts from the year 1690, suffered being watched and *whipped* by the constable, who received eight shillings and sixpence for his conspicuous trouble.[96]

The seventeenth century obsession with devils and witchcraft fuelled its own litany of cases spuriously involving 'the mad'; though now it was down to supernatural possession. Such as the 'six men and women' who 'slaughter[ed] their children, their parents or their spouses' whilst their own minds and souls were under Satanic attack.[97]

In a search for a more humane understanding, myriad opinions and voices were sought from farther afield, for the challenge was too great for a small island as ours. 'Experts' like Isaac Ray and Pinel were consulted as much as the later indigenous talent, such as Prichard, Laycock, Winslow *et al*. Underpinning it all was what constituted responsible action, and what on the other hand was considered to be no fault of a mad woman's mind. And it is arguably something that has not yet gone away.

By the dawn of the Victorian trial, authorities believed a woman's criminal act, with particular highlights, infanticide especially, was enough in itself to prove she was mad. For now it was her gender alone that led to her being considered insane. For example, in 1874, Eliza Dart was brought to trial for an attempted murder and suicide after she threw both herself and her baby in the Serpentine in London's Hyde Park. Unable to prove her empirical madness, the judge, Mr Brett, ruled that her actions were proof enough of a disordered mind.[98] As we shall see, this led to what I have come to think of as 'inverse misogyny' – when being a woman still meant gender-based bias, but now to her arguable good.

Meanwhile, women's victims too were being 'remoulded' to form a false and hideous picture, in no greater way than during the fearful rise in nineteenth century cases of infanticide deaths. The truth, today, is perhaps unexpected; women attacked other *adults* more than they did their own children. It is a fact underscored by including cases of neglect, not just deliberate murder.

Top of this list were those women whose crimes involved violence, itself anathema to her role as a nurturing mother, wife, sister and aunt. Such 'unnatural' leanings contravened her supposed purpose in life, one meant 'to embody calm, passivity and obedience'. Yet while it may be true that 'women only made up a minority of those convicted of violent crime in the Victorian period and acts of violence made up the minority of offences for which women were convicted... violent female offenders did exist to a greater extent than it may at first seem.'[99]

Domestic violence accounted for many reported and non-reported offences (the latter revealing the shame of the male and his expected character: hard-working, robust, stronger than women); while its causes – including jealousy, drunkenness and adulterous living – abounded in the insanity plea.. For example, Jane Cushion was convicted in 1866 for wounding her estranged husband, by tying his hands over his head and cutting his throat with a razor. 'I was very jealous of my husband, I did not like his going away from me; I found I could not bear it.' She was given ten years imprisonment, released after six.

In the more extreme case of actually killing her spouse, Eileen Kinsley stood trial charged only with manslaughter. During a drink-fuelled rumpus, she threw crockery at his head, causing a cut to the nose from which he bled to death while later asleep. With apparently no insanity plea offered, she was found guilty and sentenced, spending just six weeks in prison for taking his life.

Another, very Victorian problem were violent attacks by women with acid. Mary [Morrison] was one of only a few dozen...throughout the Victorian period that received heavy sentences for [such] assaults. What her victim had done to provoke such an attack, however, seemed to matter more to the courts than the felonious act.[100]

What they and many others indirectly revealed was the disturbing Victorian ideal of the peaceable woman. Violence and murder had been largely rejected by societies during the present book's five century sphere, but in the Victorian age it reappeared as a cancerous sore.

The 'idealised' woman, meanwhile, influenced, indeed shaped, historical reactions to female crime. As Lucia Zedner, present-day criminologist, observed:

> 'The comparatively low level of female convictions may be attributable to a belief in the innate non-criminality of women, but that female offenders were more likely to be stigmatised having compounded their legal transgressions by compromising their idealised roles as wives and mothers'.[101]

The further emergence of 'feeble-minded' women standing trial for their (unnatural) crimes coincided with, and perhaps even reflected, the parallel contrivance of masculine alienists, judges, juries and jurists in creating their own definition of mad or bad women.

Yet there was also something deliciously aberrant about the female offender. She displayed all the 'bad' things in life, drunkenness, temper, even being promiscuously minded. When a dash of madness was added, it only enhanced her salacious allure. In short, nineteenth century female offenders were understood to have rejected inherent misogynist leanings that demanded nice girls who *didn't* whilst welcoming those *better* girls who did.

Even those on 'their side' revealed chauvinist thinking. Such as Alfred Dymond, erstwhile Secretary of the Society for the Abolition of Capital Punishment, who gave many a pseudo-diagnosis while pleading her case.[102]

Other cases, more explicit, occurred when alleged *victims* of rape faced a new double jeopardy – that to describe the offence revealed some sexual knowledge, and implied a degree of sexual promiscuity that would weaken the claim.[103] In the 1834 case of Elizabeth Chapman, her 'plain look[s]' and 'defect in her speech such as frequently accompanies imbecility of mind' were seemingly more important to the court than the brutal truth of her treatment during her alleged multiple rape.[104]

As a final consideration, the long course of female crime and insanity saw the 'gentler sex' commandeer certain criminal offences. Witchcraft, hysteria, scolding and infanticide, all became synonymous with the reborn notion of the dangerously mad woman.[105]

In conclusion, when maternal mayhem led to a criminal action, trials heard claims of endocrine system imbalance, typically as an exculpatory factor. As late as 1938, in the Infanticide Act, this remained one of just the two needed proofs of madness for a mother to be excused for causing the death of her child.[106] Yet with so many opportunities to be labelled insane, a woman faced both patriarchal control and institutionalisation. Though it occasionally, undoubtedly worked in her favour, the norm appears to have brought no real hope, certainly not when non-legal, ruthless responses included emotional and even anatomical 'correction'. Which is what we censoriously turn to in the following chapter.

Chapter 4

'Correcting' Women

In such a history as this, disturbing factors undoubtedly rise to the surface. Nowhere was this more keenly felt – other than perhaps the Holocaust and other genocide horrors – than in the increasingly violent responses to the female insane. In both 'justification' and actual treatments, 'correcting' the woman makes for difficult reading but it is a truth that has to be told. Its entire history can be crudely summed up perhaps in the phrase, *'to incarcerate or to operate'*. And it is a topic which benefits from a strict chronological approach.

Some Early Responses

The 'correction' of women has a tortured history, so that the following serves as an introduction to what is regrettably a time-honoured theme. For example, as Burton asserted in the early 1600s, the human soul adopted three discrete parts; vegetal, sensible and rational or nutrition, perception and will. When insanity struck, the human mind having fallen to what he called fictitious perceptions, had evidently lost its rational state. Its owner, he inferred, had become no more than a beast.[1] The mistreatment of animalistic lunatics in straw-covered cells roared into view.

In near parallel ways, the regimes for 'care' were similarly brutal. In the following eighteenth century era of gents and gentility, the ongoing treatment of the crazed betrayed a nastier truth.

> 'Conditions were atrocious. There was no provision of cleanliness or comfort, much less for anything resembling therapy…asylums were custodial institutions rather than therapeutic hospitals… barbarity and ignorance were the rule.'[2]

Each incarnation was a response to prevailing ideas; at best a continuing search for deep understanding, though at worst an ignorant reaction to those unfortunate few deemed 'unfit for life'.

An holistic approach combined with magical notions rose up on the back of such rigorous thinking. Localised causes of madness were no longer enough; the human condition was a delicate system, prone to decay and disruption like a neglected machine. The fragile woman, as ever, was saddled with the reputation of carrying the greatest risk of collapse; despite the optimist's language:

'The anatomy of the nerves provides more pleasant and profitable speculations…for very many of the actions and passions that take place in our body [would] otherwise seem most difficult to explain: and from this fountain, no less than the hidden cases of diseases and symptoms, *which are commonly ascribed to the incantations of witches*, may be discovered and satisfactorily explained.'[3]

Though such early exponents retained their belief in 'nervous disorders', such as hysteric behaviour, they put safe distance between the humours and science. Blackmore's much later (1726) affirmation of the 'more soft, tender, and delicate texture of the nerves [of the female]'[4] meant hysterical conditions were a genuine ill. On such double-edged, minor advancements did the woman's position dare to improve. Nevertheless, they remained entwined by age-old ideas.

Medicines and 'remedies' were most effective, for example, when administered under auspicious cosmological conditions (akin to sowing and harvesting in tune with the moon). As late as 1597, Gerarde the herbalist advised: 'the virtues of double yellow and white batchelor's buttons, hung "in a linnen cloath about the necke of [one] that is lunaticke, in the waine of the moone, when the signe shall be in the first degree of Taurus or Scorpio".'[5]. Music, quietude and the avoidance of other patients were a melancholiac's last hope.

Extra-somatic responses still sadly included medieval abuses such as flogging the mad, which was practised at Bethlem as late as the 1700s. And even Willis himself advocated this violent response:

'The first indication, *viz*, curatory, requires threatenings, bonds, or strokes, as well as physic. For the madman…must be so handled both by the physician, and also by the servants that are prudent, that he may be in some manner kept in, either by warnings, chiding, or punishments inflicted on him, to his duty, or his behaviour, or manners.'[6]

Acceptance of such 'therapies' may have receded in time, as so too did late seventeenth century beliefs in astrology-medicine and philosophical thought. But was it to be a false dawn? Or a necessary step on the road to Enlightenment thinking? Had indeed compassion won through? As Macdonald lamented: 'The increasing presence of scientific medicine was the result of political strife and religious controversy and not the advancement of psychological theory and medical therapy.'[7]. Yet whatever the motives, the wheels of change in the treatment of madness had, albeit microscopically, shifted and turned.

But now mental conditions required opiate treatments, alongside purges and emetics, often ably assisted by blood-letting and leech. There were also individual inventions, such as the Napier's own 'controversial infusion of liquid gold'.[8] And as a relict idea, even 'earthworms and bats' remained prescribed 'cures' long into the Victorian age.[9]

One other 'treatment' remained a constant companion to these struggling medics; the power of suggestion. In the age of imagination, of witches, warlocks and Puritan hate, certain later physicians relied on nothing more than the suggestion of a fictitious but failsafe cure.[10] In effect, a placebo. To prove its worth, in the first half of the seventeenth century, two patients of John Cotta, a Northampton physician, 'developed' their respective physical ailments only after he had diagnosed them *incorrectly* with the ills they now 'had'![11]

Religion too, not just magic and mayhem, devised responses to madness, at least the sort the clerics defined. Only now any gender distinction was made even harsher, the treatment of Eve ever more cruel. In the Puritan era, early morality gave the home and the family its clear sex-defined roles. Made up of harsh expectations, unsustainable whims and, by extension, callous restraint. Little would change in the future thinking of churchmen: a woman's place in the home kept the Devil at bay.

At its heart, of course, lay this need for the sound family unit. When domestic ideals were undone, by an unyielding wife, daughter or mother, at least the insanity label would come to the patriarch's aid. Her role was set down, any deviation was brutally handled; labelled wicked or mad, she was treated the same.

By the age of the eighteenth century charlatan, the much-maligned 'mad-doctor', medicine and psychiatry were replacing the church. And as the young Victoria took the throne, a new breed of alienists brought in a 'new dawn' of the mind. Setting themselves against most other voices in the nineteenth century struggles, they attempted to repair broken women by redefining their minds. In many ways worse, as history tells us, it was those who came from within who caused the most harm. We're talking here of a new breed of 'expert', the gynaecologist turned alienist and the 'treatments' they wrought.

Characters like Isaac Baker Brown, who found a stage and a world eager to listen; Silas Weir Mitchell and his insistence on rest; and Mesmer and his electric hypnosis, each achieved notoriety and fortune from unnerving responses, in which the female 'mad' became their target of shame.

Back in the Middle Ages, modes and techniques caused their own great personal suffering, when 'successful' repair of the mad was deemed to come from thrashing the body and purging the soul. Yet there were other, more doubtful encounters: from the scold's bridle to the brank, the ducking stool to the stake. And these were, of course, largely focussed on women. Not only did she feel its humiliation and pain, most was not even done in response to what future eras would term madness. Rather, they were simply punished for being, well, women.

The cucking or ducking stool for example, has long been associated with the witch or the shrew – so, by extended inference, the mad woman as well. As Walker said, 'it is very likely that many [brutalised] scolds were really suffering … paranoia.'[12] A tradition in Cornwall related the so-called 'Ducking the Daft', in which the poor victim would be forcibly cast in a pond and thrown about until either her fury had left or her life was extinguished. If she was lucky enough to still live, she was then carried off, still dripping, to the church, where hymns and psalms were incanted to unburden her soul.

One pragmatic explanation aligns this to the one-time treatment of a former Master of Bedlam, who kept his patients 'bound in pools up to the middle and so more or less after the fit of their fury.'[13]. Though nothing could justify such dehumanisation.

Medieval diagnoses of madness in the criminal context saw not compassion but ill treatment, ostensibly to serve as an example to all: 'summarily executed, and left to rot in a gibbet at the crossroads.'[14] Non-criminal types may have resorted – or been forcibly exposed to – astrology and magic, especially in the Elizabethan age of John Dee, the queen's necromancer.[15] In contemporary literature too, in Shakespeare's *Taming of the Shrew*, Katharina reflected on the continuing medieval abuses and still, no doubt, predominant thinking:

'Saw you no more? Mark'd you not how her sister; Began to *scold* and raise up such a storm; That mortal ears might hardly endure the din?' (Act I, Sc. I).[16]

Five decades before, Dr Borde, a former Carthusian monk and London physician, published his own thoughts on handling the insane. His *Compendious Rygment or Dyetry of Helth* 'hit the shops' in 1542; in which he pronounced with all too typical blindness:

> 'I do advertyse every man [and woman] the which is madde or lunatycke or frantycke or demonyacke, to be kepte in safegarde in some close house or chamber where is lytell light; and that we have a keeper the whiche the madde man do fear.'

And yet…

> 'The patient is to have no knife or shears; no girdle (belt), except a weak list of cloth, lest he destroy himself; no pictures of man or woman on the wall, lest he have fantasies;…to have 'warm suppynges three tymes a daye, and a lytell warm meat'…Few words are to be used except for reprehension or gentle reformation.'[17]

His milder side portrayed a rare sense of humanity in this, an age of supposedly cruel intent. Or more accurately, perhaps, the pre-Enlightened age when the church's moral teachings went largely unquestioned whatever their truth.

Just as medieval madness was based on the notion of the Devil's possession, so too early 'treatments' remained unsurprisingly religion-inspired. Women and wells featured strongly:

> 'At Sturhill, in Stirlingshire, was a well famous for its healing virtues in madness. "Several persons," says Dalyell, "testified to the Presbytery of Stirling in 1668, that, having carried a woman thither, they had stayed two nights at an house hard by the well; that the first night they did bind her twice to a stone at the well, but she came into the house to them, being loosed without any help; the second night they bound her over again to the same stone and she returned loosed; and they declare also, that she was very mad before they took her to the well, but since that time she is working and sober in her wits".' [18]

Now another rank 'justification' for abusing 'mad' women had presented itself. But it was nothing to what followed. In the seventeenth century witch-hunts, cruel torture was added, some say the very worst of it kind; breast-rippers, 'strappado' and the 'witch-pricker's' arsenal of terror, and countless other devices of evil, were used by those men who sought divine retribution, by ridding themselves of the cause of their ills, Satan's lover and consort.[19]

And amidst such horrors, even as they scorched across Europe, one township in Belgium stood proud of its more compassionate ways. Long renowned for its colony of the lunacy pilgrim, the mad were kept here 'under superintendence…without restraint or precautions.'[20] And Gheel (Geel), in the province of Antwerp, soon gained its reputation for what future voices would term 'moral therapy' ideals.

Founded on the legend of St Dymphna, it brought devotees and mad people seeking its miracle cures. Her annual festival implored the Holy Virgin to rain down benevolent healing, leaving the cured free to depart as they had been at liberty to stay. Those whose minds had been missed this time around remained unconstrained until the next year's celebrations. And stay in their hundreds they most certainly did. Not for them straw-covered cells, whips, chains and beatings, but embraced by the locals, taken in by the kind-hearted residents, whose part in this humane response became internationally famed.[21]

Away from Gheel, by the reforming 1700s, attitudes and reactions had slowly, at last, started to change. Not least from the increased recognition of medical insights, putative diagnoses for the unfortunate mad. Though icons like Cheyne and Pinel may not have had all the answers, at least their therapies and remedies were generally of a more merciful kind. But what even they failed to curtail was the misappropriation of women.

Throughout history, the female mad, witches and 'naggers' found themselves drowning in an array of cruel 'treatments'; from the stocks on the green, to the Bridewell, even the surgeon. What follows summarises this 'Hobson's Choice' of brutal responses, though to begin with some earlier (and gentler) ideas preface the way.

Apparatus and Treatments

Antiquarian remedies included herb-lore and nature, many of which persisted well into the Victorian era. In the early seventeenth century, Burton like many before him, and many more since, had favoured hellebore, a plant known for its power to overcome sadness: 'they have all the symptoms of melancholy, fear, sadness, suspicion, &c. – It's hellebore reserved for them alone.'[22]

Yet as army surgeon and author, John Gideon Millingen related during Victoria's earliest years, the plant had a traditional value for madness even longer before. Its therapeutic discovery, he claimed, came from Greek legend:

> 'the daughters of Prœtus, smitten with insanity by Bacchus, were restored to reason by the shepherd Melampus, who gave them some milk drawn from goats that had eaten hellebore. It is supposed that the use of purgatives arose from this fabulous tradition, whence this plant was called *melampodium*'...causing the most 'violent evacuations' as a supreme cure for mania.[23]

Teasel and betony (a deadnettle species traditionally believed to drive away sorcery) were similarly beneficial, counter-respectively for delusions and frenzy,[24] while *Digitalis*, or foxglove, was particularly good for remedying the disrupted menses – hence its preferred use in cases of *female* madness. Other and associated conditions, however, included hysteria, epilepsy and the aforementioned amenorrhea[25] – presumably the latter from its well-known heart-strengthening properties still used today.

Along parallel lines came the ethereal realm, prevalent and still greatly feared in the seventeenth century. Herbs, potions, even love magic were all acculturated in the physick's search for a cure. The further back one looked, the more outlandish the treatments. Porter spoke of one much favoured by Burton again. For black spirits or melancholia, only a ram's head will do – or, rather, a bath in which the poor creature's brains have previously been boiled![26] Likewise, 'a roasted Mous, eaten, doth heale Franticke persons.'[27]

If these were not sufficiently obscure, to even contemporary minds, what came after raised society's eyebrows. The shape of one's face, one's head and one's goodly appearance, were now joined by religious adherence versus unspeakable habits, loose morals and sacrilegious behaviour, as both causes and symptoms of female madness. To take here just a couple in turn.

Religion had long played its part in tackling madness and, synonymous with immoral behaviour, certain personal habits came under attack. Onanism, or masturbation, especially in women, was a sure sign her mind had been lost from the world. Nor could she indulge in such evil and still try to hide it. As Mason reported, Tissot, an eighteenth century Swiss medic, observed that 'the countenance, that faithful mirror of the soul and the body, is the first to indicate [the] internal derangements [of onanism]'. The female masturbator, he wrote, is 'particularly subject to attacks of hysteria

[and] melancholy.'[28] In the same breath, Mason also records how Fowler, a hundred years later, saw countenance as a phrenological measure, betraying the signifiers of the harms of self-pleasure: 'We can not *help*...expressing all our mental operations, down even to the very innermost recesses of our souls, in and by our countenances' he warned.[29]

Yet one of the more obscure anti-madness/anti-masturbation responses was introduced in 1894, and now adorns breakfast bars all over the world! For the previously innocent cereal, developed by Kellogg, was not just devised to satisfy ravenous palates, but was intended to check the effects and temptations of what Kellogg himself labelled a hideous curse and the root of all madness. The humble cornflake was originally a supplement to curb masturbation!

Moral Management/Therapy

As at Gheel, moral management had been born as a reaction to chains, whippings and beatings, a practice never fully removed but which had at least abated as the eighteenth century closed. This new, supposedly gentler style followed two discreet yet ultimately converging trajectories: focussing attention on the *minds* of the mad, not just their bodies as past ages had done; and its eventual place in the Victorian age of hard work, self- improvement and global achievement.

As Ferriar, the Scottish physician, said at the time (1795):

'The management of the mind is an object of great consequence, in the treatment of insane persons, and has been much misunderstood. It was formerly supposed that lunatics could only be worked upon by terror; shackles and whips, therefore, became part of the medical apparatus...A system of mildness and conciliation is now generally adopted, which, if it does not always facilitate the cure, at least tends to soften the destiny of the sufferer.'[30]

Not that physical intervention suddenly became a thing of the past. Hydrotherapy, electricity and the newly invented swing-chair were all still favoured responses. The latter, designed to literally shake the melancholic free of their depression, often led to blood leaking out of her nose and ears as she was spun up to one hundred times in the course of a minute.[31]

A variation surprisingly came from the Methodist preacher turned self-styled therapist, John Wesley, who preferred his own electric machine.

Holding on to his belief in the supernatural causes of madness, including demonomania, he saw its cure in increasingly violently physicalist forms. His favoured contraption led to tasteless self-pride: 'One day, ordered several persons to be electrified'; and later proclaiming, in 1796, that 'hundreds, perhaps thousands, have received unspeakable good'.[32]

In the very same year, a more humane approach had surfaced in York. The Quaker-run Retreat quickly became a game-changing alternative to the local asylum, inspired by the latter's outright brutality witnessed in one of its own. What is less well known perhaps is that it was neither an alienist nor a mad-doctor who founded lunatic Heaven, but William Tuke, a merchant who had made his fortune in tea. He courageously put welfare and healing above restraint and control and yet, as in all things, not all would agree.[33]

From Electrocution to Scalpel

Though not gender-specific, this new moral crusade found its florescence in the commercial and economic expansion of the eighteenth and nineteenth centuries. Not that threat and menace were entirely absent: male medics still relied on intimidation and power, so that at times they were 'placid and accommodating...the next, angry and absolute.'[34] But the result, in the main, was a greater compassion.

For the female, this still hinged on her particular context: in the home, she faced even greater constraint through domestic confinement; in the courts and the prisons, a more compassionate ear, as women, mothers especially, began escaping the gallows on account of their sex; and, in certain county asylums, a more tolerant approach made life for the insane that little bit better.

Yet despite such improvements, a dark shadow of brutal oppression had crept into women's lives, perpetuated still on their alleged inferior minds. For this supposed age of yet new reason and splendour brought with it people like Silas Weir Mitchell, Anton Mesmer and the dreaded Isaac Baker Brown. If these men were unknown when they came to their notice, they were surely not missed when they faded away.

The first of the three could be said to be Franz Friedrich Anton Mesmer (1734-1815), with his theories on animal magnetism and, initially, his very public female support. His earliest European successes had stubbornly refused to be mirrored in late Georgian Britain, and it was only once celebrity physician, John Elliotson – friend and doctor to Charles Dickens – became his most ardent exponent that his methods took off.

So great did his following grow that Mesmer himself put on curative sessions, on an industrial scale. Men, but women especially, shared a (well ordered) bath into which Mesmer's acolytes thrust magnetised rods from which coursed magnetic currents. The correcting effect of their submarine power was reputed to bring one's life into balance, along with the psyche or soul.

These self-styled *baquet* sessions proved so hedonistically controversial that they and mesmerism were soon banned in France, where Mesmer had fled following an earlier scandal in his adopted Vienna (he was German). Yet so popular was he, and his bohemian methods, that his many female clients mournfully petitioned the king. A commission was thus held, but the wished-for reprieve spectacularly failed. Mesmerism, if not Mesmer, was branded a fraud – and any claims it cured illness or corrected hysteria were bluntly dismissed.[35]

In the Victorian age, and arguably courting his fame more than the health of his patients, Elliotson – with Dickens's help – put on demonstrations of Mesmer's earlier 'brilliant' notions. By displaying two sisters named Okey, and pre-empting Charcot's Tuesday hypnotic circus, he 'proved' Mesmer's simple theory that all living things were governed by an internal magnetic field which connected the body and brain. It made it a multifaceted remedy for a number of mind-body ills, even as hysteria's *arc-en-cercle* became its most particular gain.[36]

There were critics however, especially from those claiming his mostly female clients were being controlled by the mesmeriser by placing them in a hypnotic trance. Though the Okey sisters seemed to be proving their worth, being allegedly cured of their shared epilepsy, others dismissed 'these two demure little misses were transformed into precocious little minxes who joked and flirted with their audiences as well as lifting heavy weights and withstanding electric shocks.'[37]

Like Charcot, much later, unfavourable comparisons were made with charlatanism, debauchery and possibly fraud. Even allegations of keeping a brothel – akin to the earlier bagnio – were seemingly never far away. It all raised enough questions over the sobriety of the sessions that Elliotson, like his idol, was quickly 'shut down'. In this age of alienist endeavours to link madness and science, procuring mad men and women for their own cynical worth, hypnotism, trances and mesmerism became the fodder of fancy, and Elliotson faded away into the historical wasteland even as he left many women bereft.

Elliotson's earlier contribution to the insanity field had focussed on the 'science' of phrenology, itself controversially claimed to read a patient's character, mental and physical health. Its use to 'predict' whether a person was likely to go mad or to commit a serious crime rendered Elliotson, a death penalty abolitionist, particularly vocal. He claimed it made capital punishment a pointless deterrent, as villains of all hues were predisposed to executing their evil.[38]

The phrenology craze, like mesmerism later, owed much to late eighteenth century views. Credited in particular to Spurzheim and Gall. supporters like the 'alienist' Combe, and of course Elliotson himself, brought it popular fame, though its origins went way back in time. Millingen[39] narrated the 'ancient ideas', the origins of phrenological thinking. Burton, in his *Anatomy of Melancholy* spoke of parts of the 'brain-pan' which housed different conditions ('common sense, phantasie, memory'). While even earlier, as far back as the mid-1200s, Albertus Magnus, Bishop of Ratisbon (Regensburg), had 'designed a head divided into regions according to these opinions'. Others, in 1491, 1562 and 1632, apparently all followed suit. With Elliotson's adoption, the spectre of eugenics had soared into view.

The Rest Cure

Devised by Silas Weir Mitchell (1829-1914), the rest cure physically removed the 'fragile' woman from the cause of her suffering – typically, the home and those who restrained her there. Ordered to complete repose, the patient or victim, depending on viewpoint, was forbidden to leave bed, not even for toilet. She risked bed-sores and boredom as she was forcibly fed and jolted with electro-magnetic currents to prevent her muscles from wasting. The idea – to empty the brain of agitation and angst – relied on the additional verbal, coercive engagement, in which the female patient became Mitchell's personal 'toy'.

While many saw some merit in enduring such treatment, the practice had proved controversial, seemingly for isolating its patients away from their loved ones, and even brain-washing of sorts. The contemporary feminist, Charlotte Perkins Gilman, who survived a stay in Mitchell's 'clinic', afterwards wrote a withering attack on both the man and his repugnant methods. Separately too, in her novella, *The Yellow Wallpaper*, published in 1892, she confessed how both entities had pushed her to the edge of real insanity.[40]

Virginia Woolf was yet another exposed to Mitchell's techniques. Her experience of his rest cure led Woods to decry the truth in his 'treatment':

'Her reaction to the treatment highlight[ed] [its] oppressive nature…which reinforced the archaic notion that women should submit without questioning to male authority in the name of [mental and physical] health.'[41]

Mitchell however, drawing on fellow American George Beard's sex neurasthenia, believed only total rest (and female acquiescence) would cure ailments like hysteria, howsoever defined. At first lauded for its lack of brutal intrusion, the rest cure, like Mesmer's magnetic field, was soon branded a fraud. His patronization of women, by no means unusual in the Victorian era, was revealed first in his own words, that 'rest and seclusion [are] far better borne by women than by the other sex'; and then in the views of twentieth and twenty-first century critics: it was not so much a means of making 'ill' women better, but 'well' women ill.

Many despatched to receive his ministrations had been seen as in need of coercion, their self-assured, indomitable spirit mistaken for insubordinate madness.[42] And perhaps Scull best captured the point as he wrote: 'in feminist circles, [Mitchell was] the epitome of the brusque, misogynist, paternalistic Victorian nerve doctor.'[43]

The obstetrics physician, W.S. Playfair, who introduced the rest cure into Britain and harboured some intriguing ideas about the gynaecological organs and their effect on the mind, thought these young, nervous women deserved the pity and cure Mitchell's methods would bring. That they were seen to belong to a higher social standing (as Cheyne had stated); were self-driven (rebellious); and victims of gender and class expectations, he believed Mitchell could help restore the suffering female. And by that, he meant returning her home as a 'useful' family member! He sold it, in short, by suggesting it allowed them to lead lives 'much more active and satisfying than the ones they had been leading.'[44]

Another question remained; why were these women diagnosed as neurasthenics at all? From insubordinate lifestyles? Exercising their will? Or something even more deprecatory, such as a fault in their make-up? Modern researchers have conjectured an answer; sexual repression – a recoiling from anything that might penetrate their existence or their male-diagnosed bodies, whether it be food, sex, pregnancy or even miscarriage.[45] Whatever the truth, it led to some frightening reactions.

The Sordid '-otomies'

Mention the name Isaac Baker Brown and women (and men) cringe with pain and bury their heads in their hands. Between 1859 and 1867 (and probably longer), this blinkered obstetrician's response to 'insane' (or insubordinate?) women plumbed barbaric new depths. The section heading here refers to his apparent obsession with cutting, removing or otherwise adjusting every aspect of a woman's sexual form. And though not on his own in the horror, he was certainly its loudest exponent.

In his infamous title of 1866, *On the Curability of Certain Forms of Insanity etc in Females*, Baker Brown insisted on the need to correct women's functional disorders, a common enough response to her 'disruptive' biological features. Yet he betrayed his own intellectual weakness by inaccurately reading insanity in relation to the role of one's will:

> 'Ask the question, may not this 'inhibitory influence' [masturbation] originating in early life, act so powerfully on the mind as to unhinge it from that steadiness which is essential to enable it to keep the passions under control of the will; to enable, indeed, the moral tone to overcome abnormal excitement?'[46]

Of even greater resonance to the present theme, he then revealed his view of the 'errant' woman and her prescribed natural role. And justified his self-righteous techniques as a kind and 'charitable' action to prevent the young woman failing her mission by being overrun with those 'abnormal' passions.[47] He further asserted his conviction that, when so controlled, she once again became a societal asset - '[a] happy and useful [community] member'.[48]

In rather stylised terms, his views can be reflected in the following diagram, displaying an apparent preordained path for diverting women from a madness caused by moral decay:

Taking support from Brown-Séquard's belief that a woman's 'peripheral excitement' brought 'mischief' to her 'nervous centres' and so to her mind,[49] Baker Brown asserted his own conviction that the seat of female insanity lay in her sexual organs. Thus, any irritation thereof pushed her over the edge:

> 'Long and frequent observation convinced me that a large number of affections peculiar to females, depended on loss of nerve power, and that this was produced by peripheral irritation, arising originally in some branches of the pudic nerve, more particularly the incident nerve supplying the clitoris, and sometimes the small branches which supply the vagina, perineum, and anus.'[50]

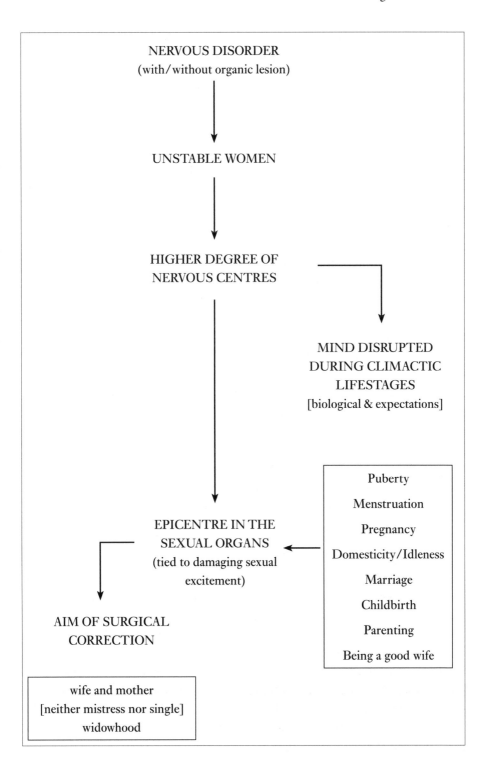

NERVOUS DISORDER
(with/without organic lesion)

UNSTABLE WOMEN

HIGHER DEGREE OF
NERVOUS CENTRES

MIND DISRUPTED
DURING CLIMACTIC
LIFESTAGES
[biological & expectations]

EPICENTRE IN THE
SEXUAL ORGANS
(tied to damaging sexual
excitement)

Puberty

Menstruation

Pregnancy

Domesticity/Idleness

Marriage

Childbirth

Parenting

Being a good wife

AIM OF SURGICAL
CORRECTION

wife and mother
[neither mistress nor single]
widowhood

Though sounding extreme, which it undoubtedly was, his view was not entirely his own. In fact, and for whatever reasons, he reinsisted this point in the very first paragraph of his Preface: 'In offering this little book to my professional brethren, I do not for one moment wish it to be understood that I claim originality in the surgical treatment herein described.' Was he aware of its professional damage?

Though to be fair, Baker Brown, having grown wary of his already corroded image, tried to justify his ideas by claiming, perhaps rightly, that his was a more humane approach than that favoured by others – such as the caustic blistering of the clitoral region. Yet two crucial points soon arose: first, that he dismissed the blistering treatment not for its cruelty but for its remedial weakness; and second that no such 'treatment' should ever have made it beyond the constraints of his mind.

His views and techniques nonetheless had their loyal supporters, insofar as he claimed for himself. He even took the liberty of naming names, of alienist medics who shared in his approach.[51] Eminent royal physician, Sir William Gull had suggestively noted: 'a most interesting instance of complete paraplegia induced by sexual excess [which paralysed the nerves]'.[52]

In return, others including some who went on to practise much later, defiantly followed his script:

> 'Before the recent advances of gynaecology, women, sane and insane, had to suffer from ills, now known to be curable…[ovarian or uterine] diseases we know are apt to entail nervous disorders, and we have seen that nervous disorders, when complicating disease of the sexual organs, are *frequently cured when the diseased organs are removed*.'[53]

Baker Brown had claimed that his supporters extended to Savage, oft-quoted and much maligned in the present title. And yet, writing many years later in Tuke's *Dictionary* opus, Savage howled opposition to Baker Brown and his work: 'To unsex a woman is surely to maim or affect injuriously the integrity of her nervous system.'[54]

So had Baker Brown got it wrong, inventing a crude, self-aggrandising endorsement? Or had Savage altered his tune? The latter's rejection of the *-otomy* came *sixteen years* after Baker Brown's death by which time was he simply saving his reputation? He was neither the first nor the last to distance himself from Baker Brown's 'fame'.

After publishing his earlier book, *On Some Diseases of Women Admitting of Surgical Treatment* (1854), *The Times* newspaper had heralded Baker Brown for '[bringing] insanity within the scope of surgical treatment.'[55]. But after issuing his 1866 treatise, even they turned on the doctor. As a net of iniquity ensnared their once bright, shining star, they audaciously questioned whether the operations he performed had been legal at all!

Not everybody agreed. None other than *The Lancet* posthumously applauded the 'enthusiastic and audacious' Baker Brown, for his 'brilliant dexterity and the power he displayed in the use of his left hand when operating on the female perineum.'[56] Others, however loudly, condemned both the man and his ways. But Baker Brown had always met them head-on:

'I hope to be able to show that a far more humane and effectual method is that which I constantly practise, and for the last six or seven years have openly and consistently advocated. Of course, from the very novelty of these views, I have been met with many objections, such as unsexing the female, preventing the normal excitement consequent on marital intercourse, or actually, as some most absurdly and unphilosophically assert, causing sterility; whereas my cases will show fact to be directly converse to all these theories.'[57]

Going much further, and just two pages on:

'Lastly, objections have been advanced against the morality of the operation [*otomy*], and *I am here at a loss* to give an answer, for I can hardly conceive how such a question can be raised against a method of treatment which has for its object the cure of a disease, *that is rapidly tending to lower the moral tone*, and which treatment is dictated by the loftiest and most moral considerations. I may here observe, that *before commencing treatment, I have always made a point of having my diagnosis confirmed by the patient or her friends.*'[58]

Note how he fails to cite husbands!

Had he needed, and were he not already dead, he would have balked at the 'support' (in its way) from the American father of neurasthenia, George Beard, for though he condemned him, he appeared to share strident attitudes towards treating the volatile woman, especially her sexual make-up. 'The orgasm in coitus is analogous to the sensation experienced in vigorous scratching to one troubled with itching,' he observed, reducing even the marital act to an unpleasant sore. 'The functions of the human body,' he added, 'that are last in order of development are the reproductive and productive'.

This was important:

> [Thus] when the nervous system is attacked by enfeebling disease [eg madness]… reproduction, should first suffer; and it is found that [it does] so suffer, and oftentimes before any other function is disturbed, *although such disturbance is not always observed by the patient*'. So that he felt he knew better than the patient themselves: 'moderate impairment of the sexual system may exist for a long time unobserved by one who does not habitually exercise that function'

The ramifications of his ideas – not to mention his jaundice – were rapidly exposed:

> 'A decline in manner, the first stage of moral decline, is always, or is almost always, the first observable symptom of insanity, since it appeals to the senses far more directly and clearly than simple suspension or perversion of the intellectual powers. *It is certain that insanity without moral decline is inconceivable*; and in that sense all insanity is moral insanity. I never give a certificate of insanity in any case unless I can find severe evidence of moral decline, and *I always specify moral decline in my certificates for commitment.*'[59]

Where he extricated himself was in creating no small distance from figures like Baker Brown, decrying the removal of the ovaries or the surgical 'repair' of a 'lacerated cervix' as a flawed understanding of the seat of neuroses. Such peer-sourced criticism had already cost Baker Brown, even within months of his 1866 *oeuvre*, and just a few short years before he finally died in 1873. Though not for the reasons one today might expect.

Baker Brown was 'struck off' from the Obstetrical Society not for his tendentious approaches, but on account of his brazen self-interest and unseemly hunt for a profit. As Vaughan has recorded, he plunged the medical world into 'uncomfortable disarray…[by] self-promotion, profiteering and allegedly making false claims. [Though in] this, surely, he was never alone.'[60]

After his death, one-time professional colleagues now presented his work as a tasteless affront, against both themselves and their work, rather more than the women he 'serviced'. Some even facetiously claimed that female masturbation – Baker Brown's favourite justification – might indeed bring on certain physical ailments, but her fall to temptation and descent into madness were not caused by the 'seat of their pleasure', but the hands that they used. These 'criminal' appendages, they said, were what should be castrated![61]

It remained plausibly true that his one-time supporter, *The Times*, had instigated his dismissal proceedings, when they reported Baker Brown to the Lunacy Commission after he outlandishly claimed to cure insane women through circumcision.[62] Yet it was for corporate reasons that he finally fell, and the world of women 'lost' his irreversible treatments. Had they not, clitoridectomy, labiaplasty and divers other abuses would have surely continued. When, at last, his exclusion arrived, years too late for his unfortunate victims, he left a legacy of shame, pain and the misogynistic savage. But in Britain at least, it all ended simply because the man himself, not his work, had threatened the fragile egos within his nascent profession.

A Final Tilt at the Problem

One of the last on the scene was one Edward Tilt. According to Arnold, Tilt's invidious fear of the menstrual cycle led him to recommend its retardation for as long as one could. From the cradle to grave, he cautioned those he thought were in power – men – to assist their women's demise into their volatile periods. Ice cold showers, wearing drawers and latterly avoiding novels and feather beds, both considered to 'hasten sexual maturity', should be joined by ice-water injections and labial leeches. And absolutely no sex.[63]

Showalter understood, whether or not she agreed, insisting Tilt had fervently believed that female adolescence was a 'miniature insanity'.[64]

Twentieth Century Horrors

Twentieth century treatments, though not exclusive to women, brought a new sense of horror. Medical understanding and motivations may have changed, but the trauma of what some considered 'right treatment' retained its unpalatable presence. In 1946, Walter Freeman, American psychiatry surgeon, began attacking human skulls with his surgical ice-pick, announcing the procedure as a courageous new dawn.

The prefrontal lobotomy had begun when Portuguese neurologist, Egas Morinz, as far back as the tense 1930s, devised his two-man 'leucotomy' approach; one medic entered the victim's frontal lobes from the side, while another sliced the exposed brain tissue the two considered at fault. A decade later, Freeman launched his transorbital lobotomy, working alone and perfecting his unilateral method by driving his unconventional tool up through the eye socket and into the brain.

Originally conceived as a cure for depression, or more lately psychosis, the results were at best mixed, at worst ineffectual, and throughout surely risky. Its perception in the world was so utterly brutal that directors and exploitative films long ago consigned it as the work of the crazed.[65] Footage and mimicry have raised the wandering zombie to its new status as an uncomfortable icon. Nor did Freeman's own reputation do much for its image after he allegedly destroyed the brain of Rosemary Kennedy, 23, the future US President's sister, in a 'botched' operation that followed his pioneering technique. It left her emotionally and intellectually paralysed, and prone to outbursts of violence.[66]

With its popular demise, another seemingly less intrusive solution came to epitomise caring. And although its florescence began after the latest date in this book, its origins once again reached back to an earlier age. The use of chemicals for controlling all forms of madness became the go-to solution for a faster-paced world with its age-old constraints; never enough time, and not enough money. Thus the 'chemical cosh' it created remains with us still.

It perhaps all began in the late 1800s when another Viennese medic, Julius Wagner von Jauregg, suggested inducing a fever might recover a mad woman's mind. He employed an array of 'febrile agents', exposing his unfortunate patients to a pathogenic cocktail of typhoid, malaria, even rat bites, all designed to bring on 'the sweats'. Uncontrolled patient reactions were then supposed to be arrested by antidotes, such as quinine, leaving the patient free of infection yet cured of her preceding dementia.[67] Though thought a success at the time, hindsight has since called into serious question both its efficacy and its moral correctness, especially it seems when allegations of von Jauregg's advocacy of Nazi-inspired eugenics surfaced after his death.

From Bedlam to County

As soon as the Middle Ages had ended, a lunatic's family found new ways of discharging their lunacy care obligations. When Bethlem had first opened its doors, in 1247, it was a hospital not an asylum, but it remained for centuries a rare exception to the home-based confinement of the familial mad. As the years slipped by, alternative options began to emerge. Norwich's 'Bethel', London's St Luke's and one or two others, were eventually followed by the Georgian private madhouse explosion, which were themselves superseded by the mid-nineteenth century arrival of the County Asylum.

Private Madhouses

Porter, as always, curated an elegant record of lunacy care up to the Georgian arrival; or, as he terms it, that late era's epiphany. Indeed, much of this section depends on his words.[68] Driven by the likes of Pinel, Tuke and Chiarugi, the Italian psychiatric reformer, he claimed the new madhouse took the care of 'The Other' away from the wise-women, quacks, star-gazers and churchmen. Now came a new deal; the bricks-and-mortar approach to handling the crazed. Removing their kind from society's eyes, institutions were developed to both study and house,[69] as they became both an inevitable wish and a dangerous ploy.

The turning point for such Georgian responses came through the insanity of George III. As Tuke insisted: 'There can be little doubt that the intense interest excited by the [king's] madness…aroused a general feeling in England in regard to the management of receptacles for the insane, and commiseration for their miserable lot.'[70] And with it came a raft of new measures, including swing chairs, Mesmerism and 'heroic' purges.[71] According to Porter again, these were not entirely devoid of compassion; indeed motivations were frequently kind. After all, thrashing the straw-bedded mad was never a cruel, simplistic brutality, it was a genuine, periodic belief.

Nonetheless, while family-centred abuse and wrongful confinement had remained real enough, now they were augmented by the pecuniary greed of the new rogue madhouse keepers, many of whom only had eyes for a profit, and early philanthropic responses came too often to nought. Defoe, the writer and spy, expressed his heartfelt concern, one shared by many: 'In my humble opinion all private mad-houses should be suppressed at once, and it should be no less than felony to confine any person under pretence of madness without due authority.'[72] If only he had been around in the 1880s!

Eventually a new-founded institutional care bucked the trend, designed with far greater compassion. The Retreat in York, Ticehurst in Sussex and the *re*-reformed Bethlem offered new, tangible hope.[73] A rare centre for women, Norman House in Fulham, attracted special attention.: 'I was delighted with the manner in which they were treated.'[74] Though the commentator was male, it was hoped it displayed an improved situation.

Yet optimism was fickle. What remained an unspoken question was how and by whom were these lunatics judged? The greater individualism of the Georgian age (with its lesser society focus) led to unpleasant, often divisive abuses: 'It was extremely easy – as Defoe [again] protested – to put [one's] relatives away.'[75] It would be a century yet before life within walls would improve on an industrial scale.

Hospitals

Bethlem had, until the late fourteenth century, offered little in the way of care for the mentally ill (arising in large part from its shared uncertain grasp on the insanity problem). Originating on a site in Bishopsgate, London, the well-intentioned Priory of the Order of St Mary of he Bethlehem (hence its name's later bastardisation) had sought to offer 'shelter to the poor, the sick and the homeless.'[76] But in soon after acquiring the mad and the frenzied, any hoped-for centre of humanitarian healing were supplanted with 'manacles … chains … locks …. keys….and stocks', all listed in an inventory from the year 1398.[77]

By the early to mid–1600s, plugging a new gap of care created by the loss of ecclesiastical and civic foundations,[78] Bethlem had provided respite for those afflicted by madness; not just its 'patients' but their long-suffering families. Yet its harsh reputation had not dwindled away. Still unregulated, save for the most cursory inspections, it retained a sorry reputation for abuses, malpractice and wrongful confinement. In 1620, for instance, its keeper, Helkiah Crooke, was exposed as a gross *mis*-manager of all things Bethlem: its patients, his staff, even the building itself.[79] Around the same time, its governors had served the same purpose at the nearby Bridewell (the penal centre for London) so that, just like the convict, a Bedlamite inmate was forced to pay money to secure their release.[80] As many arrivals had become recent inheritors of fortune[81] – doubtless a pre-certification abuse that never really stopped plaguing asylum admissions – the profits thereafter were seductively good.

In 1676, at the height of the witch scares, Bethlem moved to its new site in Moorfields. Women still faced frequent ill-treatment, such as those witnessed by a visiting magistrate to the old York Asylum, who physically retched at 'the stench of thirteen poor women encased in an eight foot square cell'.[82] Bethlem was seemingly worse.

While the gentler sex was regarded as the troublesome, more volatile gender, the view was exemplified yet again in 'visitation' statistics; numbers which counted *twice* the number of women to men suffering Bethlem's male-fashioned abuses.[83] Allegations of female sexual misconduct were regularly borne out by the number of births ,[84] though how many were caused by 'warden connection' and whether forced or desired, remained largely unknown.

By the mid eighteenth century, improvements had, allegedly, at last made Bethlem more humane; inmates were treated to 'therapeutic ideals' of exercise, roominess, quietness and decency. Although its key claim to improvement, that 'each patient was to have a cell, a bed, *and clean straw*', still offends our own modern compassion.[85] In truth, perhaps, it revealed a Georgian response that proved too little, too late?

In 1758, its physician, John Monro, whose family had run Bethlem for well over a century, entered an unpleasant spat with his fellow 'mind-doctor' at nearby St Luke's. In his *Treatise on Madness*, William Battie had insulted Monro's father for his closed-door mismanagement and misuse of medieval-style treatments. In rebuking the claims, Monro's son sought to enlighten his opponent, insisting incurable madness meant all one could do was to 'manage' its victims. His myopia proved surely ill-timed, as emerging Enlightenment views demanded more progressive solutions.[86] To make matters worse, Battie's own institution had recently gained favour for its more humane treatment and its myriad cures.

In its third incarnation, Bethlem moved to St George's Fields in Southwark in around 1815. Just one year later, several extensions had enlarged both its size and its patient capacity, so that it additionally housed madmen (and women) of the 'worst' criminal kind.[87]

Its antecedent despair was never forgotten. Tuke recalled its cruel reputation for whippings, beatings and fetters, as he too poured out his sorrow:

> '[Inmates] were too often under the charge of brutal keepers… chained to the wall or…their beds, where they lay in dirty straw, and frequently, in the depth of winter, without a rag to cover them. It is difficult to understand why and how they continued to live; why their caretakers did not, except in the case of profitable patients, kill them outright; and why, failing this - which would have been a kindness compared with the prolonged tortures to which they were subjected - death did not come sooner to their relief.'[88]

His summary of those three built stages of Bethlem was similarly doleful:

> 'The first hospital was the Bedlam of Sir Thomas More, Tyndale, and Shakespeare, who uses the word six times in his plays. More

described a lunatic thus: "All beit he had bene put up in Bedelem, and afterward by beating and correction gathered his remembraances to him to come again to himselfe, being thereupon set at liberty, and walkinge aboute abrode, his old fansies beganne to fall againe in his heade". The second Bethlem, that of Hogarth, ended in disgrace in 1815, the absurdly antiquated medical treatment and the actual inhumanity practised there deserving no better fate than that of the Bastile. The third Bethlem, although for some years a great improvement on its predecessors, was far from creditable to its governors and staff. But a change came. For the last forty years it has advanced rapidly, and has for some considerable time been an honour to the land, a school of medicine, and the moans of conferring an enormous amount of benefit upon those who enter its kindly portal and enjoy the advantages of the skilful treatment pursued there.'[89]

Despite all these accounts of misery and suffering, there exists an alternative view, one I share here. It speaks of a more benevolent, keenly self-regulated centre, more akin to its Crusade-inspired origins that met its thirteenth century need. As a sanctuary which, as soon as the 1400s, became a place where the insane were not simply a chargeable asset, locked up and tethered in straw, but who were actively cured. Even its distasteful reputation for spectator gawping was called into question, the same author proffering the idea that while money was indeed handed over, it was as charitable *alms* rather than to purchase a disparaging 'day pass' for the 'circus' inside.[90]

If in any way true, this may have had more to do with its accepting only the curably mad. Or that it kept its incurable lunatics hidden in 'out of way' places whenever outsiders' eyes were given (paid) access inside.[91]

Whatever the truth, by 1677 it ran its own welfare-style policy: 'None of the Officers or Servants shall at any time beat or abuse any of the Lunatics in the said hospital neither shall offer any force unto them but upon absolute Necessity for the better government of the said lunatics.'[92] A case in support of this view occurred in 1710.

Sarah Carter was 'called before the committee she appearing in [its] judgement...to be restored to her senses...[and] discharged from this hospital'. She was sent away not without hope but with financial support: 'thirty shillings' for 'necessary apparell (*sic*) & clothing', as well as transport costs home.[93]

Finally, as though confirming such long ago hope, its new in-house *Museum of the Mind* has since captured its remarkable transition.

An often overlooked *early* public asylum, Bethel, had opened at Norwich in 1713. Of particular note was its female founder, Mary Chapman, responding to her own deliverance from hereditary madness.[94] For its female inmates, its name (meaning 'sanctuary') and their benefactor's shared gender, probably did much to becalm the unfortunate few.

St Luke's Hospital had, from its 1751 founding, provided enviable standards compared to Bethlem's overcrowding and lack of care or reform; sadly in contrast to Battie's continued passion for somatic responses (purging, depleting etc). In 1786, it relocated to Old Street where, sixty-five years later, Charles Dickens – no stranger to social lunacy problems – recorded its famed Christmas Dance for both inmates and staff in a 1852 issue of *Household Words*. Regrettably, his account reinforced the image of the fragile female. St Luke's, he proclaimed, was extremely adept at 'proving … insanity is more prevalent among women than among men', a view he backed up with endless statistics: 'Of the eighteen thousand seven hundred and fifty-nine inmates… received in the century of [St Luke's] existence, eleven thousand one hundred and sixty-two have been women, and seven thousand five hundred and eighty-seven, men'. He added, with ever less tact: 'Female servants are, as is well known, more frequently afflicted with lunacy than any other class of persons'! Nonetheless, so positive and strong was its reputation for caring, that St Luke's inspired scores of similar establishments all over the country.[95]

Nearly half a century after the first St Luke's opened, as we saw, Tuke's York Retreat threw wide its doors in 1796. It met with instant success. 'The operation as practiced …was simple: religious segregation for purposes of moral purification.'[96] A throwback, perhaps, that the female of the species was far more susceptible to immoral decay.

County Asylums

The earliest county asylums arising from one of the two pivotal 1845 Acts emerged against the backdrop of those more exclusive hospital centres. That progress had happened now became an inescapable truth. Despite its early, periodic shortcomings, towards gender especially, an erupting new network brought a paradigm shift in lunacy care. Regulation had earlier come with the Madhouses Act (1774), as a direct response to the terrors of wrongful confinement. While Pinel and Conolly's crusades, in which both eulogised 'moral management' over physical confinement, had inspired their respective nations (France and Britain) to fight for such change.

Until the two 1845 Acts for housing the mad and observing their welfare, many incarcerations had been but short-lived responses by panic-struck families unable to cope. Without institutions, many insane had suffered heartless reactions well into the long nineteenth century, as they remained tied 'to the leg of a table, tied to a post in an outhouse, or…shut up [in an attic].'[97]

The misuse of long-term confinement meanwhile, of 'nuisance' women especially, had yet to arrive. But arrive it soon did. A reversal in admission statistics shows how, unlike eighteenth century cases, more women than men were now being locked on account of their mind.[98] Disraeli's warnings of 'lies, damn lies and statistics' spring freely to mind. Authoress Sarah Wise, for example, cited prominent sociologist Joan Busfield: 'female admission figures were no higher than male, and discharge rates differed little.'[99]

The handling of women remained a tiresome problem – not least for the inmates themselves. Though even the roughest intentions were often undeniably noble. 'Low spirited' or 'mopish' female patients were made to get up, and be shut out of their cells 'so that they may not creep back again to their beds' and to undertake needlework when they were not otherwise busy, 'rather than let them walk idle up and down the house showing it to strangers and begging for money.'[100]

The introduction of madhouse inspections in the 1774 act had not then extended to the early public asylums. And before 1845, with the parallel introduction of the Lunacy Commission, such lax monitoring had become the unscrupulous keepers' device for avoiding exposure.[101] Early township adopters included Manchester, Liverpool and Newcastle-upon-Tyne, though often from private subscription, leading to scurrilous claims of back-door privatization. One such occurred at the first Hereford asylum which, having opened in 1799 as part of the existing General Hospital, was soon offloaded through what appears to have been an early attempt at a twentieth century style Private Finance Initiative.

The tide, however, had inexorably turned. This had been achieved in a number of ways, so that now the difference between the private madhouse and public asylum had never been starker. In clientele too, the earlier periods featured well-heeled inmates (not all by any means, but disproportionately so), whereas in post-1845 Britain, some *ninety per cent* were now paupers by class.[102]

What remained stubbornly consistent, however, was female mistreatment. Like all gone before them, the public asylum remained yet another means of overpowering troublesome women.

Away from asylums, contemporary lunacy care involved the degrading workhouse, which in its earliest years of the late 1600s had provided temporary respite for the unreachably mad. St Peter's in Bristol was an early example, where concerns about overcrowding and the damaging intermingling of inmates, the sane and insane, have since been refuted.[103] Women's wards and wings in other civic establishments reinforced expectations of gender and a woman's preordained role. Not just in sex segregation (though no doubt this was occasioned, for ease of control and avoiding more obvious 'mishaps'), but in clothing, workload and 'moral therapy' too. All designed to return the curable female to her idealised role as the domestic angel.

Daily life within was equally sexist. While male inmates undertook manual work, tending the gardens and running the farm, ladies undertook sewing, cleaning and cooking, for these were much-needed skills in the Victorian home.[104] Locked up in their cells, restricted in labours, their 'excessive confinement' replicated real-life constraints. Perhaps unsurprisingly, they led to *five times* more women than men being locked up in padded refraction.[105]

There remained one more centre for female oppression, creating and brutalising the female mad. The patriarchal abode, her home, which she shared with her father, husband or brother; the one place that should have been her haven. Instead, it resembled in its stonework and corridors and dominant menfolk the *pre*-Victorian chains, cells and straw beds that many had heard of but had hoped were no more.[106] Had so little improved?

From Hell to Vienna

During the seventeenth century, reactions to witchcraft and hysteria had brought down the horrors of Hell on the feminine sex – meaning both gender *and* passion. Edward Jorden (1603) spoke of the need for marital relations, to keep the fragile woman more stable in mind because, in the young especially (meaning, of course, single), 'the passive condition of womankind is subject unto more [mental] diseases'. Later eighteenth and nineteenth century Methodists stuck to their Wesleyan master's insistence, that mad women especially should be removed of the Devil. So was there no little hope for a road out of Hades?

Fast forward to the dawning twentieth century, and a new pivotal figure emerged, only to 'manage' her kind again. Sigmund Freud, yet another mind 'expert' from Vienna, arrogated the female mind in his search for the source of its 'ills'. Going much deeper, delving into what he termed the psychosexual stages, he too saw her problem as an internalised issue. But it was her darkest most thoughts, not Satan, that he sought to expel.

His 'talking remedy', or psychoanalysis, became the forerunner of counselling, as he attempted to extract her repressed sexual feelings, rather than hunting for more tangible traits. In simplest terms, his views hinged on three discrete factors: the unconscious influences on his client's behaviour, to the patient often unknown; her subconscious resistance, from well-hidden defences; and a transference of her deep-seated emotions onto other pivotal figures, such as those causing her pain.[107]

His case célèbre 'Dora' (Ida Bauer) revealed, to Freud at least, her early-onset hysteria. Having himself once been a student of Charcot, he diagnosed Dora's subconscious love for her suffering mother, and her jealous rejection of her father's mistress whom she saw as a snake in the grass. Best known for his Oedipus complex, the less well-known Electra condition focussed on a girl's unnatural love for her natural father.

At the same time, he added, she was subconsciously lusting after her father's best male friend. So that, though over-simplified here, one got the point. However, as Dora herself ended the therapy early, Freud's accuracy and prognosis were never empirically tested.[108]

Any modernity of thinking was at times undermined by his re-using old, controversial techniques, including phrenological massage and even hypnosis. But he also felt moved to reinterpret the hysteria condition so that, along with Charcot's 'Augustine' and several others, his sexualised portrayal of the unstable female suited the mores of the time even as it advanced its inventor's career.

Not that Freud believed his own hype. With just a small number of cases, and even more limited outcomes, Freud himself forever questioned his work. Now since largely debunked, he fortunately failed to witness their final demise, dying on 23 September 1939. His legacy has remained at best controversial, rejected by others as an extreme perversion.

A decade after his death, mad women and hysterics faced a new form of oppression: their almost solitary treatment in a chemical age. We have already encountered 'Mother's Little Helper', but it was, in truth, only one in an expanding stable, including paraldehyde, barbiturates, chlordiazepoxide (Librium), chlorpromazine (Thorazine *or* Lagactil) and others.[109] Had a woman's lot ever really improved?

Chapter 5

Suffering Women: the 'Unfortunate' Sex

As we have seen throughout the earlier chapters, in the realms of medicine, law, insanity and crime, and both domestic and wrongful confinement, little ever meaningfully changed for the suffering woman. Except perhaps to get worse. This final chapter attempts a general discussion, informed by the different themes we've encountered, of what it meant to be female over five hundred years. Seldom afforded a mind of her own, she was indeed the 'unfortunate' sex...

'She wasn't mad...[but] repressed'.

While not every stated case of female madness was inherently false, many certainly were, often originating in gender oppression. In a patriarchal past, such causes, conditions, and (mis)diagnoses brought mishap and mayhem for both her nature and mind. In this sat her sorrow, her 'lot' in the world. A dulling, typically domestic existence, especially but not solely for the nineteenth century woman, frequently sent her into a spiral of madness, so that to rebel or accept an unwanted position was to either declare herself mad, or to secure it for real.

Elizabeth Garrett Anderson spoke for many in 1874, as she focussed on Maudsley and his sexist dismissal of female talent:

> '[His damaging claims] could be outnumbered ...by those in which the break-down of nervous and physical health seems... to be distinctly traceable to want of adequate mental interest and occupation...Thousands of young women, strong and blooming at eighteen, become gradually languid and feeble under the depressing influence of dullness ...till in a few years they are morbid and self-absorbed, *or even hysterical*.'[1]

To abandon their lot, women risked being labelled as mad, often bad, and sent off inside. The less numerous madhouses and the ubiquitous homesteads may have previously served as her prisons, but the county asylum often made matters worse. Treatments within may have begun to improve, but being sent there just for resisting oppression made them chambers of hell. Underpinning it all was the discouraging male.

Misogyny in all forms (viz. gender control)

Once locked away, if it indeed involved an asylum, the paternal role of the warder, physician or superintendent replaced her father or husband, sometimes even her brother, as her unwanted master, the latter empowered on account of their sex. Thus: '[the] cornerstone of Victorian psychiatry claimed male dominance was therapeutic. The doctor ruled the asylum like a father ruled his family.'[2] While such uninvited control pervaded all eras, not just the nineteenth century peak, and consistently hindered all walks of life. The passage of time only altered its nature.

Indeed, long before Victoria's reign, religion had coerced and shaped views of madness and women. Theologians cited God as the sole, divine saviour from her mind-centred suffering, as though he had been testing His creation against the Devil himself (cf medieval/early post-medieval attitudes towards demonic possession and other supernatural forces as already discussed. 'Eminent [seventeenth century] clergymen shared the popular belief that mental turmoil had a supernatural dimension.' While 'the most famous preachers of the age fostered the [equally] popular belief that spiritual and mental afflictions were identical.' Women thus 'existed at the point of convergence between the natural and supernatural orders, and [were] subject to both kinds of powers [and the dangerous sort]'.[3]

In the later, Republican era, any mention of demons and demonic possession was replaced with talk of Original Sin and the need for repentance.[4] The Puritan fathers proclaimed the only way to salvation was to seek miserable pardon for the intransigent, rib-stealing, biblical Eve. The resulting witch-craze, and its conjectured convergence with female madness, brought a new sink of oppression – as male inquisitional tyrants accused first women of madness, and then those classed insane as having bartered their souls.

Others, though, had arguably greater compassion. To them it was religion itself that produced the source of the problem; that and its uncomfortable bedfellow, melancholic decay. For how could anyone, *woman especially* meet the high expectations laid down by the church? Little wonder that religious demands for female perfection engendered such ecclesiastical pain.

For example Richard Napier, treating none other than the niece of one Archbishop Abbot, found how she was 'always praying and studying', had grown low in her spirits, and that 'her faith was [so] weakened...[that] she was [truly] persuaded...she had sinned against God'. While another, Elizabeth Whitter, had grown 'gloomy and [anxious]', the result of 'her untutored enthusiasm for Biblical study: '[She b]usieth herself with reading the scriptures, and not well understanding the meaning, [is] all fearful of her [unlikely] salvation.'[5]

This new Puritan obsession with personal cleansing, with their absent compassion for the wayward of mind, left mainstream religions to engage with the new world of science; though the woman still suffered from misogynist but now empirical thought. Born not of medical or technological breakthrough, she remained judged by social and political change,[6] leaving both sane *and* mad women suffering the patriarch's whim.

A century later brought the private Georgian madhouses. Rejected by Porter as a new 'consumer society', one in which supply made demand, they advertised their services as pseudo-Utopian centres existing purely for the 'correction' of women. While their invariably masculine 'hosts' insisted they remained the best gender to help.

Such male self-promotion even invaded the home: 'a good natured man-midwife pays the utmost attention to ladies in certain situations...' ran the masculine mantra in an unkind observation from 'celebrity' historian, Johann von Archenholz,[7] while later gynaecology 'experts' unveiled brutal procedures, claimed as 'treatments' for 'madness' and recalcitrant female minds.[8]

A new means of apportioning blame was duly created, based not on pre-programmed woe (i.e. Original Sin), but on new nerve-centred ideas of yet more 'medical' *men*. And in their searches for insight, who better to help experts like Cheyne *et al* than the seat of sensibility herself, the fragile woman? Diet, nature and idle rich-living now added to the dangers for the female mind.

At length, even as Victoria ascended the throne, another masculine breed moved centre-stage. Alienists, of so many hues and persuasions, were compassionate, sexist, unreconstituted, as they set down their own rules on women, madness and latterly insanity crime. Here morality and moral weakness drew particular attention, so that the rogue Maudsley wept: '[these women] are examples illustrating the retrograde metamorphosis of mind...[brought about] in the course of...[evolutionary] degeneration.'[9]. Likened to beasts, even Rousseau's 'noble savage', their weakened intellect and reduced capacity for learning led them to overstretch their condition and bring on the worst sorts of behaviour.

The most influential outlets thus became every court in the land, masculine places where a woman's departure from her 'natural order' drew genuine tears. Male juries, male judges, male lawyers, even male civil servants, all joined alienist endeavours to rescue the woman and help her eke out 'her best'. If she had 'fallen', even murdered her children, men became slow to condemn and quick to excuse. It was simply put down to her mind having conflicted with nature.

For example, when Elizabeth Potter drowned her hours-old infant, she received a six-month sentence for mere concealment. Even then, certain male correspondents felt she had suffered enough:

> 'In what mental condition was [she] at the time she committed the offence of concealment? I answer, she was not in a rational state of mind…The insanity which attends the puerperal condition is peculiar. It may continue for a few hours, for a few days, for weeks, or for months. It varies in intensity, sometimes being only manifested by incoherency of language, or eccentricity of behaviour; sometimes exhibiting a suicidal or homicidal propensity, so that the patient cannot be left for a moment….lest she should attempt the life of herself or infant.'[10]

Such masculine rhetoric, of course, found its outlet across a widening media; where women were appropriated like elsewhere as a social concern. Prejudicial, pre-verdict commentary of trials brought unwanted outcomes. For example, Esther Lack who was declared guilty before her trial for killing her children;[11] or Mary Ann Brough, labelled the evil adulteress, after brutally murdering six of her children, possibly to cover the shame of an illicit affair.[12] Elsewhere the problem expanded, but always cajoling the 'special nature' of woman, at worst feeding the very monster of male-centric control. Of the seemingly endless, frequently crass examples of reinforcing their weakness, Alfred Dymond[13] and A Female Matron[14], actually Frederick W. Robinson, spring readily to mind. The former appropriated the fragile female criminal mind, in his efforts to abolish the capital sentence; while Robinson related the more 'colourful' cases of female inmates in the prisons he served, occasionally inciting mental decay as the cause of their crimes.

Even post-modern academics have ridden their wake. Jordanova's assessment of Jules Michelet, and his apparent insistence in the perceived seat of the 'unstable' woman was clearly to her a marriage of imagination and masculine science. For instance, Michelet's use of anatomical plates showing her gynaecological 'gifts' as defining women's mental condition.[15] Her perspective is surely built on men's past attitudes towards women, themselves founded on account of the woman's so-say corruptible form. Internally, physically, spiritually - upset in her balance as she suffered poisoned influence from her 'organs of life'. The wandering womb may have disappeared by the long nineteenth century, but ideas of its effect were still very alive.

From such a gender perspective, biological determinism can be viewed as a largely masculine barrier to a woman's progress and freedom. Many have since highlighted its presence, especially during the Georgian era: 'British women in the eighteenth century whose abilities to exercise rational thought and logical leadership in any domain, whether it be home or the political arena, were…restricted by biological determinism.'[16] In truth, has it always been thus?

Yet even modern female writers appear to fall foul of the determinist trap. In the recent past Woods, citing others, cautiously wrote that:

'biological factors may help in part explain female depression. [Its] rise…during puberty could be due to gonadal hormonal changes, but it is difficult to separate this from the social issues surrounding puberty. While genetic factors play a significant role in the liability to develop depression… some researchers have pointed to structural differences between male and female brains, specifically the gender differences between the neurotransmitter systems noradrenaline and serotonin. Despite research into these biological factors a clear answer is not apparent. Major depression and mood disorders are 'likely a complex interaction of several factors' both biological and social.'[17]

When it came to eating, they were seemingly no better off; anorexia nervosa 'has historically been less about the fear of getting fat and more about a fear of sexuality and adulthood. She further observed how the Brontë sisters of nineteenth century fame used fasting as a feminine wile in securing their desires.[18] The contrast with the suffragette hunger strikers is of promising interest for other specialists to follow.

An Unfortunate Business - Cohabitation and Marriage

Relationships and marriage have sadly become synonymous with the suffering woman and, as referenced throughout, has been frequently linked with the madness debates. To read a contemporary guide to domestic and marital bliss underlines the subordinate role the woman was expected to serve.[19]

In the context of madness, additional disturbing effects were brought into play. A wife's non-right to reject her husband's sexual advances led, in 1886, to the Men and Women's Club dual gender debating society (advanced for its time) claiming marriage itself spelt very grave danger. Either, they said, for a woman losing her sexual freedom (and risk being labelled insane), or from her husband's disinterest; so that the former provided grounds for divorce, but the latter did not. The most extreme of reactions in both cases was her total mental collapse.[20]

A similar threat came to those women believed to be pre-destined to madness, resulting in unrestrained censure for getting married at all! Fielding Blandford was a loud advocate:

> 'One thing is certain, that women who have already had attacks of insanity should abstain from marriage and the concealment of such a history from an intended husband and his friends is a most serious and reprehensible step.'[21]

On the other hand, remaining single was seen as often more dangerous still; because women could simply not function without men in their lives. And what of her unruly passions? If not 'able' to marry, non-procreational sex further led to moral decay. The resulting suppression of her latent sexual feelings would lead her to either pre-marital affairs or destructive self-pleasure, both of which were certain roads to absolute madness.[22] The alienist Savage even admonished those who ignored the dangers of remaining a spinster (or avoiding consummation of marriage) and its role in the causes of madness. 'We believe,' he opined, '[insanity] is predisposed to in some cases by prolonged and intimate courtship, in which there is a frequent stimulus to the passion with no gratification.'[23] It thus followed, *de facto*, that marriage and sex could themselves prevent madness.

Foucault went further and based his possibly legitimate diatribe on what he saw as the unhealthy suppression of personal desire as exercised in the repressive asylum: '[They] denounce everything that opposes the essential virtues of society: celibacy – "the number of girls fallen into idiocy is seven times greater than the number of married women."…'

Which, for Foucault, meant only one thing: '"we can…deduce that marriage constitutes for women a kind of preservative against the two sorts of insanity which are most inveterate and most often incurable"; debauchery, misconduct, and "extreme perversity of habits; vicious habits such as drunkenness, limitless promiscuity, an apathetic lack of concern can gradually degrade the reason and end in outright insanity".' [24]

While away from the bedroom, such 'relationship laws' led to feigned cases of madness, either by a desperate woman or a villainous man, though it must also be acknowledged that scurrilous claims were frequently made by devious women, seeking personal gain or occasionally professional pride. In certain real-life cases, a wife's genuine madness became the unwelcome result. In a hearing for separation brought by one Mary Kelly against her husband, Reverend James Kelly of St George's in Liverpool, the litany of evidence included expert medical witness:

> 'She could not eat; she hardly slept at all; she was subject to constant trembling and fainting; she awoke involuntarily screaming at night, and her nervous system was so shattered that [I] declared paralysis or even madness to be imminent.' [25]

The causes were manifold, yet of singular flavour. Having no occupation, ostracised by both her husband and son, deprived of her freedom and friends outside the home, prevented even from fulfilling her role as housewife and mother (truly her right?!), and made inferior to servants, she grew penniless and friendless;

> 'the daily life of this lady was little better than an imprisonment, the solitary silence of which was broken only by the language of harsh rebuke, foul words, and epithets of insult, indignity, and shame. What wonder that, under so grievous an oppression, her [mental] health again gave way?' [26]

Such hideous mistreatment had its historical origins. Long before the asylum expansion of the mid- to late-1800s, 'women were…admitted to private asylums on slender evidence, notably those who contravened expectations concerning their modesty, conduct, duties or behaviour or those who would not bend to their husbands' will'.

In 1763, William Battie recounted the woman whose husband saw little difference between the asylum and the nearby prison, expecting either to punish his wife. When told to take her back home, he retorted that 'he understood [this place] to be a…place of correction.'[27]

In the 1766 case of Hannah Mackenzie, 'Peter [her husband] sought to confine his wife after he attempted to make Hannah's niece, with whom he was having an adulterous affair, mistress of the household. Hannah fled when [the same] Dr Battie…was brought to the house, but [she] was tricked into returning and locked in her bedchamber, supervised by a female keeper and restrained in a straitjacket. Thereafter she was conveyed to Peter Day's Paddington madhouse.'[28] She escaped after drawing the attention of the boy living next door.

A plethora of cases, such as Rosina Bulwer-Lytton who embarrassed her husband MP after he had her first thrown from their home and afterwards locked up in Wyke House asylum; or Georgina Weldon, whose attempted incarceration was ridiculously botched, and who exposed alleged profiteering by alienists like Winslow the younger; have been well-recounted elsewhere.[29] And while they reveal how the insane (*viz.* rebellious) woman was at last finding her outlet, eventually securing the vote was but one albeit significant strand.

Suffragism

In Victorian society alone, being a woman meant having no persona at all. The draconian coverture was a presumption in law (and elsewhere?) that a married woman was under her husband's protection; that, like children and madmen, she had no legal recourse.[30] It's first (overdue) revocation came with the 1870 Married Woman's Property Act, so that, at last and at least, she may keep her own earnings!

The 1857 Matrimonial Causes Act too, which 'provided for divorce through the law courts rather than the previous solitary, financially precluding private Parliamentary petition.' And three decades later, under the 1888 Local Government Act, 'unmarried women *who were ratepayers* were allowed to vote' in county elections, which from this point took on administration of local asylums.'[31] In short, now it was not just her gender but personal wealth that gave her a voice.

It is surely safe to assume that the all-too-recent suffragette movement was both justified *and* resisted on misogynist terms. This year (2018) sees its centenary celebration, rightly commemorating the special things it achieved. Yet winning the vote amplified many other, unsettling issues.

'With women, madness lay in essential constitutional weakness'... in effect [she was] predisposed to insanity.'[32] To rail against status quo meant only one thing - she had taken a complete leave of her senses!

A 'network of gendered meanings involved the construction of women as passive subjects, 'heavily determined by social forces, the antithesis of the autonomous, rational masculine self'', Ward had pronounced as a new millennium dawned.[33]

Thus still considered insane, suffragettes faced imprisonment, abuse and being force-fed through a tube, even though even alienist advice had long warned against such a tack (e.g. Sutherland's liberating advice: '[t]he forcible or artificial feeding of the insane should never be resorted to if it can possibly be avoided.')[34] But then no-one really believed there was madness involved.

Success eventually came in two particular statutes: the 1918 Representation of the People Act and the Parliament (Qualification of Women) Act in the same year; the latter giving women the right to sit and vote in the House of Commons. Not that misogynist abuse ceased as her vote was allowed. Institutionalisation remained but one continuing ploy. Certain societal sections (largely but not exclusively male) breathed new life into age-old abuses. No longer able to declare the woman a witch, or claim she was in league with the Devil, the threatened male now turned his attention on her supposed immoral living. From condemning affairs, courting in public, through to Freud's couch-focussed fantastical nightmares of deep-rooted sex, women's 'rediscovered' corruption was yet again to be found in her thoughts. They may have won the vote, but their minds were still not their own.

In the five hundred years leading up to today, the woman's lot in the world has been mediocre at best, brutal at worst. From words, thoughts and deeds, including physical horrors, the genuinely mad, and those accused of the same, have suffered alike from their want of a voice. Yet looking back now, one still has to wonder; has there been a danger throughout of distorting the truth? As much as new thinking is to be encouraged and welcomed, is there the risk – and I write this as a male melancholic neurasthenic – that, as in so many contexts, a post-modern realignment of madness has thrown a blanket of mis-meaning on a past that was never intentionally there? An inherent weakness in all historical study is that we view the past through our post-modern lens. By holding on to this warning, history is best able to speak for itself.

This book now ends ahead of arguably the single biggest change in the subject of women and madness. The removal of 'hysteria' from American texts at the start of the Fifties,[35] to a new 'women's movement' just one decade later, were joined by a new breed of *female* experts, who leapt into the traditionally masculine realm.[36] Just one hundred years before, ' feminist writings [had] considered the socio-cultural status of women and voiced the need to provide female branches of law, psychology and medicine in order to better understand their own kind: '[through] our steady insistence on proclaiming sex-distinction,' wrote Gilman, ' we have grown to consider most human attributes as masculine attributes, for the simple reason that they were allowed for men and forbidden to women.'[37] She had demonstrated perfectly the pitiful absence in the history of female madness – the women themselves.

It is thus appropriate, after all that has been written, to leave the last words to a woman:

> 'Psychotherapy treatment options are now recommended, sometimes in conjunction with other measures, to treat the many conditions once broadly called female hysteria. It is important that these options are made available to women throughout their many life stages. While in the United States we might take this and other victories of the feminist movement for granted, we need to ensure that progress continues.
>
> 'The continuing battle for women's psychological rights may not be as clear-cut as the suffragist movement or the fight for reproductive freedoms, but it is no less important. In literature it is important for women to let their voices be heard, particularly in cultures that do not encourage them to speak out. By demystifying 'female' psychological conditions and distancing them from historically supported stigma we can move into an era where women's psychological wellbeing is free from moral and political assumptions.'[38]

Hear, hear!

Appendix 1

A Token of Madness

I might have chosen any true story about the saddest madness of all; when love went one way. The following captured both the attitudes of the time, and the apparently *factual* cause of a woman's mental decay:

'About the year 1780, a young East Indian, whose name was Dupree, left his fatherland to visit a distant relation, a merchant, on Fish Street Hill. During the young man's stay, he was waited on by the servant of the house, a country girl, Rebecca Griffiths, chiefly remarkable for the plainness of her person, and the quiet meekness of her manners. The circuit of pleasure run, and yearning again for home, the visitor at length prepared for his departure; the chaise came to the door, and shaking of hands, with tenderer salutations, adieus, and farewells, followed in the usual abundance.

'Rebecca, in whom an extraordinary depression had for some days previously been perceived, was in attendance, to help to pack the luggage. The leave-taking of friends and relations at length completed, with a guinea squeezed into his humble attendant's hand, and a brief 'God bless you, Rebecca', the young man sprang into the chaise, the driver smacked his whip, and the vehicle was rolling rapidly out of sight, when a piercing shriek from Rebecca, who had stood to all appearance vacantly gazing on what had passed, alarmed the family, then retiring into the house. They hastily turned round: to their infinite surprise, Rebecca was seen wildly following the chaise. She was rushing with the velocity of lightning along the middle of the road, her hair streaming in the wind, and her whole appearance that of a desperate maniac!

'Proper persons were immediately dispatched after her, but she was not secured till she had gained the Borough; when she was taken in a state of incurable madness to Bethlehem Hospital, where she died some years after. The guinea he had given her was her richest treasure, her only wealth and never suffered, during life, to quit her hand; she grasped it still more firmly in her dying moments, and at her request, in the last gleam of returning reason the lightning before death, it was buried with her…

'It was Mr. Dupree's only consolation, after her death, that the excessive homeliness of her person, and her retiring air and manners, had never even suffered him to indulge in the most trifling freedom with her. She had loved hopelessly, and paid the forfeiture with sense and life.'

[Transcribed from *Old and New London* v6: 359; in the author's collection]

Appendix 2

The Unsuitable Suffragette Mind

The inevitable collapse of Rule: Feminism, the Suffragettes and the Unsuitable Mind

The following extract came from an article entitled 'Feminism in France', in which comparisons were drawn between the suffragists there and their 'sisters' in England. Its woeful rhetoric on her perceived mental constraints appeared in an age when the lunatic asylum retained its hideous threat for those speaking their mind:

'The fact that 'feminism' figures in Murray's dictionary and is defined as 'the qualities of females' justifies the statement that the word has been incorporated into the English language…[and yet] 'Female Suffrage' is merely a means to an end, and therefore a very incomplete definition of ideas and aspirations which find favour with the Suffragists. Those aspirations clearly point to the dethronement of virility in the councils of the State and the substitution in its place of all those 'female qualities' which are embodied in the expression 'feminism'.

'The difference between the 'hyenas in petticoats' – to borrow a phrase of Horace Walpole's – who have from time to time disgraced the annals of France, and incendiary viragoes who have recently gained an infamous notoriety in England, is merely one of degree and opportunity.

'Once…the Parliamentary vote be acquired,…feminism, in a more or less extreme form, will follow as a natural consequence. It is all the more certain to do so because the *moderate* suffragists themselves often exhibit, although in a far less prominent degree than the *extremists*, those *defects of character and intellect which render it undesirable that direct political power should be conferred on women.*

'Further, in common with all thoughtful anti-feminists… the leading characteristics of women… disqualify them from political life. [I quote] with approval the words of M. Thomas, who in 1772 published a remarkable essay in which he said: "Read history; you will find that women always display an excess of pity or an excess of vindictiveness. They are wanting the calm strength that tells them when and where to stop".'

[Transcribed from *The National Review*, November 1913; in the author's collection (my *emphasis*)]

Endnotes

Introduction

1. Ludmilla Jordanova, *Sexual Visions* (Hemel Hempstead, 1989), p. 76 (fn 25).
2. Roy Porter, *Mind-Forg'd Manacles* (London, 1990), p. 18.
3. Daniel Hack Tuke (ed), *A Dictionary of Psychological Medicine* (Philadelphia 1892), vol. 1, pp. 1-26.
4. Roy Porter, *Mind-Forg'd Manacles* (London, 1990), p. 19.
5. Michael Macdonald, *Mystical Bedlam* (Cambridge, 1988), p. 169.
6. *Ibid.*, p. 173.
7. For varying 'takes' on the medical humours, compare Catharine Arnold, *Bedlam* (London, 2009) and Harvard Online (n.d.).
8. Andrew Scull, *Madness. A Very Short Introduction* (Oxford, 2011), pp. 12-13.
9. *Ibid.*, pp. 13-14.
10. Tania Woods, *From Female Sexuality and Hysteria to Feminine Psychology: The Gender Of Insanity in Literature* (n.d.), p. 5 (my *emphasis*).
11. Roy Porter, *Mind-Forg'd Manacles* (London, 1990), p. 45.
12. *Ibid.*, p. 80.
13. Anne Digby, Women's Biological Straitjacket. In Mendus, S. and J. Rendall (eds), *Sexuality and Subordination: Interdisciplinary Studies of Gender in the Nineteenth Century* (London, 1989), p. 193.
14. Crimean nurse, Florence Nightingale, became a rebellion sensation long before her fame for caring. Her essay, *Cassandra* (London, 1852), vigorously rejected her solitary, family existence even at great risk to her mental health.
15. Elaine Showalter, *The Female Malady* (London, 1987), p. 8.
16. Title of Robert-Fleury's (1876) painting, celebrating Pinel's adoption of moral management over physical restraint of the insane.
17. Isaac Ray, *Treatise on the Medical Jurisprudence of Insanity* (Boston 1838), in which he extolled the use of open space and country surroundings for calmly (and successfully) treating the mad.

18. Compare the differing responses to an apparently philanthropic decision. See Elaine Showalter, *The Female Malady* (1987: 8), for her feminist perspective, versus Michel Foucault, *Madness and Civilization* (New York 1988; eg 245, 247, 266), for his male psychologist's viewpoint.
19. Elaine Showalter, *The Female Malady* (London, 1987), p. 62.
20. Quoted in Freedman and Hellerstein's 'documentary account of women's lives in nineteenth-century England': Hellerstein *et al* (eds), *Victorian Women* (Brighton, 1981), p. 118.
21. Judith R. Walkowitz, *City of Dreadful Delights. Narratives of Sexual Danger in Late-Victorian London*, (London, 1994), p. 135.
22. In Hellerstein *et al* (eds), *Victorian Women* (Brighton, 1981), p. 129.
23. William Acton, *The Functions and Disorders of the Reproductive Organs* (4th Edition) (Philadelphia, 1867), p. 144 (my *emphasis*).
24. *Ibid.*, p. 178.
25. From course notes at University of Warwick, *From Cradle to Grave: Health, Medicine and Lifecycle in Modern Britain (H1278)* (2018).
26. Andrew Scull, *Hysteria* (Oxford, 2011), p. 100 (my *emphasis*).
27. Elaine Showalter, *The Female Malady* (London, 1987), p. 126.
28. Lyn Pykett, Women Writing Woman: nineteenth-century representations of gender and sexuality. In J. Shattock (ed), *Women and Literature in Britain 1800-1900* (Cambridge, 2001), p. 79.
29. Jacqueline Pearson, Women Reading, Reading Women. In H. Wilcox (ed), *Women and Literature in Britain 1500-1700* (Cambridge, 1998), p. 86.
30. William S. Playfair in Tuke (ed), *A Dictionary of Psychological Medicine* (Philadelphia 1892), vol. 2, p. 851.
31. See Elizabeth Garrett Anderson, Sex in Mind and in Education: A Reply. In Leighton, M. E. and L. A. Surridge (eds), *The Broadview Anthology of Victorian Prose 1832-1901* (Ontario, 2012), pp. 200-03.
32. See Hilary Marland, *Women and Madness* (2013). Others may take a dissimilar view, for example see Anna Shepherd, *Institutionalizing the Insane in the Nineteenth Century* (London, 2014).
33. Both cases cited in Andrew Roberts' *The Lunacy Commission*, an online repository of all things lunacy and legislation and much else besides. See bibliography for access.
34. Elizabeth Foyster, At the Limits of Liberty: Married Women and Confinement in Eighteenth-Century England, *Continuity and Change* 17 (2002), Abstract.
35. Derek Clear *at al* (eds), *Deviance, Disorder and the Self* (n.d.).
36. Quoted in *ibid.*

37. Roy Porter, *Mind-Forg'd Manacles* (London, 1990), pp. 148-49.

38. Derek Clear *at al* (eds), *Deviance, Disorder and the Self* (n.d.).

39. Akinobu Takabayashi, *Surviving the Lunacy Act of 1890: English Psychiatrists and Professional Development during the Early Twentieth Century* (2017).

40. Andrew Roberts, *The Lunacy Commission. Its Origin, Emergence and Character* (1981).

41. Quoted in Clear *at al* (eds), *Deviance, Disorder and the Self* (n.d.), Introduction.

42. See Roger Smith, *Trial by Medicine* (Edinburgh, 1981), pp. 21-22.

43. Quoted in Andrew Roberts, *The Lunacy Commission. Its Origin, Emergence and Character* (1981).

44. Quoted in Clear *at al* (eds), *Deviance, Disorder and the Self* (n.d.),

45. Louise Lowe, *The Bastilles of England* (London, 1883), p. 3.

46. Clear *at al* (eds), *Deviance, Disorder and the Self* (n.d.), Introduction.

47. Michel Foucault, *Madness and Civilization* (New York, 1988). p. 270.

48. Patricia Allderidge, Bedlam: fact or fantasy? In Bynum *et al* (eds), *The Anatomy of Madness* (London, 1985), vol. 2, p. 19.

49. Roy Porter, *Mind-Forg'd Manacles* (London, 1990), p. 105.

50. Elaine Showalter quoted in *Ibid*.

51. Katharine Hodgkin (ed), *Women, Madness and Sin in Early Modern England. The autobiographical writings of Dionys Fitzherbert*, p. 67.

52. *Ibid.*, p. 59.

53. After George Cheyne, the first physician to highlight the impact of poor diet and idleness on the nerves and from which he introduced the world to vegetarianism, especially as a cure for an "attack of the vapours".

54. Quoted in Roy Porter, *Mind-Forg'd Manacles* (London, 1990), p. 49.

55. Vivienne Parry, *Were the `Mad' Heroines of Literature Really Sane?* (2010).

Chapter 1: Engendered Madness

1. Bynum *et al* (eds), *The Anatomy of Madness* (London, 1985), v1, 12-13, (original *emphasis*).

2. Thomas Adams, *Mystical Bedlam* (London, 1615), p. 50.

3. *Ibid*.

4. *Ibid.*, pp. 122-23.

5. Henry Maudsley, Sex in Mind and in Education, *Popular Science Monthly* 5 (1874), p. 200.

6. Quoted in Elaine Showalter, *The Female Malady* (London, 1987), pp. 122-23.

7. George M. Beard, *Sexual Neurasthenia [Nervous Exhaustion]. Its Hygiene, Causes, Symptoms, and Treatment* (New York, 1884), p. 15 (my *emphasis*).

8. *Ibid.*, pp. 28-29.

9. Tania Woods, *From Female Sexuality and Hysteria to Feminine Psychology: The Gender Of Insanity in Literature* (n.d.).

10. Quoted in Elaine Showalter, *The Female Malady* (London, 1987), p. 122.

11. *Ibid.*

12. Ludmilla Jordanova, *Sexual Visions* (Hemel Hempstead, 1989), p. 73.

13. Taken from Gooch's *On Some of the Diseases Peculiar to Women; with Other Papers* (1831), quoted in Susan Hogan, The Tyranny of the Maternal Body: Madness and Maternity, *Women's History Magazine* 54 (2006), p. 23.

14. Quoted in *Ibid.*

15. Hilary Marland, *Dangerous Motherhood* (London, 2004), p. 38.

16. After Susan Hogan, The Tyranny of the Maternal Body: Madness and Maternity, *Women's History Magazine* 54 (2006), p. 24.

17. Henry Maudsley, *Pathology of Mind* (London, 1895), p. 208.

18. *Ibid.*, p. 415

19. Citing Edward Shorter in Susan Hogan, The Tyranny of the Maternal Body: Madness and Maternity, *Women's History Magazine* 54 (2006), pp. 24-25.

20. See Science Museum Online's useful web pages for an introductory discussion to the topic. Details in bibliography.

21. Quoted in Leslie Abshire, *Art Mimics Life: Witches and Magic in Early Modern Art* (2014).

22. *Ibid.*, (*my emphasis*).

23. See University of Warwick, *From Cradle to Grave: Health, Medicine and Lifecycle in Modern Britain* (2018).

24. Heinrich Kramer, *Malleus Maleficarum* (1486), trans. Rev. M. Summers (1928).

25. *Ibid.*

26. Catharine Arnold, *Bedlam* (London, 2009), p. 55.

27. Quoted in Lucy Williams, *Wayward Women* (Barnsley, 2016), p. 97.

28. Sharon M. Setzer (ed), *A Letter to the Women of England and the Natural Daughter* (Canada, 2003), Introduction.

29. *Ibid.*, pp. 242-44.

30. Judith R. Walkowitz, *City of Dreadful Delights. Narratives of Sexual Danger in Late-Victorian London*, (London, 1994), pp. 22-23. See also Judith R. Walkowitz, *Prostitution and Victorian Society: Women, Class, and the State* (New York, 1980).

31. Quoted in Reva B. Siegel, 'The Rule of Love': Wife Beating as Prerogative and Privacy, *Faculty Scholarship Series*, Paper 1092 (1996), p. 2152 (fn 131).

32. In 1838, Mary Cruse escaped being charged with the attempted murder of her 7 year old child after counsel contended such a capital offence would see her acquitted through her *husband's coercion*, whether actual or not. Instead she was convicted of common assault, and sentenced to just 1 month in prison. The law has since been reformed, though only in part. See David J. Vaughan, *Mad or Bad* (Barnsley, 2017), pp. 64-68.

33. Taken from Andrew Roberts, *The Lunacy Commission. Its Origin, Emergence and Character* (1981).

34. The History of Parliament, Jane Campbell: Parliamentary Divorce Pioneer (2016).

35. John S. Mill, *The Subjection of Women* (London, 1869), pp. 56-57.

36. Cited in Ludmilla Jordanova, *Sexual Visions* (Hemel Hempstead, 1989), pp. 76-77.

37. *Ibid.*; pp. 77-78.

38. *Ibid.*, pp. 52-53. For an early feminist rejection, see Mary Wollstonecraft, *A Vindication of the Rights of Women: with Strictures on Political and Moral Subjects* (Boston, 1792).

39. Quoted in Radojka Startup, *Damaging Females: Representations of Women as Victims and Perpetrators of Crime in the Mid Nineteenth Century* (2000), p. 311, fn 58.

40. Quoted in Tania Woods, *From Female Sexuality and Hysteria to Feminine Psychology: The Gender of Insanity in Literature* (n.d.), p. 37 (my *emphasis*).

41. Ben Griffin, *The Politics of Gender in Victorian Britain* (Cambridge, 2012), p.39.

42. *Ibid.*, pp. 37-39.

43. Leonore Davidoff and Catherine Hall quoted in *ibid.*, p. 40.

44. Quoting Tush in *ibid*,. p. 40.

45. John Stuart Mill, *The Subjection of Women* (London, 1869), pp. 81-82.

46. Roy Porter, *Mind-Forg'd Manacles* (London, 1990), p. xi.

47. Cited in *ibid.*, p. 23.

48. William G. Willoughby in Tuke (ed), *A Dictionary of Psychological Medicine* (Philadelphia 1892), 1892 vol. 2, p. 1276.

49. *Ibid.*, pp. 1276-77.

50. Paraphrased from Michael Macdonald, Women and Madness in Tudor and Stuart England, *Social Research* 53/2 (1986), p. 267.

51. Rutherford Macphail in Tuke (ed), *A Dictionary of Psychological Medicine* (Philadelphia 1892), 1892 vol. 1, p. 135.

52. *Ibid.*, p. 139.

53. C. E. Beevor in *ibid.*, p. 157.

54. Crochley Clapham in *ibid.*, pp. 164–68.

55. Thomas Laycock, *A Treatise on the Nervous Diseases of Women* (London, 1840).

56. Crochley Clapham in Tuke (ed), *A Dictionary of Psychological Medicine* (Philadelphia 1892), 1892 vol. 1, pp. 164–68.

57. See, for example, James Cowles Prichard, *A Treatise on Insanity and Other Disorders Affecting the Mind* (Philadelphia, 1837).

58. James Fitzjames Stephen, *A History of the Criminal Law of England* (London, 1883), vol. 2, p. 97.

59. Robert Burton (1577–1640) was a scholar, cleric and accepted father of English psychiatry. His famous quotes include 'on the shoulders of giants' (long before Sir Isaac Newton) and 'what cannot be cured must be endured' (long before Salman Rushdie). Cited here in Michael Macdonald, *Mystical Bedlam* (Cambridge, 1988), p. 180.

60. Roy Porter, *Mind-Forg'd Manacles* (London, 1990), p. 58.

61. For example, David J. Vaughan, 'Healthy Impulses to Crime' - Crime, Insanity & the Elusive Free Will. In *Mad, Bad and Desperate* (2016).

62. James Fitzjames Stephen, *A History of the Criminal Law of England* (London, 1883), vol. 2, p. 138.

63. Quoting Griesinger, Andrew Scull's 'founding father of German psychiatry', in *ibid.*

64. Richard Blackmore on Willis, quoted in Roy Porter, *Mind-Forg'd Manacles* (London, 1990), p. 177.

65. *Ibid.*, p. 178.

66. For example, see Nancy J. Hirschmann, *Gender, Class, and Freedom in Modern Political Theory* (Princeton, 2008).

67. Roy Porter, *Mind-Forg'd Manacles* (London, 1990), pp. 188–91.

68. Richard Blackmore, *A Treatise of the Spleen and Vapours* (London, 1725). Quoted in Roy Porter, *Mind-Forg'd Manacles* (London, 1990), p. 177.

69. Roy Porter, *Mind-Forg'd Manacles* (London, 1990), pp. 19–20.

70. Cited in Andrew Scull, *Hysteria* (Oxford, 2011), pp. 35–36.

71. See Catharine Arnold, *Bedlam* (London, 2009), pp. 29–31.

72. Daniel Hack Tuke (ed), *A Dictionary of Psychological Medicine* (Philadelphia 1892), vol. 1, pp. 174, 352.

73. In *ibid.*, p. 619.

74. Andrew Scull, *Madness. A Very Short Introduction* (Oxford, 2011), pp. 17–18.

75. Bynum *et al* (eds), *The Anatomy of Madness* (London, 1985), vol. 1, p. 3.

76. Quoted in Catharine Arnold, *Bedlam* (London, 2009), p. 57.

77. Quoted in Louise Jackson, Witches, wives and mothers: Witchcraft Persecutions and Women's Confessions in Seventeenth-Century England. In Levack (ed), *New Perspectives on Witchcraft, Magic and Demonology vol. 4. Gender and Witchcraft*, p. 261.

78. Michael Macdonald, *Mystical Bedlam* (Cambridge, 1988), p. 204.

79. *Ibid.*, p. 121.

80. *Ibid.*, p. 208.

81. After *ibid*.

82. Charles Mackay, *Memoirs of Extraordinary Popular Delusions and the Madness of Crowds* (London, 1852), vol. 2, p. 102 (my *emphasis*).

83. Bynum *et al* (eds), *The Anatomy of Madness* (London, 1985), vol. 1, p. 3.

84. Roy Porter, *Mind-Forg'd Manacles* (London, 1990), p. 108.

85. James Fitzjames Stephen, *A History of the Criminal Law of England* (London, 1883), vol. 2, p. 431

86. Daniel Hack Tuke, *Chapters in the History of the Insane in the British Isles* (London, 1882), pp. 36-37.

87. James Fitzjames Stephen, *A History of the Criminal Law of England* (London, 1883), vol. 2, p. 207.

88. Its "co-author", Dominican friar Jacob Sprenger, was only posthumously added to its 1519 reissue, now largely dismissed.

89. Heinrich Kramer, *Malleus Maleficarum* (1486), trans. Rev. M. Summers (1928).

90. Michael Macdonald, *Mystical Bedlam* (Cambridge, 1988), p. 210.

91. Daniel Hack Tuke, *Chapters in the History of the Insane in the British Isles* (London, 1882), p. 36.

92. Beatriz Qunitanilla, Witchcraft or Mental Illness?, *Psychaitric Times* (2010).

93. Andrew Scull, *Hysteria* (Oxford, 2011), pp. 1-5.

94. *Ibid.*, pp. 15-19.

95. Nigel Walker, *Crime and Insanity in England* (Edinburgh, 1968), vol. 1, p. 47.

96. Daniel Hack Tuke, *Chapters in the History of the Insane in the British Isles* (London, 1882), p. 38.

97. Michael Macdonald, Women and Madness in Tudor and Stuart England, *Social Research* 53/2 (1986), p. 278.

98. Ronald C. Sawyer quoted in *ibid*.

99. *Ibid.*, p. 215.

100. Jacqueline Broad, Cavendish, van Helmont, and the Mad Raging Womb. In Hayden, J. A. (ed), *The New Science and Women's Literary Discourse: Prefiguring Frankenstein*, p. 66.

101. Michael Macdonald, *Mystical Bedlam* (Cambridge, 1988), p. xiv.

102. *Ibid.*, p. 209.

103. *Ibid.*, p. 213 (my *emphasis*).

104. Bynum *et al* (eds), *The Anatomy of Madness* (London, 1985), vol. 1, p. 3, fn. 15.

105. William Battie, *A Treatise on Madness* (London, 1758), quoted in Michael Macdonald, *Mystical Bedlam* (Cambridge, 1988), p. 171.

106. James Fitzjames Stephen, *A History of the Criminal Law of England* (London, 1883), vol. 2, pp. 431-35.

107. Charles Mackay, *Memoirs of Extraordinary Popular Delusions and the Madness of Crowds* (London, 1852), vol. 2, p. 158 (my *emphasis*).

108. Roy Porter, *Mind-Forg'd Manacles* (London, 1990), p. 81.

109. *Ibid.*, pp. 108-09.

110. George Cheyne, *The English Malady* (London: 1733), quoted in Roy Porter, *Mind-Forg'd Manacles* (London, 1990), p. 52 (original *emphasis*).

111. Quoted in Andrew Scull, *Hysteria* (Oxford, 2011), p. 50.

112. BBC Radio 4 Online, *George Cheyne and His Work* (2003).

113. Bynum *et al* (eds), *The Anatomy of Madness* (London, 1985), vol. 1, p. 90.

114. Thomas Laycock, On the reflex function of the brain. In *The British and Foreign Medical Review* 19 (1845), pp. 298-311.

115. Thomas Laycock, *A Treatise on the Nervous Diseases of Women* (London, 1840). See also Bynum *et al* (eds), *The Anatomy of Madness* (London, 1985), vol. 1, pp. 94, 95.

116. Roy Porter, *Mind-Forg'd Manacles* (London, 1990), p. 60.

117. For example, Michel Foucault, *Madness and Civilization* (New York, 1988), pp. vi-vii.

118. Roy Porter, *Mind-Forg'd Manacles* (London, 1990), p. 110.

119. *Ibid.*, pp. 111.

120. Bethlem Museum of the Mind online, *From Melancholia to Prozac: Depression Throughout History* (2013).

121. Andrew Scull, *Madness. A Very Short Introduction* (Oxford, 2011), pp. 3-4.

122. Roy Porter, *Mind-Forg'd Manacles* (London, 1990), p. 31 (my *emphasis*).

123. Catharine Arnold, *Bedlam* (London, 2009), p. 217.

124. *Ibid.*, pp. 217-18 (my *emphasis*).

125. Roy Porter, *Mind-Forg'd Manacles* (London, 1990), p. 24.

126. *Ibid.*, p. xi.
127. *Ibid.*, p. 33.
128. Michael Macdonald, Women and Madness in Tudor and Stuart England, *Social Research* 53/2 (1986), p. 262.
129. Quoted in Roy Porter, *Mind-Forg'd Manacles* (London, 1990), p. 34.
130. Tania Woods, *From Female Sexuality and Hysteria to Feminine Psychology: The Gender of Insanity in Literature* (n.d.), p. 3.
131. Jacqueline Broad, *Cavendish, van Helmont, and the Mad Raging Womb* (2016), p. 54.
132. *Ibid.*, p. 63.
133. Daniel Hack Tuke in Tuke (ed), *A Dictionary of Psychological Medicine* (Philadelphia 1892), vol. 1, p. 241.
134. *Ibid.*, p. 677.
135. Roger Smith, *Trial by Medicine* (Edinburgh, 1981), p. 143.
136. Lucia Zedner quoted in Arlie Loughnan, Gender, 'Madness' and Crime: the Doctrine of Infanticide. In Loughnan, A., *Manifest Madness: Mental Incapacity in the Criminal Law* (Oxford, 2012), p. 214.
137. Joel P. Eigen quoted in *ibid.*, p. 214 (my *emphasis*).
138. John Haslam, *Observations on Insanity* (London, 1798), p. 106 *et seq.*
139. Lyttelton Forbes Winslow, *The Insanity of Passion and Crime* (London, 1912), pp. 279-313.
140. Alfred Swaine Taylor, *Principles and Practice of Medical Jurisprudence* (London, 1865), p. 1099.
141. Thomas Claye Shaw in Tuke (ed), *A Dictionary of Psychological Medicine* (Philadelphia 1892), vol. 1, p. 354 (my *emphasis*).
142. Lucy Williams, *Wayward Women* (Barnsley, 2016), p. 83 (my *emphasis*).
143. Havelock Ellis in Tuke (ed), *A Dictionary of Psychological Medicine* (Philadelphia 1892), vol. 2, pp. 1154-56.
144. In *ibid.*, vol. 1, p. 177.
145. Michael Macdonald, *Mystical Bedlam* (Cambridge, 1988), p. 126.
146. *Ibid.*, p. 146.
147. Andrew Scull, *Madness. A Very Short Introduction* (Oxford, 2011), pp. 14-15.
148. *Ibid.*, p. 7.
149. Michael Macdonald, *Mystical Bedlam* (Cambridge, 1988), p. 142.
150. *Ibid.*, p. 149.
151. George Fielding Blandford in Tuke (ed), *A Dictionary of Psychological Medicine* (Philadelphia 1892), vol. 2, p. 999.

152. Samuel Wilks, *Lectures on Diseases of the Nervous System* (London: 1878), p. 367.

153. George H. Savage in Tuke (ed), *A Dictionary of Psychological Medicine* (Philadelphia 1892), vol. 2, p. 775.

154. *Ibid.*, p. 776.

155. In Tuke (ed), *A Dictionary of Psychological Medicine* (Philadelphia 1892), vol. 2, p. 984.

156. Judith R. Walkowitz, *City of Dreadful Delights. Narratives of Sexual Danger in Late-Victorian London*, (London, 1994), p. 155.

157. James Fitzjames Stephen, *A History of the Criminal Law of England* (London, 1883), vol. 2, p. 133.

158. In Tuke (ed), *A Dictionary of Psychological Medicine* (Philadelphia 1892), vol. 2, pp. 873-74.

159. Wendy Wallace, Sent to the Asylum: The Victorian Women Locked Up Because They Were Suffering From Stress, Post Natal Depression and Anxiety, *Mail Online* (2012).

160. George M. Robertson in Tuke (ed), *A Dictionary of Psychological Medicine* (Philadelphia 1892), vol. 1, p. 564.

161. Quoted in Roy Porter, *Mind-Forg'd Manacles* (London, 1990), p. 27 (fn. 143).

162. Smith-Rosenberg and Rosenberg quoted in Andrew Scull, *Hysteria* (Oxford, 2011), p. 72.

163. *Ibid.*, p. 72.

164. Horatio Robinson Storer, *The Causation, Course, and Treatment of Reflex Insanity in Women* (Boston, 1871), p. 78.

165. Michael Macdonald, *Mystical Bedlam* (Cambridge, 1988), p. 126 (my *emphasis*).

Chapter 2 – The Hysteria Hysterics

1. Helen King, Once Upon a Text. Hysteria from Hippocrates. In Gilman *et al* (eds), *Hysteria Beyond Freud* (Berkeley, 1993), Chapter 1.

2. Andrew Scull, *Hysteria* (Oxford, 2011), p. 3.

3. Michael Macdonald, *Mystical Bedlam* (Cambridge, 1988), p. 211.

4. *Ibid.*, p. 199.

5. Quoted in Jacqueline Broad, *Cavendish, van Helmont, and the Mad Raging Womb* (2016), p. 73.

6. Andrew Scull, *Hysteria* (Oxford, 2011), p. 14.

7. *Ibid.*, pp. 28-29.

8. *Ibid.*, p. 45.

9. *Ibid.*, pp. 48-49.

10. For example, see Andrew Combe, *Observations on Mental Derangement* (Edinburgh, 1831), pp. 117-20.
11. Quoted in Andrew Scull, *Hysteria* (Oxford, 2011), p. 51.
12. Cited in *ibid.*, p. 33.
13. *Ibid.*, p. 35.
14. Samuel Wilks, *Lectures on Diseases of the Nervous System* (London: 1878), p. 362 (my *emphasis*).
15. Elaine Showalter, *The Female Malady* (London, 1987), p. 138.
16. Hilary Evans and Robert E. Bartholomew, *Outbreak! The Encyclopedia of Extraordinary Social Behavior* (New York, 2009), p. 292.
17. Daniel Hack Tuke (ed), *A Dictionary of Psychological Medicine* (Philadelphia 1892), vol. 2, p. 723.
18. *Ibid.*, vol. 1, p. 696.
19. Andrew Combe, *Observations on Mental Derangement* (Edinburgh, 1831), p. 199 (original *emphasis*).
20. Nigel Walker, *Crime and Insanity in England* (Edinburgh, 1968), vol. 1, p. 48.
21. Jacqueline Broad, *Cavendish, van Helmont, and the Mad Raging Womb* (2016), pp. 66-67.
22. In Tuke (ed), *A Dictionary of Psychological Medicine* (Philadelphia 1892), vol. 1, pp. 627-28.
23. Charcot's degrading display of "hysterical" women has received broad condemnation in post-1950s literature, amongst them Andrew Scull, *Hysteria* (Oxford, 2011), p. 122.
24. Daniel Hack Tuke (ed), *A Dictionary of Psychological Medicine* (Philadelphia 1892), vol. 1, pp. 627-41.
25. *Ibid.*, p. 629.
26. *Ibid.*, p. 630.
27. *Ibid.*, p. 631.
28. *Ibid.*, p. 632.
29. *Ibid.*, p. 637.
30. Ibid., p. 640.
31. Samuel Wilks, *Lectures on Diseases of the Nervous System* (London: 1878), p. 38.
32. Andrew Scull, *Hysteria* (Oxford, 2011), p. 113.
33. In Tuke (ed), *A Dictionary of Psychological Medicine* (Philadelphia 1892), vol. 1, p. 640.
34. Andrew Scull, *Hysteria* (Oxford, 2011), pp. 119-20.
35. Cf Beatriz Pichel, *The Backstage of Hysteria: Medicine in the Photographic Studio* (2017).

36. For a useful spread of opinion, see Andrew Scull, *Hysteria* (Oxford, 2011); Andrew Scull, *Madness. A Very Short Introduction* (Oxford, 2011); Elaine Showalter, *The Female Malady* (London, 1987); Michel Foucault, *Madness and Civilization* (New York, 1988).
37. F. C. Skey quoted in Andrew Scull, *Hysteria* (Oxford, 2011), p. 93.
38. Henry Maudsley quoted in *ibid*.
39. Cf Charlotte Perkins Gilman (Stetson), The Yellow Wallpaper, *New England Magazine* 11/5 (1892), pp. 647-57.
40. Andrew Scull, *Hysteria* (Oxford, 2011), p. 182.
41. *Ibid.*, p. 45.
42. Andrew Combe, *Observations on Mental Derangement* (Edinburgh, 1831), p. 168.
43. Alexander Crichton, *Inquiry into the Nature and Origin of Mental Derangement* (London 1798), pp. 137-38 (my *emphasis*).
44. In Tuke (ed), *A Dictionary of Psychological Medicine* (Philadelphia 1892), vol. 2, p. 936, (my *emphasis*).
45. In ibid., p. 1350 (my *emphasis*).
46. Thomas Laycock, *A Treatise on the Nervous Diseases of Women* (London, 1840).
47. Lyttelton Forbes Winslow, *The Insanity of Passion and Crime* (London, 1912), p. 5.
48. *Ibid.*, pp. 283-84.
49. See Horatio B. Donkin in Tuke (ed), *A Dictionary of Psychological Medicine* (Philadelphia 1892), vol. 1, pp. 618-27.
50. *Ibid.*, p. 619.
51. Elaine Showalter, *The Female Malady* (London, 1987), p. 131 *et seq*.
52. Andrew Scull, *Hysteria* (Oxford, 2011), p. 7.
53. Conolly Norman in Tuke (ed), *A Dictionary of Psychological Medicine* (Philadelphia 1892), vol. 2, p. 768.
54. George H. Savage in *ibid.*, p. 775.
55. Horatio B. Donkin in *ibid.*, vol. 1, p. 621.
56. Samuel Wilks, *Lectures on Diseases of the Nervous System* (London: 1878), p. 367.
57. *Ibid.*
58. *Ibid.*, p. 369.
59. Cf Thomas Laycock, *A Treatise on the Nervous Diseases of Women* (London, 1840).
60. Jacqueline Broad, *Cavendish, van Helmont, and the Mad Raging Womb* (2016), p. 55.

61. Nigel Walker, *Crime and Insanity in England* (Edinburgh, 1968), vol. 1, p. 46.
62. Andrew Scull, *Hysteria* (Oxford, 2011), p. 55.
63. Helen Goodman, 'Madness and Masculinity': Male Patients in London Asylums and Victorian Culture (London, 2015).
64. David J. Vaughan, Centres of Lunacy. In *Mad, Bad and Desperate* (2015).
65. Still a relatively emerging idea covered *inter alia* in Andrew Scull, *Hysteria* (Oxford, 2011); Andrew Scull, *Madness. A Very Short Introduction* (Oxford, 2011); Elaine Showalter, *The Female Malady* (London, 1987); Catharine Arnold, *Bedlam* (London, 2009).
66. For example, Sarah Jaffray, Hysteria, *Wellcome Collection* (2017).
67. For example, Andrew Scull, *Hysteria* (Oxford, 2011), p. 96.
68. Quoted in Lyn Pykett, Women Writing Woman: nineteenth-century representations of gender and sexuality. In J. Shattock (ed), *Women and Literature in Britain 1800-1900* (Cambridge, 2001), p. 83.
69. Quoted in Judith R. Walkowitz, *Prostitution and Victorian Society: Women, Class, and the State* (New York, 1980), p. 173.
70. Henry Rayner quoted in J. P. Williams, Psychical Research and Psychiatry in Late Victorian Britain: Trance as Ecstasy or Trance as Insanity. In Bynum *et al* (eds), *The Anatomy of Madness* (London, 1985), vol. 1, p. 234.
71. Quoted in Roy Porter, *Mind-Forg'd Manacles* (London, 1990), p. 186.
72. Sarah Jaffray, Hysteria, *Wellcome Collection* (2017).

Chapter 3 – Maternal Mayhem

1. Robert Barnes in Tuke (ed), *A Dictionary of Psychological Medicine* (Philadelphia 1892), vol. 1, p. 234.
2. Daniel Hack Tuke in *ibid.*, vol. 2, p813.
3. Alfred Swaine Taylor, *Principles and Practice of Medical Jurisprudence* (London, 1865), p. 873.
4. For a recent, pertinent account of this pivotal case, see David J. Vaughan, *Mad or Bad* (Barnsley, 2017), pp. 48-54.
5. In Tuke (ed), *A Dictionary of Psychological Medicine* (Philadelphia 1892), vol. 2, pp. 801-02.
6. Cited in *ibid.*, p. 803.
7. Séverin Icard, *La Femme Pendant la Période Menstruelle. Psychologie Morbide et de Médecine Légale* (Paris, 1890), p. 266.
8. In Tuke (ed), *A Dictionary of Psychological Medicine* (Philadelphia 1892), vol. 1, p. 218 (my *emphasis*).
9. Andrew Combe, *Observations on Mental Derangement* (Edinburgh, 1831), p. 147.

10. Currier's then new title, *The Menopause*, reviewed in Hughes (ed), *The Alienist and Neurological Quarterly Magazine* 18 (1897), p. 460.

11. Susan Hogan, The Tyranny of Expectations of Post-Natal Delight: Gendered Happiness, *Journal of Gender Studies* 26 (2016), p. 53, note 1.

12. John Haslam, *Observations on Madness and Melancholy* (2nd Edition) (London, 1809), pp. 245–46.

13. Kristine Swenson, Review of Hilary Marland's Dangerous Motherhood: Insanity and Childbirth in Victorian Britain, *Bulletin of the History of Medicine* 81/2 (2007), pp. 455–56.

14. Lyttelton Forbes Winslow, *The Insanity of Passion and Crime* (London, 1912), Contents.

15. Andrew Combe, *Observations on Mental Derangement* (Edinburgh, 1831), p. 94.

16. Susan Hogan, The Tyranny of the Maternal Body: Madness and Maternity, *Women's History Magazine* 54, pp. 21–30.

17. Thomas Clouston quoted in *ibid.*, p. 23.

18. Robert Gooch, *On Some of the Most Important Diseases Peculiar to Women* (London, 1831), p. 54.

19. George H. Savage in Tuke (ed), *A Dictionary of Psychological Medicine* (Philadelphia 1892), vol. 2, pp. 1025–36.

20. John C. Bucknill and Daniel Hack Tuke, *A Manual of Psychological Medicine* (2nd Edition) (London, 1862), p. 258.

21. In Tuke (ed), *A Dictionary of Psychological Medicine* (Philadelphia 1892), vol. 2, p. 997.

22. George H. Savage in Tuke (ed), *A Dictionary of Psychological Medicine* (Philadelphia 1892), vol. 2, p. 1041.

23. *Ibid.*, pp. 1041–42.

24. James Cowles Prichard, *A Treatise on Insanity and Other Disorders Affecting the Mind* (Philadelphia, 1837), p. 222.

25. Radojka Startup, *Damaging Females: Representations of Women as Victims and Perpetrators of Crime in the Mid Nineteenth Century* (2000), p. 38 (my *emphasis*).

26. According to Hilary Marland, *Women and Madness* (2013).

27. John Haslam, *Observations on Madness and Melancholy* (2nd Edition) (London, 1809), p 247.

28. *Ibid.*, pp. 247–48.

29. *Ibid.*, pp. 248–49.

30. John C. Bucknill and Daniel Hack Tuke, *A Manual of Psychological Medicine* (2nd Edition) (London, 1862), p. 256.

31. The same James MacDonald of Bloomingdale Asylum, quoted in *ibid.*, pp. 258-59.

32. James Cowles Prichard, *A Treatise on Insanity and Other Disorders Affecting the Mind* (Philadelphia, 1837), p. 226.

33. *Ibid.*, pp. 226-29.

34. Lyttelton Forbes Winslow, *The Insanity of Passion and Crime* (London, 1912), p. 297.

35. Radojka Startup, *Damaging Females: Representations of Women as Victims and Perpetrators of Crime in the Mid Nineteenth Century* (2000), throughout.

36. Hilary Marland, *Dangerous Motherhood* (London, 2004), p. 6.

37. In Tuke (ed), *A Dictionary of Psychological Medicine* (Philadelphia 1892), vol. 2, p. 1036.

38. Roger Smith, *Trial by Medicine* (Edinburgh, 1981), p. 162.

39. David J. Vaughan, Crime, Insanity and Sex: 3 - From Motherhood to En-gender-ed Madness. In *Mad, Bad and Desperate* (2014).

40. Roger Smith, *Trial by Medicine* (Edinburgh, 1981), p. 153. See also *The English Reports*, vol. 175, 1309-11.

41. Alfred Swaine Taylor, *Principles and Practice of Medical Jurisprudence* (London, 1865), p. 1122.

42. David J. Vaughan, *The Secret Life of Celestina Sommer. A Very Victorian Murder* (2014).

43. Isaac Ray, *Treatise on the Medical Jurisprudence of Insanity* (Boston 1838), p. 207.

44. Andrew Scull, *Madness. A Very Short Introduction* (Oxford, 2011), p. 10.

45. Quoted in Radojka Startup, *Damaging Females: Representations of Women as Victims and Perpetrators of Crime in the Mid Nineteenth Century* (2000), p. 312.

46. Arlie Loughnan, Gender, 'Madness' and Crime: the Doctrine of Infanticide. In Loughnan, A., *Manifest Madness: Mental Incapacity in the Criminal Law* (Oxford, 2012), p. 202.

47. *Ibid.*, pp. 202-03.

48. Old Bailey Proceedings Online (Version 7.2), *The Proceedings of the Old Bailey* (2017-2018).

49. *Old Bailey Proceedings Online* (www.oldbaileyonline.org, version 8.0, 23 April 2018), February 1747, trial of Hannah Perfect (t17470225-1).

50. Arlie Loughnan, Gender, 'Madness' and Crime: the Doctrine of Infanticide. In Loughnan, A., *Manifest Madness: Mental Incapacity in the Criminal Law* (Oxford, 2012), p. 204.

51. *Ibid.*, p. 206.

52. Informed *inter alia* by Nigel Walker, *Crime and Insanity in England* (Edinburgh, 1968), vol. 1, p. 46.
53. Michael Macdonald, *Mystical Bedlam* (Cambridge, 1988), p. 128.
54. Cited in Nigel Walker, *Crime and Insanity in England* (Edinburgh, 1968), vol. 1, p. 127 (fn. 8).
55. *Old Bailey Proceedings Online* (www.oldbaileyonline.org, version 8.0, 23 April 2018), September 1674, trial of Young Wenches (t16740909-2).
56. Quoted in Andrew Mangham, Murdered at the Breast': Maternal Violence and the Self-Made Man in Popular Victorian Culture, *Critical Research* 16/1 (2004), pp. 23-24.
57. See *inter alia* Nigel Walker, *Crime and Insanity in England* (Edinburgh, 1968), vol. 1, p. 126.
58. Quoted in Hellerstein *et al* (eds), *Victorian Women* (Brighton, 1981), p. 205.
59. Quoted in Radojka Startup, *Damaging Females: Representations of Women as Victims and Perpetrators of Crime in the Mid Nineteenth Century* (2000), p. 283 (fn. 8).
60. David J. Vaughan, *Mad or Bad* (Barnsley, 2017), pp. 55-58.
61. Andrew Mangham, Murdered at the Breast': Maternal Violence and the Self-Made Man in Popular Victorian Culture, *Critical Research* 16/1 (2004), p. 25.
62. Her Majesty's Stationery Office, *Report of the Capital Punishment Commission; together with the minutes of evidence and appendix* (London, 1866), pp. 290-91.
63. Quoted in Andrew Mangham, Murdered at the Breast': Maternal Violence and the Self-Made Man in Popular Victorian Culture, *Critical Research* 16/1 (2004), p. 23.
64. Nigel Walker, *Crime and Insanity in England* (Edinburgh, 1968), vol. 1, p. 136.
65. *Ibid.*, pp. 134-35.
66. Quoted in Arlie Loughnan, Gender, 'Madness' and Crime: the Doctrine of Infanticide. In (Oxford, 2012), p. 217.
67. Nigel Walker, *Crime and Insanity in England* (Edinburgh, 1968), vol. 1, pp. 135-36.
68. Radojka Startup, *Damaging Females: Representations of Women as Victims and Perpetrators of Crime in the Mid Nineteenth Century* (2000), pp. 297-300.
69. Quoted in Alfred Dymond, *The Law on its Trial* (London, 1865), p. 176 (original *emphasis*).
70. *Ibid.*, pp. 174-78.
71. *Weekly Mail.*

72. Taken from David J. Vaughan, Surrogate Woes. In *Mad, Bad and Desperate* (2016).

73. Lucy Williams, *Wayward Women* (Barnsley, 2016), pp. 91-95. For Dyer, see Angela Buckley, *Amelia Dyer and the Baby Farm Murders* (Reading, 2016); David J. Vaughan, *Mad or Bad* (Barnsley 2017).

74. Anon, *Jeanne Weber l'Ogresse de la Goutte d'Or* (2014).

75. Radojka Startup, *Damaging Females: Representations of Women as Victims and Perpetrators of Crime in the Mid Nineteenth Century* (2000), p. 45 (fn. 88).

76. *Ibid.*, p. 219.

77. *Ibid.*, p. 53.

78. Alfred Swaine Taylor, *Principles and Practice of Medical Jurisprudence* (London, 1865), p. 1123.

79. John C. Bucknill and Daniel Hack Tuke, *A Manual of Psychological Medicine* (2nd Edition) (London, 1862), pp. 232-36.

80. John Baker in Tuke (ed), *A Dictionary of Psychological Medicine* (Philadelphia 1892), vol. 2, p. 726.

81. Quoted in Roger Smith, *Trial by Medicine* (Edinburgh, 1981), p. 226.

82. John Baker in Tuke (ed), *A Dictionary of Psychological Medicine* (Philadelphia 1892), vol. 2, p. 728.

83. Cited in *ibid.*, p. 727. See also Charles C. H. Marc, *De la Folie Considérée Dans Ses Rapports Avec les Questions Médico-Judiciaires* (Paris, 1840).

84. L. H. Wootton, 6. Sociology, *The British Journal of Psychiatry* 68/280 (1922), p. 97.

85. Roy Porter, *Mind-Forg'd Manacles* (London, 1990), p. 115.

86. James Fitzjames Stephen, *A History of the Criminal Law of England* (London, 1883), vol. 2, p. 210.

87. Quoted in Whan B. Kim, On Trichotillomania and Its Hairy History, *JAMA Dermatology* 150/11 (2014), p. 1179.

88. Cited in Haggett, Looking Back: Masculinity and Mental Health - the Long View, *The Psychologist* 27 (2014), pp. 426-29.

89. James Fitzjames Stephen, *A History of the Criminal Law of England* (London, 1883), vol. 2, p. 150.

90. Andrew Scull, *Madness. A Very Short Introduction* (Oxford, 2011), pp. 67-68.

91. Nigel Walker, *Crime and Insanity in England* (Edinburgh, 1968), vol. 1, p. 38.

92. *Ibid.*, p. 35.

93. Quoted in *ibid.*, pp. 44-45.

94. *Ibid.*, p. 37.
95. *Ibid.*, p. 42.
96. Cited in *ibid.*, p. 45.
97. Michael Macdonald, *Mystical Bedlam* (Cambridge, 1988), p. 202.
98. Cited in Nigel Walker, *Crime and Insanity in England* (Edinburgh, 1968), vol. 1, p. 119.
99. Lucy Williams, *Wayward Women* (Barnsley, 2016), p. 82.
100. All cases and more detailed in *ibid.*
101. Cited in Radojka Startup, *Damaging Females: Representations of Women as Victims and Perpetrators of Crime in the Mid Nineteenth Century* (2000), pp. 20-21.
102. See Alfred Dymond, *The Law on its Trial* (London, 1865) for a plethora of cases.
103. Garthine Walker quoted in Radojka Startup, *Damaging Females: Representations of Women as Victims and Perpetrators of Crime in the Mid Nineteenth Century* (2000), p. 181.
104. Radojka Startup, *Damaging Females: Representations of Women as Victims and Perpetrators of Crime in the Mid Nineteenth Century* (2000), pp. 182-84.
105. *Ibid.*, p. 22.
106. Nigel Walker, *Crime and Insanity in England* (Edinburgh, 1968), vol. 1, pp. 125, 132.

Chapter 4 – 'Correcting' Women

1. Michael Macdonald, *Mystical Bedlam* (Cambridge, 1988), pp. 178-79.
2. Quoted in Roy Porter, *Mind-Forg'd Manacles* (London, 1990), p. 4.
3. Willis quoted in Andrew Scull, *Hysteria* (Oxford, 2011), p. 27 (my *emphasis*).
4. In *ibid.*, p. 40.
5. Quoted in Daniel Hack Tuke, *Chapters in the History of the Insane in the British Isles* (London, 1882), p. 31.
6. Quoted in Michael Macdonald, *Mystical Bedlam* (Cambridge, 1988), p. 196.
7. *Ibid.*, p. 197.
8. *Ibid.*, p. 191.
9. Daniel Hack Tuke, *Chapters in the History of the Insane in the British Isles* (London, 1882), p. 33.
10. Michael Macdonald, *Mystical Bedlam* (Cambridge, 1988), pp. 193-94.
11. *Ibid.*, p. 182.
12. Nigel Walker, *Crime and Insanity in England* (Edinburgh, 1968), vol. 1, p. 48.

13. Daniel Hack Tuke, *Chapters in the History of the Insane in the British Isles* (London, 1882), pp. 11-12.
14. Catharine Arnold, *Bedlam* (London, 2009), p. 24.
15. For example, see Michael Macdonald, *Mystical Bedlam* (Cambridge, 1988), p. 175.
16. My *emphasis*. See Nigel Walker, *Crime and Insanity in England* (Edinburgh, 1968), vol. 1, p. 48.
17. Quoted in Daniel Hack Tuke, *Chapters in the History of the Insane in the British Isles* (London, 1882), p. 27.
18. Quoted in *ibid.*, p. 16.
19. Plausible explanations for the role of hysteria in witchcraft have been discussed. Others more qualified than I have written reams on the subject, for example: Jessica O'Leary, Where there are many women there are many witches: The Social and Intellectual Understanding of Femininity in the Malleus Maleficarum (1486), *Reinvention: an International Journal of Undergraduate Research* 6/1 (2013); Julian Goodare, *The European Witch-Hunt* (Abingdon, 2016); Willow Winsham, *Accused: British Witches Throughout History* (Barnsley, 2016).
20. Daniel Hack Tuke in Tuke (ed), *A Dictionary of Psychological Medicine* (Philadelphia 1892), vol. 1, p. 239.
21. Jules Morel in *ibid.*, p. 547.
22. Robert Burton, *The Anatomy of Melancholy* (1638), p. 756.
23. Millingen, J. G. 1837, *Curiosity of Medical Experiences* v2 (London, 1837), pp. 235-36.
24. Catharine Arnold, *Bedlam* (London, 2009), p. 32.
25. For example, Daniel Hack Tuke in Tuke (ed), *A Dictionary of Psychological Medicine* (Philadelphia 1892), vol. 1, p. 388.
26. Roy Porter, *Mind-Forg'd Manacles* (London, 1990), p. 169. For the more macabre reader, check out the original source.
27. Quoted in Catharine Arnold, *Bedlam* (London, 2009), p. 32.
28. Quoted in Diane Mason, *The Secret Vice* (Manchester, 2008), p. 51.
29. Quoted in *ibid.* (original *emphasis*).
30. Quoted in Roy Porter, *Mind-Forg'd Manacles* (London, 1990), p. 212.
31. *Ibid.*, p. 221.
32. Nigel Walker, *Crime and Insanity in England* (Edinburgh, 1968), vol. 1, pp. 126-28.
33. Roy Porter, *Mind-Forg'd Manacles* (London, 1990), pp. 223-24. For an alternative perspective, read Michel Foucault, *Madness and Civilization* (New York, 1988).

34. William Pargeter quoted in *ibid*., p. 213.
35. Andrew Scull, *Hysteria* (Oxford, 2011), pp. 59-61.
36. *Ibid*., p. 57.
37. Wendy Moore, Research Notes: a Chance Discovery, *Wellcome Collection* (2017).
38. Alan Gauld, *A History of Hypnotism* (Cambridge, 1992), p. 207.
39. John G. Millingen, *Curiosity of Medical Experiences* (2nd Edition) (London, 1839), p. 135.
40. Andrew Scull, *Hysteria* (Oxford, 2011), p. 94.
41. Tania Woods, *From Female Sexuality and Hysteria to Feminine Psychology: The Gender of Insanity in Literature* (n.d.), p. 37.
42. *Ibid*., esp. pp. 37-38.
43. Andrew Scull, *Hysteria* (Oxford, 2011), p. 103.
44. Elaine Showalter, *The Female Malady* (London, 1987), p. 140.
45. *Ibid*.
46. Isaac Baker Brown, *On the Curability of Certain Forms of Insanity, Epliepsy, Catalepsy and Hysteria in Females* (London, 1866), p. 12.
47. *Ibid*.
48. *Ibid*., p. 13.
49. *Ibid*., Preface.
50. *Ibid*., p. 7.
51. The list makes for interesting reading and reveals some 'startling' names, including Dr George Savage, Bethlem and celbrity psychiatrist; Sir James Simpson, Scottish obstetrician and discoverer of chloroform as a human anaesthetic; and no less than two of his sons! See *ibid*., p. 13.
52. *Ibid*., p. 6.
53. Robert Barnes, On the Correlations of the Sexual Functions and Mental Disorders of Women, *British Gynaecological Journal* 6 (1890), (my *emphasis*).
54. George H. Savage in Tuke (ed), *A Dictionary of Psychological Medicine* (Philadelphia 1892), vol. 2, p. 876.
55. See David J. Vaughan, Butcher Baker Brown - His Unnerving Demise. In *Mad, Bad and Desperate* (2017).
56. Quoted in Andrew Scull, *Hysteria* (Oxford, 2011), p. 76.
57. Isaac Baker Brown, *On the Curability of Certain Forms of Insanity, Epliepsy, Catalepsy and Hysteria in Females* (London, 1866), pp. 9-10.
58. *Ibid*., p. 12 (my *emphasis*).
59. All taken from George M. Beard, *Sexual Neurasthenia [Nervous Exhaustion]. Its Hygiene, Causes, Symptoms, and Treatment* (New York, 1884), pp. 67-68 (my *emphasis*).

60. David J. Vaughan, Butcher Baker Brown – His Unnerving Demise. In *Mad, Bad and Desperate* (2017).

61. Catharine Arnold cited in *ibid*.

62. Andrew Scull, *Hysteria* (Oxford, 2011), p. 81.

63. Catharine Arnold, *Bedlam* (London, 2009), pp. 219-20.

64. Elaine Showalter, T*he Female Malady* (London, 1987), p. 56.

65. Andrew Scull, *Madness. A Very Short Introduction* (Oxford, 2011), pp. 79-82.

66. Burton Feldman, *The Nobel Prize* (New York, 2001), pp. 287-88.

67. Andrew Scull, *Madness. A Very Short Introduction* (Oxford, 2011), p. 79.

68. Roy Porter, *Mind-Forg'd Manacles* (London, 1990), pp. 169-74.

69. Compare two alternative views: *ibid* vs. Michel Foucault, *Madness and Civilization* (New York, 1988).

70. Daniel Hack Tuke (ed), *A Dictionary of Psychological Medicine* (Philadelphia 1892), vol. 1, p. 24.

71. Roy Porter, *Mind-Forg'd Manacles* (London, 1990), p. 175.

72. Quoted in *ibid*., p. 148.

73. *Ibid*., pp. 12-13.

74. Edward Wakefield in the Report from the Committee on Madhouses in England (1815). Quoted in *ibid*., pp. 156-57.

75. Quoted in *ibid*., p. 11.

76. Catharine Arnold, *Bedlam* (London, 2009), p. 11.

77. *Ibid*., p. 22.

78. Referencing the Post-Reformation in Roy Porter, *Mind-Forg'd Manacles* (London, 1990), pp. 121-22.

79. *Ibid*., p. 123.

80. Nigel Walker, *Crime and Insanity in England* (Edinburgh, 1968), vol. 1, p. 43.

81. Catharine Arnold, *Bedlam* (London, 2009), p. 46.

82. Roy Porter, *Mind-Forg'd Manacles* (London, 1990), p. 10.

83. Catharine Arnold, *Bedlam* (London, 2009), p. 43.

84. *Ibid*., p. 44.

85. Roy Porter, *Mind-Forg'd Manacles* (London, 1990), p. 127 (my *emphasis*).

86. *Ibid*., pp. 128-29.

87. Roger Smith, *Trial by Medicine* (Edinburgh, 1981), p. 22.

88. Daniel Hack Tuke, *Chapters in the History of the Insane in the British Isles* (London, 1882), pp. 43-44.

89. Daniel Hack Tuke in Tuke (ed), *A Dictionary of Psychological Medicine* (Philadelphia 1892), vol. 1, p. 25.

90. Patricia Allderidge, Bedlam: fact or fantasy? In Bynum *et al* (eds), *The Anatomy of Madness* (London, 1985), vol. 2, pp. 19, 21–22.
91. Roy Porter, *Mind-Forg'd Manacles* (London, 1990), p. 126.
92. Quoted in Patricia Allderidge, Bedlam: fact or fantasy? In Bynum *et al* (eds), *The Anatomy of Madness* (London, 1985), vol. 2, p. 28.
93. Reported in Roy Porter 1990, *Mind-Forg'd Manacles* (London, 1990), pp. 126–27.
94. *Ibid.*, pp. 129–30.
95. *Ibid.*, p. 131.
96. Paul A. Erickson and Liam D. Murphy (eds), *Readings for a History of Anthropological Theory* (Fifth Edition) (Toronto, 2016), p. 398.
97. Quoted in Roy Porter, *Mind-Forg'd Manacles* (London, 1990), p. 119.
98. For comparative views, see *inter alia* Anna Shepherd, *Institutionalizing the Insane in the Nineteenth Century* (London, 2014) and Helen Goodman, 'Madness and Masculinity': Male Patients in London Asylums and Victorian Culture (London, 2015).
99. Sarah Wise, *An Inconvenient People. Lunacy, Liberty and the Mad-Doctors in Victorian England* (London, 2013), p. 393.
100. Patricia Allderidge, Bedlam: fact or fantasy? In Bynum *et al* (eds), *The Anatomy of Madness* (London, 1985), vol. 2, p. 29.
101. Roy Porter, *Mind-Forg'd Manacles* (London, 1990), p. 135.
102. For a well-crafted assessment, see *ibid.*, pp. 129–31, 163.
103. *Ibid.*, p. 118.
104. Western Libraries, *Restoring Perspective. Life and Treatment at the London Asylum* (n.d.).
105. Elaine Showalter, *The Female Malady* (London, 1987), p. 81.
106. *Ibid.*
107. A Clare, Freud's Cases: the Clinical Basis of Psychoanalysis. In Bynum *et al* (eds), *The Anatomy of Madness* (London, 1985), vol. 1, p. 274.
108. *Ibid.*, p. 279.
109. See, for example, Jonathan M. Meyer and George M. Simpson, From Chiorpromazine to Olanzapine: A Brief History of Antipsychotics, *Psychiatric Services* 48/9 (1997), pp. 1137–39; and Andrew Scull, *Madness. A Very Short Introduction* (Oxford, 2011), pp. 104–21.

Chapter 5 – Suffering Women: The 'Unfortunate' Sex

1. Quoted in Lyn Pykett, Women Writing Woman: nineteenth-century representations of gender and sexuality. In J. Shattock (ed), *Women and Literature in Britain 1800–1900* (Cambridge, 2001), p. 80 (my *emphasis*).

2. *Ibid.*
3. An excellent entry into the role of the Devil and madness is provided in Michael Macdonald, *Mystical Bedlam* (Cambridge, 1988).
4. *Ibid.*, p. 9.
5. *Ibid.*, p. 221.
6. *Ibid.*, p. 178.
7. Quoted in Roy Porter, *Mind-Forg'd Manacles* (London, 1990), p. 165.
8. Andrew Scull, *Hysteria* (Oxford, 2011), p. 74.
9. After Roger Smith, *Trial by Medicine* (Edinburgh, 1981), p. 55.
10. Correspondence to the *Daily News*, 11 August 1854. Quoted in David J. Vaughan, Elizabeth Potter was the Subject of Puerperal Derangement. In *Mad, Bad and Desperate* (2016).
11. Roger Smith, *Trial by Medicine* (Edinburgh, 1981), p. 223.
12. David J. Vaughan, *Mad or Bad* (Barnsley, 2017), pp. 55-58.
13. Alfred Dymond, *The Law on its Trial* (London, 1865).
14. A Prison Matron, *Female Life in Prison* (London, 1862).
15. Ludmilla Jordanova, *Sexual Visions* (Hemel Hempstead, 1989), p. 74.
16. Marjean D. Purinton, Lee: the New Science and Female Madness. In Hayden, J. (ed), *The New Science and Women's Literary Discourse: Prefiguring Frankenstein* (New York, 2011), p. 186.
17. Tania Woods, *From Female Sexuality and Hysteria to Feminine Psychology: The Gender of Insanity in Literature* (n.d.), p. 10.
18. *Ibid.*, pp. 11-15.
19. For a recent exemplary discussion, see Mimi Matthews, *19th Century Marriage Manuals: Advice for Young Wives* (2015).
20. Judith R. Walkowitz, *City of Dreadful Delights. Narratives of Sexual Danger in Late-Victorian London*, (London, 1994), p. 155.
21. In Tuke (ed), *A Dictionary of Psychological Medicine* (Philadelphia 1892), vol. 2., p. 1001.
22. For example, Diane Mason, *The Secret Vice* (Manchester, 2008), pp. 33-34.
23. In Tuke (ed), *A Dictionary of Psychological Medicine* (Philadelphia 1892), vol. 2., p. 775.
24. Michel Foucault, *Madness and Civilization* (New York, 1988), p. 258 (quoting Pinel).
25. Quoted in Hellerstein *et al* (eds), *Victorian Women* (Brighton, 1981), p. 262.
26. *Ibid.*
27. Nigel Walker, *Crime and Insanity in England* (Edinburgh, 1968), vol. 1, p. 44.
28. Hilary Marland, *Women and Madness* (2013).

29. For example, see respectively Sarah Wise, *An Inconvenient People* (London, 2013); and Judith R. Walkowitz, *City of Dreadful Delights. Narratives of Sexual Danger in Late-Victorian London*, (London, 1994).
30. Andrew Roberts, *The Lunacy Commission. Its Origin, Emergence and Character* (1981).
31. *Ibid.*, (my *emphasis*).
32. Joel P. Eigen quoted in Arlie Loughnan, Gender, 'Madness' and Crime: the Doctrine of Infanticide. In (Oxford, 2012), p. 214.
33. Quoted in *ibid*.
34. In Tuke (ed), *A Dictionary of Psychological Medicine* (Philadelphia 1892), vol. 1, p. 494.
35. Tania Woods, *From Female Sexuality and Hysteria to Feminine Psychology: The Gender of Insanity in Literature* (n.d.), p. 19.
36. *Ibid.*, p. 3.
37. Edles & Appelrouth quoted in *ibid.*, p. 38.
38. *Ibid.*, p. 39.

Further Reading

Antiquarian Sources

Adams, T. 1615, *Mystical Bedlam: or the World of Mad-Men*, London: Clement Knight

Jorden, E. 1603, *A Briefe Discourse of a Disease Called the Suffocation of the Mother*, London: Windet

Willis, T. (trans. S. Pordage) 1684 (1681), *An Essay of the Pathology of the Brain and Nervous Stock: In Which Convulsive Diseases Are Treated Of*, London: Dring, Leigh and Harper

Original Sources

A Prison Matron (Robinson, F. W.) 1862, *Female Life in Prison* (2 vols.), London: Hurst and Blackett

Acton, W. 1867, *The Functions and Disorders of the Reproductive Organs* (4th Edition), Philadelphia: Lindsay and Blakiston

Anon 1864, Child-Murder and its Punishment. In *Social Science Review*, New Series (2), 452-59, http://bit.ly/2lTVtkA

Baker Brown, I. 1866, *On the Curability of Certain Forms of Insanity, Epilepsy, Catalepsy and Hysteria in Females*, London: Robert Hardwicke

Barnes, R. 1890, On the Correlations of the Sexual Functions and Mental Disorders of Women, *British Gynaecological Journal*, 6, 390-430

Battie, W. 1758, *A Treatise on Madness*, London: J. Whiston and B. White

Beard, G. M. 1884, *Sexual Neurasthenia [Nervous Exhaustion]. Its Hygiene, Causes, Symptoms, and Treatment*, New York: E. B. Treat

Blackmore, Sir R. 1725, *A Treatise of the Spleen and Vapours; or, Hypochondriacal and Hysterical Affections*, London: Pemberton

Bucknill, J. C. and D. H. Tuke 1862, *A Manual of Psychological Medicine* (2nd Edition), London: John Churchill

Cheyne, G. 1733, *The English Malady; or a Treatise on the Spleen and the Vapours*, London: Strahan and Leake

Clouston, T. S. 1882, Female Education. From a Medical Point of View, Edinburgh: Macniven and Wallace

Combe, A. 1831, *Observations on Mental Derangement*, Edinburgh: John Anderson

Crichton, A. 1798, *Inquiry into the Nature and Origin of Mental Derangement*, London: Cadell and Davis

Dymond, A. 1865, *The Law on its Trial: or, Personal Recollections of the Death Penalty and its Opponents*, London: Alfred W. Bennett

Gooch, R. 1831, *On Some of the Most Important Diseases Peculiar to Women*, London: J. Murray

Hale, Sir M. 1736, *The History of the Pleas of the Crown* (2 vols.), London: F. Gyles

Haslam, J. 1798, *Observations on Insanity. With Practical Remarks on the Disease, and an Account of the Morbid Appearances on Dissection*, London: F. & C. Rivington

Haslam, J. 1809, *Observations on Madness and Melancholy* (2nd Edition), London: J. Callow

Her Majesty's Stationery Office (HMSO) 1866, *Report of the Capital Punishment Commission; together with the minutes of evidence and appendix*, London

Hughes, C. H. (ed) 1897, *The Alienist and Neurological Quarterly Magazine* 18

Icard, S. 1890, *La Femme Pendant la Période Menstruelle. Psychologie Morbide et de Médecine Légale*, Paris: Alcan

Krafft-Ebing, R. von (trans. C. G. Chaddock) 1894 (1886), *Sexualis Psychopathia. With Especial Reference to Contrary Sexual Instinct: A Medico-Legal Study*, London: F. J. Rebman

Laycock, T. 1840, *A Treatise on the Nervous Diseases of Women; Comprising an Inquiry into the Nature, Causes, and Treatment of Spinal and Hysterical Disorders*, London: Longman, Orme, Brown, Green, and Longmans

Laycock, T. 1845, 'On the reflex function of the brain'. In *The British and Foreign Medical Review* 19: 298–311

Lowe, L. 1883, *The Bastilles of England: or, the Lunacy Laws at Work*, London: Crookenden & Co.

Mackay, C. 1852, *Memoirs of Extraordinary Popular Delusions and the Madness of Crowds* (vol. II), London: Office of the National Illustrated Library

Marc, C. C. H. 1840, *De la Folie Considérée Dans Ses Rapports Avec les Questions Médico-Judiciaires*, Paris: J. B. Baillière

Maudsley, H. 1874, Sex in Mind and in Education, *Popular Science Monthly* (5), 198-215

Maudsley, H. 1895, *Pathology of Mind*, London: Macmillan & Co.

Mill, J. S. 1869, *The Subjection of Women*, London: Longmans, Green, Reader & Dyer

Millingen, J. G. 1837, *Curiosity of Medical Experiences* v2, London: Richard Bentley

Millingen, J. G. 1839, *Curiosity of Medical Experiences* (2nd Edition), London: Richard Bentley

Mitchell, S. W. 1881, *Lectures on Diseases of the Nervous System, Especially in Women*, Philadelphia: Henry C. Lea's Son & Co.

Prichard, J. C. 1837, *A Treatise on Insanity and Other Disorders Affecting the Mind*, Philadelphia: E. L. Carey & A. Hart

Ray, I. 1838, *Treatise on the Medical Jurisprudence of Insanity*, Boston: Charles C. Little and James Brown

Stephen, Sir J. F. 1883, *A History of the Criminal Law of England* (3 vols.), London: Macmillan & Co.

Storer, H. R. 1871, *The Causation, Course, and Treatment of Reflex Insanity in Women*, Boston: Lee and Shepard

Taylor, A. S. 1865, *Principles and Practice of Medical Jurisprudence*, London: John Churchill & Sons

Tuke, D. H. (ed) 1892, *A Dictionary of Psychological Medicine* (2 vols.), Philadelphia: P. Blakiston, Son & Co.

Tuke, D. H. 1882, *Chapters in the History of the Insane in the British Isles*, London: Kegan Paul, Trench & Co.

Walford E. c. 1881, *Old and New London Illustrated. A Narrative of Its History, Its People and Its Places* v6, London: Cassell, Petter and Galpin

Wilks, S. 1878, *Lectures on Diseases of the Nervous System*, London: J. & A. Churchill

Wollstonecraft, M. 1792, *A Vindication of the Rights of Women: with Strictures on Political and Moral Subjects*, Boston: Thomas and Andrews

Modern Sources

Allderidge, P. 1985, Bedlam: fact or fantasy? In Bynum *et al* (eds), *The Anatomy of Madness* v2, 17-33, London: Tavistock Publications

Anderson, E. G. 2012, Sex in Mind and in Education: A Reply. In Leighton, M. E. and L. A. Surridge (eds), *The Broadview Anthology of Victorian Prose* 1832-1901, 200-03, Ontario: Broadview

Arnold C. 2009 (2008), *Bedlam. London and Its Mad*, London: Simon & Schuster

Buckley, A. 2016, *Amelia Dyer and the Baby Farm Murders*, Reading: Manor Vale Associates

Bynum, W. F. 1985, The nervous patient in eighteenth- and nineteenth-century Britain: the psychiatric origins of British neurology. In Bynum *et al* (eds), *The Anatomy of Madness* v1, 89-102, London: Tavistock Publications

Bynum, W. F., Porter, R. and M. Shepherd (eds) 1985, *The Anatomy of Madness. Essays in the History of Psychiatry* (2 vols.), London: Tavistock Publications

Clare, A. 1985, Freud's Cases: the Clinical Basis of Psychoanalysis. In Bynum *et al* (eds), *The Anatomy of Madness* v1, 271-88, London: Tavistock Publications

Digby, A. 1989, Women's Biological Straitjacket. In Mendus, S. and J. Rendall (eds), *Sexuality and Subordination: Interdisciplinary Studies of Gender in the Nineteenth Century*, 192-219, London: Routledge

Eigen, J. P. 1998, Criminal Lunacy in Early Modern England: Did Gender Make a Difference?, *International Journal of Law and Psychiatry*, 21 (4), 412

Ellis, H. 1908, *Studies in the Psychology of Sex. Sexual Inversion*, Philadelphia: F. A. Davis Company

Erickson, P. A. and L. D. Murphy (eds) 2016, *Readings for a History of Anthropological Theory* (Fifth Edition), Toronto: University Press

Evans, H. & R. E. Bartholomew 2009, *Outbreak! The Encyclopedia of Extraordinary Social Behavior*, New York: Anomalist Books

Feldman, B. 2001, *The Nobel Prize. A history of genius, controversy, and prestige*, New York: Arcade Publishing

Foucault, M. (trans. R. Howard) 1988 (1965), *Madness & Civilization. A History of Insanity in the Age of Reason*, New York: Vintage Books

Freedman, E. B. and E. O. Hellerstein 1981, The Adult Woman: Personal Life (Introduction). In Hellerstein *et al* (eds), *Victorian Women. A Documentary Account of Women's Lives in Nineteenth-Century England, France, and the United States*, Brighton: The Harvester Press

Gauld, A. 1992, *A History of Hypnotism*, Cambridge: University Press

Gilman, S. L. 1996 (1982), *Seeing the Insane*, Nebraska: Bison Books

Goldberg, A. 1999, *Sex, Religion and the Making of Modern Madness*, New York: Oxford University Press

Goodare, J. 2016, *The European Witch-Hunt*, Abingdon: Routledge

Goodman, H. 2015, 'Madness and Masculinity': Male Patients in London Asylums and Victorian Culture. In Knowles and Trowbridge (eds), *Insanity and the Lunatic Asylum in Nineteenth Century*, 149-66, London: Pickering & Chatto

Griffin, B. 2012, *The Politics of Gender in Victorian Britain: Masculinity, Political Culture and the Struggle or Women's Rights*, Cambridge: University Press

Hellerstein, E. O., Hume, L. P. & K. M. Offen (eds) 1981, *Victorian Women. A Documentary Account of Women's Lives in Nineteenth-Century England, France, and the United States*, Brighton: The Harvester Press

Hirschmann, N. J. 2008, *Gender, Class, and Freedom in Modern Political Theory*, Princeton: University Press

Hodgkin, K. (ed) 2016 (2010), *Women, Madness and Sin in Early Modern England. The autobiographical writings of Dionys Fitzherbert*, London: Routledge

Hogan, S. 2016, The Tyranny of Expectations of Post-Natal Delight: Gendered Happiness, *Journal of Gender Studies*, 45-55, http://dx.doi.org/10.1080/09589236.2016.1223617

Houston, R. A. 2000, *Madness and Society in Eighteenth-Century Scotland* (Oxford Studies in Social History), Oxford: University Press

Jackson, L. 1995, Witches, wives and mothers: witchcraft persecution and women's confessions in seventeenth-century England, *Women's History Review*, 4 (1), 63-84

Jackson, L. 2001, Witches, wives and mothers: Witchcraft Persecutions and Women's Confessions in Seventeenth-Century England. In Levack, B. P. (ed), *New Perspectives on Witchcraft, Magic and Demonology vol. 4. Gender and Witchcraft*, 257-77, London: Routledge

Jordanova, L. 1989, *Sexual Visions: Images of Gender in Science and Medicine Between the Eighteenth and Twentieth Centuries*, Hemel Hempstead: Harvester Wheatsheaf

Kilday, A-M 2013, *A History of Infanticide in Britain, c. 1600 to the Present*, Basingstoke: Palgrave Macmillan

King, H. 1993, Once Upon a Text. Hysteria from Hippocrates. In Gilman *et al* (ed), *Hysteria Beyond Freud*, 3-90, Berkeley: University of California Press

Loughnan, A. 2012, Gender, 'Madness' and Crime: the Doctrine of Infanticide. In Loughnan, A., *Manifest Madness: Mental Incapacity in the Criminal Law*, 202-25, Oxford: University Press

Macdonald, M. 1986, Women and Madness in Tudor and Stuart England, *Social Research* 53 (2), 261-81

Macdonald, M. 1988 (1981), *Mystical Bedlam. Madness, Anxiety, and Healing in Seventeenth-Century England*, Cambridge: University Press

Mangham, A. 2004, 'Murdered at the Breast': Maternal Violence and the Self-Made Man in Popular Victorian Culture, *Critical Research* 16(1), 20-34, http://bit.ly/2lVsexE

Marland, H. 2004, *Dangerous Motherhood: Insanity and Childbirth in Victorian Britain*, London: Palgrave Macmillan

Mason, D. 2008, *The Secret Vice. Masturbation in Victorian Fiction and Medical Culture*, Manchester: University Press

Moore, W. 2017, Research Notes: a Chance Discovery, *Wellcome Collection*, http://bit.ly/2ADxbzG [acessed November 2017]

Mounsey, C. 2001, *Christopher Smart: Clown of God*, London: Associated University Presses

Parry-Jones, W. Ll. 1972, *The Trade in Lunacy: A Study of Private Madhouses in England in the Eighteenth and Nineteenth Centuries*, London: Routledge & Kegan Paul

Pearson, J. 1998 (1996), Women Reading, Reading Women. In H. Wilcox (ed), *Women and Literature in Britain 1500-1700*, 80-99, Cambridge: University Press

Porter, R. 1985, 'The Hunger of Imagination': Approaching Samuel Johnson's melancholy. In Bynum *et al* (eds), *The Anatomy of Madness* v1, 63-88, London: Tavistock Publications

Porter, R. 1990 (1987), *Mind-Forg'd Manacles: A History of Madness in England from the Restoration to the Regency*, London: Penguin Books

Purinton, M. D. 2011, Lee: the New Science and Female Madness. In Hayden, J. (ed), *The New Science and Women's Literary Discourse: Prefiguring Frankenstein*, 183-200, New York: Palgrave Macmillan

Pykett, L. 2001, Women Writing Woman: nineteenth-century representations of gender and sexuality. In J. Shattock (ed), *Women and Literature in Britain 1800-1900*, 78-98, Cambridge: University Press

Russett, C. E. 1991 (1989), *Sexual Science: The Victorian Construction of Womanhood*, Massachusetts: Harvard University Press

Scull, A. 2011a, *Madness. A Very Short Introduction*, Oxford: University Press

Scull, A. 2011b, *Hysteria. The Disturbing History*, Oxford: University Press

Setzer, S. M. (ed) 2003, *A Letter to the Women of England and the Natural Daughter*, Canada: Broadview Literary Texts

Shepherd, A. 2014, *Institutionalizing the Insane in the Nineteenth Century*, London: Pickering & Chatto

Showalter, E. 1987 (1985), *The Female Malady. Women, Madness and English Culture, 1830-1980*, London: Virago Press

Small, H. 1998 (1996), *Love's Madness: Medicine, the Novel, and Female Insanity, 1800-1865*, Oxford: Clarendon Paperbacks

Smith, R. 1981a, *Trial by Medicine. Insanity and Responsibility in Victorian Trials*, Edinburgh: University Press

Smith, R. 1981b, The Boundary Between Insanity and Criminal Responsibility in 19th Century England. In Scull (ed), *Madhouses, Mad-Doctors, and Madmen: the Social History of Psychiatry in the Victorian Era*, 363-84, London: The Athlone Press

Startup, R. 2000, *Damaging Females: Representations of Women as Victims and Perpetrators of Crime in the Mid Nineteenth Century*, PhD Thesis

Vaughan, D. J. 2017a, *Mad or Bad. Crime and Insanity in Victorian Britain*, Barnsley: Pen & Sword History

Walker, N. 1968, *Crime and Insanity in England. One: The Historical Perspective*, Edinburgh: University Press

Walkowitz, J. R. 1980, *Prostitution and Victorian Society: Women, Class, and the State*, New York: Cambridge University Press

Walkowitz, J. R. 1994 (1992), *City of Dreadful Delights. Narratives of Sexual Danger in Late-Victorian London*, London: Virago Press

Williams, J. P. 1985, Psychical Research and Psychiatry in Late Victorian Britain: Trance as Ecstasy or Trance as Insanity. In Bynum *et al* (eds), *The Anatomy of Madness* v1, 233-54, London: Tavistock Publications

Williams, L. 2016, *Wayward Women. Female Offending in Victorian England*, Barnsley: Pen & Sword History

Winsham, W. 2016, *Accused: British Witches Throughout History*, Barnsley: Pen and Sword History

Winslow, L. F. 1912, *The Insanity of Passion and Crime*, London: John Ouseley

Wise, S. 2013, *An Inconvenient People. Lunacy, Liberty and the Mad-Doctors in Victorian England*, London: Vintage

Online Resources

Abshire, L. 2014, *Art Mimics Life: Witches and Magic in Early Modern Art*, http://bit.ly/2ClI2k6 [accessed November 2017]

Anon 2014, *Jeanne Weber l'Ogresse de la Goutte d'Or*, http://bit.ly/2CKuN09 [accessed January 2018]

BBC Radio 4 Online 2003, *George Cheyne and His Work*, http://bbc. in/2p0f1rn [accessed November 2017]

Bethlem Museum of the Mind 2013, *From Melancholia to Prozac: Depression Throughout History*, http://bit.ly/2vgr0lB [accessed October 2017]

Broad, J. 2016 (2011), Cavendish, van Helmont, and the Mad Raging Womb. In Hayden, J. A. (ed), *The New Science and Women's Literary Discourse: Prefiguring Frankenstein*, 47-63, http://bit.ly/2GNzzqZ [accessed October 2017]

Burton, R. 2004 (1638), *The Anatomy of Melancholy* (3 vols.), http://bit. ly/2CNmctD [accessed October 2017]

Clear, D., ffytche, M., Homberger, M., Lister, J. and T. Loughran (eds) nd, *Deviance, Disorder and the Self*, http://bit.ly/2ANdTK2 [accessed December 2017]

Dickens, C. 1852, A Curious Dance Round a Christmas Tree, *Household Words* 4 (95), 385-89, http://bit.ly/2FoFtiQ [accessed February 2018]

Foyster, E. 2002, At the Limits of Liberty: Married Women and Confinement in Eighteenth-Century England, *Continuity and Change* (17), 39-62, doi:10.1017/S0268416002004058 [accessed Nov 2017]

Gilman, C. P. 1892, The Yellow Wallpaper, *New England Magazine* 11 (5), 647-57 http://bit.ly/2HnWw4U [accessed February 2018]

Haggett, A. 2014, Looking Back: Masculinity and Mental Health - the Long View, *The Psychologist* 27, 426-29, http://bit.ly/2HQhdXU [accessed December 2017]

Harvard Online nd, *Contagion: Historical Views of Diseases and Epidemics*, http://bit.ly/2BpkCbT [accessed January 2018]

Hogan, S. 2006, The Tyranny of the Maternal Body: Madness and Maternity, *Women's History Magazine* 54, 21-30, http://bit.ly/2Fs4dH0 [accessed September 2017]

Jaffray, S. 2015, Hysteria, *Wellcome Collection*, http://bit.ly/2CaShXS [accessed October 2017]

Kim, W. B. 2014, On Trichotillomania and Its Hairy History, *JAMA Dermatology* 150 (11), 1179, http://bit.ly/2HQvhRc [accessed February 2018]

Kramer, H. and J. Sprenger (trans. Rev. M. Summers) 1928 (1486), *Malleus Maleficarum*, http://bit.ly/2F2zSBS [accessed October 2017]

Marland, H. 2013, *Women and Madness*, http://bit.ly/2CNn4LD [accessed September 2017]

Matthews, M. 2015, *19th Century Marriage Manuals: Advice for Young Wives*, http://bit.ly/2HU4iUT [accessed January 2018]

Meyer, J. M. and G. M. Simpson 1997, From Chiorpromazine to Olanzapine: A Brief History of Antipsychotics, *Psychiatric Services* 48 (9), 1137-39, http://bit.ly/2Ft3plm [accessed February 2018]

Old Bailey Proceedings Online (Version 7.2) 0, *The Proceedings of the Old Bailey*, http://bit.ly/2HPbhOF [accessed throughout 2017-2018]

O'Leary, J. 2013, 'Where there are many women there are many witches': The Social and Intellectual Understanding of Femininity in the Malleus Maleficarum (1486), *Reinvention: an International Journal of Undergraduate Research* 6 (1), http://bit.ly/2HSoXZg [accessed December 2017]

Parry, V. 2010, *Were the 'Mad' Heroines of Literature Really Sane?*, https://bbc.in/2HhEalS [accessed December 2017]

Pichel, B. 2017, *The Backstage of Hysteria: Medicine in the Photographic Studio*, http://bit.ly/2iA1YJA [accessed October 2017]

Quintanilla, B. 2010, Witchcraft or Mental Illness?, *Psychaitric Times*, http://bit.ly/2liubTM [accessed November 2017]

Roberts, A. 1981, *The Lunacy Commission. Its Origin, Emergence and Character*, http://bit.ly/2EoWDQ4 [accessed October 2017]

Science Museum Online nd, Women and Psychiatry, *Brought to Life. Exploring the History of Medicine*, http://bit.ly/2Dx04Ty [accessed November 2017]

Siegel, R. B. 1996, 'The Rule of Love': Wife Beating as Prerogative and Privacy, *Faculty Scholarship Series*, Paper 1092, 2117-2207, http://bit.ly/2HUd8lv [accessed February 2018]

Swenson, K. 2007, Review of Hilary Marland's Dangerous Motherhood: Insanity and Childbirth in Victorian Britain, *Bulletin of the History of Medicine* 81 (2), 455-56, http://bit.ly/2CbXUoA [accessed November 2017]

Takabayashi, A. 2017, *Surviving the Lunacy Act of 1890: English Psychiatrists and Professional Development during the Early Twentieth Century*, http://bit.ly/2CeSEQl [accessed February 2018]

The English Reports, *The English Reports (1900-1930)*, 176 vols., Edinburgh: Green, http://bit.ly/2DK1fvT [accessed January 2018]

The History of Parliament 2016, Jane Campbell: Parliamentary Divorce Pioneer, http://bit.ly/2CYD37Z [accessed October 2017]

University of Warwick 2018, *From Cradle to Grave: Health, Medicine and Lifecycle in Modern Britain (HI278)*, http://bit.ly/2Fx0gkw [accessed January 2018]

Vaughan, D. J. 2014a, *The Secret Life of Celestina Sommer. A Very Victorian Murder*, http://amzn.to/2dbFBmg [accessed February 2018]

Vaughan, D. J. 2014b, Crime, Insanity and Sex: 2 - Getting Hysterical About Hysteria. In *Mad, Bad and Desperate*, http://bit.ly/2EIawcF [accessed February 2018]

Vaughan, D. J. 2014c, Crime, Insanity and Sex: 3 - From Motherhood to En-gender-ed Madness. In *Mad, Bad and Desperate*, http://bit.ly/2BGJ1xa#MARY_MCNEIL_CASE_5 [accessed September 2017]

Vaughan, D. J. 2015, Centres of Lunacy. In *Mad, Bad and Desperate*, http://bit.ly/2sKewU3 [accessed January 2018]

Vaughan, D. J. 2016a, 'Healthy Impulses to Crime' - Crime, Insanity & the Elusive Free Will. In *Mad, Bad and Desperate*, http://bit.ly/2pcu3dM [accessed December 2017]

Vaughan, D. J. 2016b, Elizabeth Potter was the Subject of Puerperal Derangement. In *Mad, Bad and Desperate*, http://bit.ly/2Ft76aK [accessed December 2017]

Vaughan, D. J. 2016c, Surrogate Woes. In *Mad, Bad and Desperate*, http://bit.ly/2ApEPO4 [accessed December 2017]

Vaughan, D. J. 2017b, Butcher Baker Brown - His Unnerving Demise. In *Mad, Bad and Desperate*, http://bit.ly/2mezrZa [accessed September 2017]

Wallace, W. 2012, Sent to the Asylum: The Victorian Women Locked Up Because They Were Suffering From Stress, Post Natal Depression and Anxiety, *Mail Online*, http://dailym.ai/2svWotn [accessed November 2017]

Western Libraries nd, *Restoring Perspective. Life and Treatment at the London Asylum*, http://bit.ly/2rpfowG [accessed November 2017]

Woods, T. nd, *From Female Sexuality and Hysteria to Feminine Psychology: The Gender of Insanity in Literature*, http://bit.ly/2FuMGhG [accessed December 2017]

Wootton, L. H. 1922, 6. Sociology, *The British Journal of Psychiatry* 68 (280), 97-98, http://bit.ly/2qsVoZQ [accessed January 2018]

Index

Abortion, 8
Acid attacks, 83-4
Adam Bede, 11, 65-6
Adolescence, 35-7, 103
Alcoholism (and *Delirium Tremens*),
    34, 79, 83, 84, 119
Alienists, xv, 16, 32, 71, 72, 88, 115
Anderson, Elizabeth Garrett, xx, 113
Anglicanism, 26
'Archangel Raphael', 25
Aristotle, xiii
Ashmore, Jane (pyromaniac), 79
Astrology, xii, 25, 87, 89
Austen, Jane, 28

Baby farming, 77-8
Bacchus, 92
Baillie, Joanna, 26
Baker Brown, Isaac, 89, 97-103
Baquet (Mesmer), 54, 95
Barebones Parliament, 80
Battie, William, 107, 109, 120
Bauer, Ida ('Dora'), 112
Beard, George M., 2, 3, 97, 101-102
Bedlamites, xi, 106
'Bethel', Norwich, England, 105, 109
Bethlem (Bethlehem, Bedlam), xi, xv, 34,
    39, 51, 65, 80, 87, 89, 104-109, 123
    an alternative view, 108
Beveridge, William Henry, xviii
Biological determinism, 117
Blackmore, Richard, xxiv, 18, 87
Blackstone, William, 9
Blackstone's *Commentaries on the
    Laws of England*, 9
Blandford, George Fielding, 62, 118
Borde, Andrew, 90
Bracton, Henry de, 80, 81

Bramwell, Baron George William, 71
British Medical Journal, xxii, 71
Brixey, Martha, 57
Broadmoor, 76
Brough, Mary Ann (infanticide), 72, 116
Browne, William A. F., xxi
Brown-Séquard, Charles-Édouard, 98
Bucknill & Tuke, 63, 79
Bulwer-Lytton, Rosina, xxii, 8, 120
Burton, Robert, 17, 32-3, 35, 86, 91, 92, 96

Caithness, Scotland, 27
Capital punishment, xxii, 69, 71,
    77, 84, 96, 116
Causes of madness,
    marriage/relationships, 35, 37, 60, 99,
        118-20
    nerves, xxiv, 27-8
    nervous disorder, 2, 18-19, 39
    reproductive apparatus, 4
Cavendish, Margaret, Duchess of
    Newcastle, 52
Charcot, Jean-Martin [see also Hysteria],
    45, 54, 95, 112
Cheltenham Ladies College, 43
'Chemical Cosh', the, 5, 104, 112
Cheyne, George, xiv, 3, 20, 27-8, 39,
    42, 49, 54, 80, 115
Chiarugi, Vincenzo, 105
Cibber, Caius Gabriel, xv
Clarke, Maria (infanticide), 74-5
Class madness, 3, 11, 27, 62, 80,
    97, 109, 110
Clouston, Thomas, xix, 4, 60
Coke, Edward, 80-1
Combe, Andrew, 49, 58, 60, 96
Compassion, 21, 26, 94, 114
    mental price of, 2

Concealment, 69-71
  'benefit of linen', 70
  importance of marriage, 70-1
  '*lude*' women, 70
Conolly, John, 110
Contagious Diseases Act (1864), 9
Cotta, John, 41, 88
County Asylums, 109-10
Court of King's Bench, xx
Creationism and 'Original Sin', 1, 8, 19,
  20-1, 114, 115
Crichton, Alexander, 49
'Criminal Lunatics Act' (1800), 82
Criminal Procedure Act (1853), 9
Crooke, Helkiah (Keeper of Bedlam), 106
Currier, Andrew F., 58

Darwin, Charles Robert, 3, 11
Defoe, Daniel, 105, 106
Dickens, Charles, 94, 95, 109
  a Christmas Dance, 109
Diminished Responsibility, 74
Divorce, 37, 118, 120
Dix, Dorothea, xxiii
Domestic oppression, x, xvi, 3, 10, 12-13,
  39, 94, 97, 105, 111, 119
  American War of Independence, 13
  religious endorsement, 13
  'the Angel in the House', xiv, xvii
  the 'home and the hearth', xvi, xviii, 13, 59
Domestic violence, 64, 83
Donkin, Horatio, 21, 51
Dornoch, Scotland, 27
Dymond, Alfred, 84, 116

Early Modern, 22
Education, xviii-xix, 1,
Eighteenth century, 3, 9, 17, 27, 86
Eliot, George, 11, 65
Elizabeth I, 89
Elliotson, John, 94-6
Ellis, Havelock, 34
Enlightenment, the, xv, 19, 26, 27, 29, 88
Esquirol, Jean-Étienne, 57
Eugenics, xvii, 96, 104

'Female Correction', ix-x, 9, 86-112, 120
Feminism, x, 12, 51, 67, 96, 97, 122

Ferriar, John, 64, 93
Force-feeding, 121
Foucault, Michel, 106
Fourteenth century, xxiii, 30-1, 118-19
Freeman, Walter, 103-104
Freud, Sigmund, 5, 47, 111-12, 121

Galen, xiii, 15, 18, 35, 42
Gender stereotypes and
  applications, 1-39, 88
  brutalisation, 48, 94, 97-104
  separation (of genders), 6-7, 111
  slavery, 10
  subjugation of woman,
    3, 8, 10, 115-16, 117
  the 'weaker sex', xxiii, 17
  under husband's control, 9
  unsuited for competition, xix, 2, 34
General Paralysis of the
  Insane (GPI), xii, 9, 16
George III (madness of), 105
Georgian, xxiv, 67, 94, 105, 117
Gerarde (herbalist), 87
Gheel, 91, 93
Gilman, Charlotte Perkins, 12, 96, 122
Gleizes, Louise ('Augustine'), 45-6, 112
'Great Confinement', the (Foucault), 30-1
Great Staughton, Huntingdonshire, 82
Griesinger, Wilhelm, 80, 81
Gull, William, 100
Gynaecological madness [see also Baker
  Brown], ix, xvi, xviii, 3, 24, 31, 34, 37,
  39, 56, 62
  ovarian insanity, 38

Hale, Matthew, 80, 81, 82
Haslam, John, 34, 62-3
Henry VIII, 23, 80
Hereford Asylum, 110
Hippocrates, ix, xiii, 15, 18, 31, 35, 40
Hogarth, William, 108
Home Secretary's Mercy, 73
Homicide Act (1957), 74
Hopkins, Matthew, 24
Hospitals, 106-107
Humours, the, xiii-xiv, xxiii, 15, 16, 35
Huntingdon, Cambridgeshire, England, 26
Hyde Park, London, 83

Hysteria and its elements, ix, xiv, xvi, 1, 21, 29, 31, 35, 40-55
  Adhesiveness, 49
  Amativeness, 49
  anorexia nervosa, 48, 117
  arc-en-cercle, 46, 50, 95
  as a mental or physical problem, 42
  as a social disease, 44, 51-2
  as a symptom, 50
  blamed on class and/or diet, 42, 115
  blamed on hypochondria, 42
  blamed on imagination, 43-4, 49
  blamed on imitation, 43
  blamed on self-pity, 42-3, 47, 53
  blamed on sexual energy, 42, 44, 118
  Charcot, 45-7
  chorea (St Vitus's Dance) [see also 'Jumpers of Cornwall'], 29, 40, 44, 47
  defined, 47-53
  excusing crime, 50-1, 116
  globus hystericus, 48
  hereditary, 45
  hypnosis, 47, 54, 95, 112
  in men, 53
  male pity for, 46, 53-4
  non gender specific, 45
  parc-de-cercle, see *arc-en-cercle*
  'shell-shock', 53
  'Suffocation of the Mother', 25, 41
  the 'wandering' *or* 'mad, raging womb', ix, 33, 40, 41, 52, 116
  to escape domestic oppression, 54
  treatments for, 37, 41-2, 46-7, 49, 50, 54-5, 95, 97, 122
  witchcraft, 24

Icard, Séverin, 57-8
Iconographie Photographique de la Salpêtrière, 47
Industrial Revolution (and its effects), 11
Infanticide, 8, 11, 65-78
  cases, 74-7
  legal leniency, 65-6, 72-74, 94, 116
  nineteenth century crisis, 71-4
  Nottingham Cases, 71-2
Infanticide Act (1922), 74
Infanticide Act (1938), 85

Insane Prisoners Act (1840), xxii
Insane Prisoners Amendment Act (1864), xxii

Jealousy, 15, 37, 62, 83
Jervis, Lord Chief Justice John, 74-5
John Dee, 89
Johnson, Dr Samuel, 14
Jordanova, Ludmilla, 3
Jorden, Edward, 24-5, 41, 111
Jumpers of Cornwall, 43-4

Kellogg's Cornflakes, 93
Kennedy, Rosemary, 104
Kleptomania, 79
Kramer, Heinrich, 24

l'Ogresse de la Goutte d'Or, 78
Lack, Esther (child murder), 116
Law, Mrs (infanticide), 65
Laycock, Thomas, 2, 16, 29, 50, 82
Liberalism, 19
Life Stages
  (from puberty to widowhood), 35-6
Liverpool, 75-7
Local Government Act (1888), 120
Locke, John, 18
Lombroso, Cesare, 78
Louis XIV of France ('Louis the Great'), 30
Lowe, Louisa, xxii-xxiii
Lunacy Act (1890), xxi
Lunacy Commission, 103, 110
Lunatic Asylums Act (1845), 109, 110
Lunatics Care and Treatment Act (1845), 109, 110

MacDonald, James
  (Bloomingdale Asylum), 61
'Mad-doctor', xxi, xxiii, 88, 94
Madhouses Act (1774), xxi, 109
Madness, 14-20, 31-9
  biblical sanction, 1-2, 7, 8, 24
  'brain madness', 16
  cacodemonomania, 21
  childbirth, 38
  climactic insanity, xvi, 35-8
  'communicated insanity', 33
  delirium, 35

delusions, 17, 34, 62
demonic possession (and religion), 20-2, 82, 88, 90, 92, 94, 114
depression, 15, 33, 58, 59, 93, 104, 117
diet/disrupted digestion, 19, 27
dreaming/imagination, 17, 29
Electra complex, 112
epilepsy, 24, 29, 34, 35
erotomania, 32
homicidal mania, 2, 34
humoral insanity, 35
immoral living, 2-3, 4, 27, 34, 92, 115-16, 121
impulsive insanity, 16, 34, 79
inherited insanity, 33
lactational madness (and breastfeeding), 5, 10, 38, 61-2
male appropriation of, xv
mania, xiv, 16, 35
mania transitoria (ephemeral insanity), 65
marital insanity, 37
melancholia, xiv, 5, 16, 32, 34, 35, 38
misdiagnosis (esp in women), 31
moods, 35
nymphomania, xviii, 1, 103
Oedipus complex, 112
'Old Maid's Insanity', 38
paranoia, 62
physicalism, 28, 38, 80
psychosis, 104
puerperal madness, 4, 16, 38, 62-5
religious mania, 21, 115
sexual deviancy, 7, 34, 36-7, 51, 107
sexual restraint (celibacy), including dangers of, 37-8, 97, 103, 118-19
socially defined, 32, 116
somnambulism (sleep-walking), 29
trichotillomania, 80
uterine madness, xv, xvi, 4-5, 34, 39, 57
vanity, 2, 11, 39
virginity, 10, 36-7
Madness and marriage, 35, 37-8, 41-2, 99, 118-20
Maidstone, 79
Malleus Maleficarum, 7, 24
Man-midwife, 115
Marc, Charles C. H., 79

Married Women's Property Acts (1870/1882), 10, 120
Masturbation (onanism), 92-3, 98, 118
Maternal mayhem, ix, 4, 38, 56-85
Matrimonial Causes Act (1857), 9-10, 120
Maudsley, Henry, xviii-xix, xx, 2, 4-5, 48, 113, 115
McNeil, Mary (infanticide), 65
Medical assessment, 9
Medico-Psychological Association, xxi
Medieval, 4, 20-2, 34-5, 48, 89
Men and Women's Club, the, 37-8, 118
Menstrual Madness, 16, 31, 34, 56-8, 66, 79, 99, 103
Mesmer, F. F. Anton, 54, 89, 94-6
Mesmerism [see also baquet], 94-5, 105
Michelet, Jules, 10, 117
Mill, Harriet, 10
Mill, John Stuart, xvii, 10, 13-14
Millingen, John Gideon, 92, 96
Misogyny, x, xvii, 1, 6, 11-12, 32, 73, 114, 118-20, 121
Mitchell, Silas Weir, 28, 89, 94
Monro, John, 107
More, Thomas, 81-2
Morinz, Egas, 103-104
Mother's Little Helper, 5, 112
Murder, 11, 17, 29, 34, 50, 51-2, 56-7, 65-7, 68, 70-1, 78-9, 83-4, 116

Nanterre Asylum, France, 78
Napier, Richard, 22, 24, 25, 26, 35, 41, 88, 115
Neurasthenia, xvi, 2, 11, 29, 97
Nicholson, Margaret (treason), 79-80
Nightingale, Florence, xvi, 12
Nineteenth century, xvii, 1, 3, 5, 9, 11, 31, 32, 47, 104
Norman House, London (female asylum), 105

Obstetrical Society [see Baker Brown], 102
Occult, the, 25
Offences Against the Person Act (1861), 70
Okey sisters, 95
Old Bailey Proceedings Online, 67-9

Packard, Elizabeth, xxiii
Parliament (Qualification of Women) Act (1918), 121
Parliamentary responses, xx, 9
Parturition, 59, 61, 63, 66
Patriarchal abuse, ix, x, xiii, xvi, 39, 60, 88, 110, 113-14, 115, 119
Pearson, Karl, xvii
Phrenology, 44, 49, 93, 95-6
Physiognomy [see also 'Phrenology'], 15-16, 78, 92
Pinel, Philippe, xv, 82, 105, 110
Playfair, William Smoult, 28, 97
Potter, Elizabeth (infanticide), 116
Pregnancy, 59-65
    and potential for madness, 61
    Insanity of, 60-1
    mental impact, 61
Prichard, James Cowles, 2, 16, 62, 63-4, 82
Psycho-sexualisation (of women), 5, 112
Punishments, xvii, 81-2, 87-8, 89
    burning, 23
    ducking stool, 89
    scold's bridle, 89
Puritans, xix, 26, 88, 114, 115
Pyromania (incendiarism), 79

Rape, 84
Ray, Isaac, xv-xvi, xxii, 65, 82
Reason, xv, 21
'Reflex action', 16
Renaissance, the, 35, 48
Representation of the People Act (1918), 121
Reproduction, 2, 3
Ritti, Antonie, 58
Robinson, Frederick W. (A Prison Matron), 116
Robinson, Mary, 8
Rochester, Lady, 80
Rousseau, Jean-Jacque, 10-11
Royal Commission on Capital Punishment, 73
'Rule of Thumb', 9
Ryder, Mrs (infanticide), 65

Saint Dymphna, xii, 91
Salpêtrière, 45, 46

Savage, George, 51, 54, 65, 100, 118
Scold, 8
Scot, Reginald, 21
Seventeenth century, 6, 22-6, 33, 70, 82, 86, 111
Sex,
    obligations/disinterest, dangers thereof, xvii-xviii, 118
Sexless ants, xix
Sexualisation of the female insane, xv, 5, 46
Shelley, Mary, 12
Shepherd, Ann (kleptomania), 79
'Ship of Fools' (Foucault), 30
Sixteenth century, 81
Skae, David, 38
Society for the Abolition of Capital Punishment, 84
Sommer, Celestina (murder), 66
Spurzheim and Gall, 96
St Luke's, London, 105, 107, 109
Stephen, James Fitzjames, 17-18, 27, 38, 72-3, 81
Stuart, 67
Sturgeon, Elizabeth Ann, 75-7
Suffragettes, xxiv, 27-8
Suffragism, 13, 120-1
Suicide, 62, 78
Sydenham, Thomas, 42

Taming of the Shrew, 89
Taylor, Alfred Swaine, 34, 56, 65, 79
Tennyson, Alfred Lord, xvii
The History of the Pleas of the Crown (Hale), 82
The Lancet, 73, 101
The Rolling Stones, 5
The Times, xxi, 76, 101, 103
The Yellow Wallpaper, 96
Thirteenth century, 81, 104, 108
Ticehurst Asylum, Sussex, England, 105
Tilt, Edward, 54, 103
Tissot, 92-3
Treason, 79-80
Treatments, ix-x
    as a form of social construction, 32, 98
    asylum, xv, xx, 30, 31
    beating the mad, 20, 81, 82, 89, 105, 107

clitoridectomy, 98, 103
electricity, 93
emetics, blisters, purges etc, 64, 105
fever (induced), 104
herbs and plants, 46, 91-2
hydrotherapy, 54, 93
labiaplasty [see also leeches], 103
leeches, 38, 64, 103
lobotomy, 103-104
Mitchell's 'Rest Cure', 28, 46, 54, 96-7
'moral therapy', 46, 93-4, 110
poison, 46
preventing insanity, 28
private mad-house, 30, 105-106, 115
psychotherapy/psychoanalysis, 5, 112
quinine, 104
sigil, 25
'swing chair', 93, 105
transorbital lobotomy, 104
workhouse, 30, 111
Tuke, Daniel Hack, xi-xii, 15, 24,
    34, 45, 107
Tuke, William (York Retreat), xvi, 94, 105
Twentieth century, 5, 103-104, 111-12
Two Sex Model, 6, 7

Vagrancy Act (1714), xxii
van Helmont, 33, 41, 44
Victorian, xxiv, 60, 82-5
Vienna, 95, 104, 111
von Jauregg, Julius Wagner, 104

Walters, Margaret (baby farmer), 77
Weber, Jeanne (child murderess), 78
Weir, Johannes, 21
Weldon, Georgina, 8, 120
Wesley, John, 93-4
Wilks, Samuel, 43, 46, 51, 79
Willis, Thomas, 18, 20, 87

Winslow, Forbes Benignus, 34, 82
Winslow, Lyttelton Forbes, 34, 50, 54, 60,
    64, 120
Witchcraft, 26
Witchcraft Act (1541), 23
Witches & witchcraft, 6, 7, 21-2,
    22-7, 82, 114
    as a means of control, 23
    as a symbol of madness, 23, 24, 25
    James I (VI of Scotland), 23, 69, 70
    torturing of, 91
    witch's teat, 9
    women more susceptible, 6, 27
Wittmann, Blanche, 45
Wollstonecraft, Mary, 12
Woman,
    appropriation by men, 91, 116
    as the criminal gender, 80-1
    asylum admissions, 106-107, 110
    fear of, xvi, xxiv, 1-4, 6-11, 27,
        31-5, 78, 103, 121
    forced silence, xv, 33
    her natural role/make-up, xv, 2, 3, 5, 20,
        24, 33, 39, 60, 116
    inferior species, 3, 7, 26, 39
    male expectations, xv, xvii-xviii, 11, 12,
        84, 111, 117
    proneness to madness/emotional decay,
        xiv, xv, xxiii-xxiv, 2, 4, 28, 29, 31, 33-4,
        36, 39, 60-1, 109
    'The Other', 27
Woolf, Virginia, 51, 96-7
Wrongful Confinement, xv, xx-xxii, 5, 8-9,
    14, 105, 109-10, 119, 120, 121
    disincentive for, 30
Wyke House asylum, 120

York Asylum, 106
York Retreat, xvi, 94, 105, 109